INDIGENOUS ARCHIVAL ACTIVISM

INDIGENOUS ARCHIVAL ACTIVISM

MOHICAN INTERVENTIONS IN PUBLIC HISTORY AND MEMORY

Rose Miron

UNIVERSITY OF MINNESOTA PRESS

MINNEAPOLIS • LONDON

Portions of chapters 3 and 5 are adapted from "Fighting for the Tribal Bible: Mohican Politics of Self-Representation in Public History," *Native American and Indigenous Studies* 5, no. 2 (Fall 2018): 91–122.

Maps were created by Andrew Lamers.

Published by the University of Minnesota Press
111 Third Avenue South, Suite 290
Minneapolis, MN 55401–2520
http://www.upress.umn.edu

ISBN 978-1-5179-1270-3 (hc)
ISBN 978-1-5179-1271-0 (pb)

Library of Congress record available at https://lccn.loc.gov/2024000393.

Printed in the United States of America on acid-free paper

The University of Minnesota is an equal-opportunity educator and employer.

32 31 30 29 28 27 26 25 24   10 9 8 7 6 5 4 3 2 1

To future generations of the
Stockbridge-Munsee Mohican Nation,
the next recorders and rememberers

Contents

Foreword

In *Indigenous Archival Activism: Mohican Interventions in Public History and Memory*, Rose Miron has taken fifty years of the Mohican Nation Historical Committee's work and woven a remarkable historical story of resiliency. Her culturally sensitive perspective is drawn from respectful listening and working with our community. She has focused twelve years of tedious archival research balanced with interviews of Mohican tribal members and experts, along with traveling to our Mohican homelands along the Mahicannituck (Hudson) River.

Readers learn through understanding that as a result of historical trauma over generations of forced removal and loss of land, language, and lives, collecting, interpreting, and controlling Mohican history is central to Mohican identity. From old handwritten documents and poignant elder stories, Rose Miron brings archival collections to life. She states, "The creation of an archival collection that collects previously scattered sources and establishes the Mohicans as the leading experts on their own history is an essential piece of contesting dominant narratives and constructing new histories that emphasize Mohican survival and nationhood" (chapter 5). *Indigenous Archival Activism: Mohican Interventions in Public History and Memory* provides a story that is unique and is highly recommended.

Oneewe (Mohican—Thank you)
Anushiik (Munsee—We are grateful)
Mohican Nation, Stockbridge-Munsee Historical Committee

Sheila (Miller) Powless	Molly Miller
Leah Miller	Tammy Pecore
Jo Ann (Gardner) Schedler	Brent Michael Davids

A Note on Terminology

Prior to the Treaty of 1856, the U.S. government referred to the combined group of Mohican and Munsee people as the Stockbridge *and* Munsee Tribes of Indians, to signify separate groups, in spite of the fact that Mohican and Munsee people have always been relatives. After the treaty, the name was hyphenated and the singular nation has henceforth been referred to as the Stockbridge-Munsee Mohican Nation, or officially by the federal government as the Stockbridge-Munsee Community. This book is steeped in the collective history of the Munsee and Mohicans, but the majority of the events and initiatives I discuss occur in the twentieth and early twenty-first centuries, well after both the U.S. government and the tribe itself considered the Stockbridge-Munsee Mohicans a single tribal nation. Therefore, though I often shorten the full tribal name to "Mohican" or "Stockbridge-Munsee," I am always referring to the entire Stockbridge-Munsee Mohican Nation and their shared history and tribal identity, unless specifically stated otherwise. I have chosen to do this both for brevity and to reflect how tribal members typically shorten the name today.

More broadly, the public history projects and related archives I discuss in this book are primarily located within the United States. Still, I primarily use the broader terms "Indigenous" and "Native" rather than "American Indian" to be inclusive of Alaska Native and Native Hawaiian people who are also affected by U.S. archives, policies, and narratives. I hope the terms also invite readers to consider how the basic pillars of Indigenous archival activism might translate or be applied in other contexts.

Timeline of Notable Events

This is not a comprehensive timeline of Mohican history. Rather, it lays out notable events related to the preservation and recovery of Mohican history, alongside important national events that resonate with or had an impact on Mohican actions. The events below primarily occurred between 1968 and 2021, in alignment with the focus of the book.

1734 Mohican leaders allow John Sergeant Sr. to establish a Christian mission in their village Wnahktukuk (in present-day western Massachusetts), which Sergeant renamed Stockbridge. Many Munsee people, and some people from other Native nations, join the Mohicans at Stockbridge.

1745 Two-volume Bible set gifted to the Stockbridge Mohicans from the chaplain to the Prince of Wales.

1783 Over several years, white settlers worked to evict the Native people at Stockbridge. The Mohicans and some of their Munsee relatives accept an invitation from the Oneida to leave Stockbridge and live with them in New Stockbridge, New York.

1790 Hendrick Aupaumut writes "History of the Muh-he-con-nuck Indians," which is later published in part as "Extract from an Indian History."

1792 Hendrick Aupaumut records notes about his role as a diplomat to western Native nations. This journal is later published as *Narratives of an Embassy to the Western Indians*.

1804 Hendrick Aupaumut's narrative "Extract from an Indian History," the first written history of the Stockbridge Munsee and Mohican people, is published in part by the Massachusetts Historical Society.

1818 The state of New York moves to remove all Native people from within its borders. Some Munsee and Mohican people travel to White River, Indiana, to live with Myaamia and Lenape relatives. When they arrive, they learn that the Lenape had already been forced to sell their land.

1822 More Munsee and Mohican, along with Oneida and Brothertown people, leave New York in the wake of increasing white settlement. They travel to Green Bay (Oneida) and Kaukauna (Mohican, Munsee, Brothertown) in Michigan Territory (present-day eastern Wisconsin), where land was set aside for them after treaty negotiations with the Menominee and Ho-Chunk Nations.

1826 James Fenimore Cooper's *The Last of the Mohicans* is published, igniting the pervasive myth of Mohican disappearance.

1827 Hendrick Aupaumut's journal is published by the Pennsylvania Historical Society as *Narratives of an Embassy to the Western Indians.*

1830 Congress passes the Indian Removal Act.

1834 The Menominee and Ho-Chunk Nations are forced to renegotiate their land claims. The Mohicans and Munsee, along with their Brothertown relatives, are forced to move again to the eastern shore of Lake Winnebago in present-day Wisconsin.

1839 Fearing further removal, some Mohicans and Munsee elect to move to present-day Kansas. Some eventually return to Wisconsin, while others remain.

1844 More Munsee reach the village on Lake Winnebago and are welcomed into the community.

1854 John Quinney gives his famous Fourth of July speech in which he recalls the tradition of preserving and passing on Mohican history.

Electa Jones publishes *Stockbridge Past and Present,* which includes the full version of Aupaumut's "History of the Muh-he-con-nuck Indians."

1856 The Treaty of 1856 results in the Stockbridge-Munsee Mohican Nation's removal to Shawano County in the central Wisconsin townships of Red Springs and Bartelme. After this treaty, the U.S.

government begins referring to the tribe as the Stockbridge-Munsee Mohicans rather than the Stockbridge and Munsee Tribes of Indians.

1871   The Act of 1871 sells fifty-four sections of pine-forested land "for the relief of the Stockbridge and Munsee Indians," effectively eliminating the majority of the Stockbridge-Munsee reservation.

Congress ends treaty making with American Indian nations.

1887   The remaining sections of the Stockbridge-Munsee reservation are allotted into individual parcels under the General Allotment Act. Many tribal members are forced to sell their allotments out of desperation, leaving the tribe with very little land remaining.

1930   The Stockbridge-Munsee Business Committee, led by Carl Miller, is formed to support the reorganization of the Stockbridge-Munsee Community and regain land lost through allotment.

1934   Congress passes the Indian Reorganization Act.

1935   Arvid and Bernice Miller are married and begin helping the Business Committee prepare for reorganization by preserving committee minutes and correspondence and collecting and organizing historical records such as land and government records in their home.

1936   Under the Indian Reorganization Act, the Stockbridge-Munsee Mohicans regain fifteen thousand acres of their original reservation in the township of Bartelme. Though the land had been clear-cut by pine loggers, tribal members move about ten miles northwest to this land from the little remaining land they held on the eastern side of the reservation in the township of Red Springs. Only twenty-five hundred acres of this land are actually placed in trust (meaning it is protected from being sold).

1941   Arvid E. Miller elected tribal chairman.

1944   National Congress of American Indians founded; Arvid Miller is a cofounder.

1961   Native leaders gather at the American Indian Chicago Conference and publish the Declaration of Indian Purpose; Arvid Miller, Dorothy Davids, Elmer Davids, Blanche Jacobs, and Margaret Raasch all attend.

1963   Wisconsin Tribal Chairman's Association (eventually incorporated as
       the Great Lakes Intertribal Council) founded; Arvid Miller is a
       cofounder.

1968   Bernice Miller's house catches fire. Neighbors and friends save the
       documents that she and her husband collected from the fire and
       move them to an army tent in her yard. Informal Historical
       Committee formed.

       Historical Committee members make their first historical trip to the
       Mahicannituck (Hudson) River Valley.

       The American Indian Movement is founded.

1969   The Occupation of Alcatraz in California begins.

       First American Indian studies department founded at the University
       of Minnesota.

1972   Tribal Council grants space for the archival materials in the former
       tribal craft shop and formally recognizes the Historical Committee.

       First publication of *Quin'a Month'a*, the Historical Committee's
       newsletter.

       Remaining thirteen thousand acres of land regained under the
       Indian Reorganization Act are placed back in trust for the tribe;
       supported by Historical Committee research.

       Second historical trip coordinated by Historical Committee
       members.

       Historical Committee holds "teach-in" at Bowler Schools near the
       reservation.

       The American Indian Movement leads the Trail of Broken Treaties
       March.

       The D'Arcy McNickle Center, the first research center for American
       Indian studies outside of a university, founded at the Newberry
       Library in Chicago.

       Survival schools founded in Minnesota.

1973   The American Indian Movement organizes the occupation of
       Wounded Knee on the Pine Ridge Reservation in South Dakota.

1974   Archival materials moved into a new permanent space; the Library-
       Museum is officially opened to the public.

Historical Committee leads two-week, on-reservation workshop for teachers from the Bowler School District.

1975   Historical Committee initiates campaign to retrieve Bible and Communion set from the Mission House Museum in Stockbridge, Massachusetts.

Third historical trip coordinated by Historical Committee members.

Mobile exhibit on Mohican History curated by the Historical Committee, tours Wisconsin.

Indian Self-Determination and Education Act passed.

1976   Bernice Miller donates her land allotment, and a new building is constructed to house the tribal archive, library, and museum.

1977   Fourth historical trip coordinated by Historical Committee members.

1978   Muh-he-con-neew Inc. founded as the educational arm of the Historical Committee.

White House holds its Preconference on Indian Library and Information Services on or Near Reservations.

1979   First Mohican curriculum project.

The American Indian Libraries Association founded.

1980   Muh-he-con-neew Press founded as the publishing arm of the Historical Committee.

Historical Committee publishes library catalog.

1984   John Fleckner's *Native American Archives: An Introduction* is published.

1987   Fifth historical trip coordinated by Historical Committee members.

1989   Sixth historical trip coordinated by Historical Committee members.

1990   Native American Graves Protection and Repatriation Act (NAGPRA) passed by Congress.

1991   Repatriation of Bible set from the Mission House in Stockbridge.

First attempt to restore reservation boundaries set in the Treaty of 1856.

1992   Revitalization of W'Chindin ceremony.

Section 106 of the National Historic Preservation Act is amended to emphasize required consultation with Indian tribes and Native Hawaiian organizations.

1993   Second curriculum project, first stand-alone Mohican curriculum.

1995   Creation of living village Wea Tauk.

Seventh historical trip coordinated by Historical Committee members, including a reburial of repatriated ancestors.

New signage about Mohican history installed at the Lutheran Mission School in Red Springs, Wisconsin.

Aboriginal and Torres Strait Islander Protocols for Libraries, Archives, and Information Services published by the Australian Library and Information Association.

1996   Tribe prevents Wal-Mart from building store on Leeds Flat historical site in New York State.

Eighth historical trip coordinated by Historical Committee members, including a reburial of repatriated ancestors.

Creation of Institute for the Study of Native Americans of the Northeast at Columbia-Greene Community College in New York in collaboration with Mohican tribal members.

1997   Ninth historical trip coordinated by Historical Committee members, including delegation advocating for the protection of Schodack Island in New York State.

1998   "Memoir-izing Our Mohican Lives" oral history project.

Second attempt to restore reservation boundaries set in the Treaty of 1856.

1999   Booklet from the *Stories of Our Elders* oral history project published by the Historical Committee.

2000   Language and Culture Committee founded.

2001   "Many Trails of the Mohican Nation" history conference.

A Brief History of the Mohican Nation: Stockbridge-Munsee Band published by the Historical Committee.

Stockbridge-Munsee Repatriation Office and Committee established.

U.S. Indigenous Data Sovereignty Network founded at the University of Arizona.

2003   Tenth historical trip coordinated by Historical Committee members.

2004   Repatriation Office is recognized by the National Park Service and officially designated as the Tribal Historic Preservation Office.

2005   Library program for Head Start children begins.

Digitization of archival records and photographs begins.

Eleventh historical trip, coordinated by the Tribal Historic Preservation Office.

Memorandum of understanding signed with West Point Military Academy.

2006   Oral interviews for second edition of *Stories of Our Elders*.

Tribal members begin working with a linguist to revitalize the Mohican language.

Repatriation of Communion set from the Mission House in Stockbridge.

Twelfth historical trip, coordinated by Tribal Historic Preservation Office.

Posters about historical preservation and repatriation added to the "Indian Museum" behind the Mission House.

2007   "Protocols for Native American Archival Materials" published by First Archivist Circle.

2008   Third curriculum project, designed for fourth and fifth graders and accompanying training program created in conjunction with the Wisconsin Improving Teacher Quality Program.

2009   *Hear Our Stories* oral history project completed.

2010   Restoration of Mohican Burial Ground in Stockbridge.

Second edition of *Stories of Our Elders* published by the Historical Committee.

The Association for Tribal Archives, Libraries, and Museums founded.

2011   The Stockbridge-Munsee Community purchases sixty-three acres of land on the Hudson River to protect a sacred site.

2012 Designation of Stockbridge plot as additional protected burial ground.

2013 Thirteenth historical trip coordinated by Historical Committee
      members.

2015 Satellite Historic Preservation Office opened in Mohican homelands.

2016 *People of the Waters That Are Never Still: Pictorial History of the
      Stockbridge-Munsee Band of Mohicans* published.

2017 Institute of Museum and Library Services grant received to formally
      hire community linguist to support Mohican language revitalization.

      Paid "Language Manager" position created.

2018 Tribal Council creates the Department of Cultural Affairs, uniting
      staff within the Library-Museum, Language and Culture, and
      Historic Preservation units. The Historical Committee continues to
      work closely with the Department of Cultural Affairs.

      "Footprints of Our Ancestors: Mohican Walking Tour" launched in
      Stockbridge.

2019 Fourteenth historical trip coordinated by Historical Committee
      members and Department of Cultural Affairs.

      Walking tour updated to include a digital component, including
      videos of tribal members narrating Mohican history.

2021 Highway mural representing tribal members installed on Interstate
      87 in New York State.

      New signage about Mohican history installed at Mawignack Preserve
      in the Catskill Mountains.

      Satellite Historic Preservation Office moved to Williams College,
      official partnership with the college begins.

      Repatriation of John Quinney's powder horn from the Oshkosh
      Public Museum in Wisconsin.

      Return of Papscanee Island in New York State to Mohican ownership.

      Two trails on Monument Mountain renamed at the direction of the
      Department of Cultural Affairs; signage about Mohican history
      added.

      Archaeological dig for Stockbridge Meeting House and George
      Washington ox roast begins.

Mohican Miles exhibit curated by the Department of Cultural Affairs, replaces previous exhibits in the "Indian Museum" behind the Mission House in Stockbridge.

Muh-he-con-ne-ok: The Peoples of the Water That Are Never Still exhibit curated by the Department of Cultural Affairs, installed at the Berkshire Museum.

Introduction

An Archive Story

the place where the action is
> —Dorothy Davids, cofounder of the Historical Committee, describing the
> Stockbridge-Munsee Mohican library, museum, and archive in her
> unpublished "History of the Historical Library Museum"

In 1968, Bernice Miller's home in Bowler, Wisconsin, caught fire.[1] Despite growing flames and billowing smoke, her neighbors broke a window and entered the burning structure.[2] Such a dangerous endeavor suggests perhaps a child, or maybe even a pet, was left inside. But instead, the neighbors emerged with documents: important records of the Stockbridge-Munsee Mohican Nation that Miller and her late husband, Arvid E. Miller, had collected for the last thirty-plus years. Some of the documents were original Tribal Council papers that the Millers had filed, while others they collected from attics or auctions, including some dating as far back as the seventeenth century.[3] A number were transcriptions of documents related to Mohican history from other archives across the country, which Arvid had located and carefully copied by hand. Together, they narrated the history of the Stockbridge-Munsee Mohican Nation.

Why would people risk their lives for records? For the Millers and the tribal members who ran into Bernice's house that day, these materials were more than keepsakes: they documented a proud history and heritage that generations of Mohicans had fought to preserve. Arvid and Bernice Miller had always dreamed of expanding this archive into a library and museum beyond their home, and the fire became the catalyst that spurred Bernice to transform their dream into a reality and ensure these materials would be protected for generations to come. In the immediate aftermath of the near disaster, the documents were kept in an army tent outside Miller's home on

1

the Stockbridge-Munsee reservation. Thereafter, she and others petitioned the Tribal Council for a more permanent space, and in 1972 they moved the documents to an abandoned Civilian Conservation Corps building down the road from her house that had previously been used as a craft shop. As they searched for a permanent home for the materials, Miller, her sister, Dorothy Davids, and other tribal members formed the Stockbridge-Munsee Mohican Historical Committee.[4]

The formation of the committee, which has historically been made up of almost entirely women, immediately spurred what Davids called "a surge of community activity."[5] In the aftermath of the fire, these women would go on to launch what they called "The Stockbridge-Munsee Historical Project." They gathered everything they could find about Stockbridge-Munsee Mohican history; assembled these materials in an expanded, more accessible building on the Stockbridge-Munsee Mohican Nation's reservation in Wisconsin; enacted the Mohican nation's sovereign right to determine who could access these items; and used the new collection to pursue countless public history projects on and off the Mohican reservation. These projects disrupted existing misrepresentations of Stockbridge-Munsee Mohican history and sought to create new narratives that, in the committee's words, would "increase pride in and understanding of [our] own cultural and historical tradition."[6]

Indigenous Archival Activism is a history of the Historical Committee, the creation of the Mohican tribal archive, and the mobilization of that collection. It is a tribally focused story that prompts enduring questions about who has the right to collect and represent Native history as well as how power and historical violence affect the construction of historical narratives. Using archival sources such as meeting minutes, newspaper articles, and correspondence, the book traces the multidimensional work of the Historical Committee from 1968 to the early 2020s and analyzes the publications, museum exhibits, curriculum, and other types of public history projects created by the committee and the tribe's more recent Historic Preservation Office and Department of Cultural Affairs. The Mohicans' effort to build and mobilize their tribal archive reveals how Indigenous nations use historical records to strengthen tribal identity and sovereignty and highlights the role of tribal archives in Indigenous nation-building.

I argue that the creation and strategic use of tribal archives constitute an important type of Indigenous political action and nation-building that fundamentally shifts how Native history is accessed, represented, taught, and written. I collectively call these activities "Indigenous archival activism." Indigenous archival activism is anchored around three elements: access, sovereignty, and new narratives. It encompasses the actions Indigenous nations take to make their histories and historical materials more accessible to tribal members; to exercise sovereignty over the retrieval, organization, and description of their records and knowledge while using these materials to defend Indigenous nationhood; and to contest existing, and create new, narratives of Native history. Put simply, it is the act of mobilizing archives to change Indigenous narratives and representations.

My understanding of Indigenous archival activism first grows out of existing scholarship that has examined archival and collective memory practices and interventions as important forms of activism. In the context of non-Indigenous community archives, archival studies scholar Andrew Flynn defines "archival activism" as a practice that is "frequently associated with a political agenda aiming at social transformation and challenging discrimination."[7] Within Indigenous studies, historian Jennifer O'Neal has also used the phrase "archival activists" to describe those who "were at the forefront of a grassroots movement to establish and develop tribal archives, return and secure tribal history and rights during the restoration era, and establish training and best practices for the respectful care of Indigenous collections."[8] My study of Indigenous archival activism builds on the work of these scholars but is especially focused on not only the creation but also the *use* of tribal archives to craft and shape new narratives, particularly those within public history.[9]

My development of this term and particularly the three pillars—access, sovereignty, and new narratives—also stems from my own experience working in several nontribal archival contexts. First, as the program manager for the National Native American Boarding School Healing Coalition, during which I helped to plan for their digital archive project, and then as the director of the D'Arcy McNickle Center for American Indian and Indigenous Studies at the Newberry Library (where I continue to work as of this writing), I have often described greater access to records and respect for tribal sovereignty as the levers that non-Native archives can pull to ensure that tribal nations can reclaim their histories on their terms and create new, tribally centered narratives. While the book focuses specifically on *Mohican* archival activism, I hope the pillars encourage readers to consider how this framework might be used in other contexts. Within the scope of the Mohican tribal archive,

Indigenous archival activism encompasses both the creation and mobilization of the tribal archive, and because the work is so multidimensional,
the pillars also help group activities and explain why access and sovereignty
are critical factors in changing the way Mohican history, and Native history
more broadly, is taught, represented, and written. Therefore, each pillar merits additional explanation and definition.

Access encompasses Mohican efforts to recover their archival materials and
make them readily available to tribal members, as well as Historical Committee efforts to make Mohican history more accessible to tribal members
through other internal-facing projects such as publications, on-reservation
classes, language revitalization, and historical trips back to Mohican homelands. Sovereignty includes Mohican data sovereignty, the tribe's enaction
of their right to control the organization of, access to, and use of historical
records that include tribal knowledge, as well as their use of archival records
to defend their sovereignty in legal matters with the United States, including
repatriation cases, historical preservation work, language revitalization, and
land battles. Greater access to historical records enables this latter type of
sovereignty, while data sovereignty is used as a tool by the Mohican Nation
to shape existing and create new historical narratives.[10] Access to and control
over these records has enabled tribal members to contest existing misrepresentations in museums, textbooks, and scholarly narratives while also gen-
erating new Mohican-centered narratives in various contexts, ranging from
public walking tours to curriculum and beyond. Importantly however, it is
the combination of these gathered archival records and existing community
knowledge that makes new representations possible. Archival records can be
critical in filling gaps that settler-colonial violence has created, but they are
incomplete without the knowledge and interpretation of community members. This is precisely why Indigenous access to historical records and support for Indigenous data sovereignty in the classification and description of
these materials are essential for the creation of accurate and respectful new
narratives.

This book narrates how these pillars support Indigenous nation-building
and prompt a reimagined, collaborative process for writing history, one in
which Native peoples retain authority over the collection and presentation
of their own histories. As I discuss in the methodology section of this introduction, the community-based format of this project aims to highlight this
collaborative process directly. I am a non-Mohican and non-Native historian,

and this history is based in more than a decade of work with the Stockbridge-Munsee Mohican Nation. Together, we built a reciprocal relationship of trust and shaped a community-engaged methodology that has included consulting with Historical Committee members about the tribe's research interests and priorities *throughout* the project's evolution, privileging tribal voices and sources, talking with tribal members and receiving feedback about the content of this narrative, collaborating with the tribe to contribute to their research interests and priorities, and working with the tribe's Legal Department and Tribal Council to obtain permission before publishing my research in any form. I hope this book contributes to the growing tide of scholarship that centers Indigenous voices and perspectives and shifts the way scholars understand archival expertise and knowledge. My goal is that both its tracing of Indigenous engagements with public history and scholars and its reflections on my own methodology as a non-Native scholar can make a strong case for consultation and collaboration with Native nations within the scope of academic research and public history.

Stockbridge-Munsee Mohican History and Record Keeping

Though the Historical Committee was officially formed after the Miller house fire in 1968, the legacy of Mohican historical activism and record keeping dates from much earlier than the Millers and extends geographically far beyond the Mohican reservation in Wisconsin. Understanding this history must begin with a sense of who the Stockbridge-Munsee Mohican people are. Before European colonization, Mohican homelands extended over both sides of the Mahicannituck (Hudson) River and included land in what are now the states of New York, Vermont, Massachusetts, Connecticut, Pennsylvania, and New Jersey.[11] The Muhheconneok or Muhheconeew, a name that has since been shortened to Mohican, are the "People of the Waters That Are Never Still," and their identity is directly tied to this landscape, the coursing waters of the Mahicannituck.[12] The Munsee are a separate, though related, people connected to the larger Lenni-Lenape (Delaware) Nation, whose homelands also lie in the southern Mahicannituck River Valley.[13]

In 1734, Mohican leaders decided to allow a Christian mission to be established in their village Wnahktukuk (in present-day western Massachusetts) and to center their nation there. They considered the decision carefully over the course of four days and ultimately determined that the mission was their best chance of survival. It would enable their children to learn to read and write in English, and the mission town would become an important meeting place that fostered ongoing diplomatic relationships and peace in the Housatonic River Valley.[14] The first missionary, John Sergeant Sr., renamed the village Stockbridge after a village in England, and from this point on, white leaders collectively referred to the Mohicans and others who gathered at the mission (including Munsees) as the "Stockbridge Indians." However, soon after the mission was established, illegal white settlement in the town grew, and non-Native town leaders worked to evict the Mohicans from their land. In 1783 the tribe was forced to leave their homelands for the first time.

This was only the beginning of several removals forced by settler-colonial land encroachment and coercive negotiations (see Figure 1). Through each of these removals, Mohican leaders made difficult decisions about what was best for the future of their nation. After being pushed out of Stockbridge in 1783, the tribe accepted an invitation from the Oneida Nation to live with them in New Stockbridge, New York. However, as pressure for the removal of all Native people from New York State grew, groups of Mohicans and their Munsee relatives began to move west, fearing the inevitable. One group traveled to White River, Indiana, in 1818 to live with Myaamia and Lenape relatives, only to find when they arrived that the Lenape had been coerced to sell their land. Another group, including Mohican, Munsee, Oneida, and Brothertown people, left New York in 1822, traveling to present-day northeastern Wisconsin. While the Oneida settled near Green Bay, the Mohican, Munsee, and Brothertown were granted land tracts in present-day Kaukauna, Wisconsin, a small town on what is now called the Fox River where a tract of land had been set aside after negotiations with the Menominee and Ho-Chunk Nations. Interest in the Fox River as a major waterway forced the Menominee and Ho-Chunk to renegotiate their land claims with the federal government, and the Mohicans, Munsee, and Brothertown were removed yet again in 1834 to the eastern shore of what is now called Lake Winnebago.[15] By 1844, several more Munsee people had reached the village on Lake Winnebago and had been welcomed into the community.[16] The Treaty of 1856 resulted in the Stockbridge-Munsee Mohicans' sixth removal, to Shawano County in central Wisconsin, but much of the land promised in this treaty was subsequently taken through the Act of 1871, which sold fifty-four sections of pine-forested reservation land "for the relief of the Stockbridge and Munsee Indians," and the 1887 General Allotment Act, which broke up the remaining reservation into individual parcels, many of which individual tribal members sold out of desperation. By the 1920s the tribe was virtually land-less, and it was not until 1936, two years after the passage of the Indian Re-organization Act (IRA), that they were able to regain land that was stolen and completed their final removal to their current reservation.[17] This land is in the townships of Bartelme and Red Springs in Shawano County, Wisconsin, which lies on the southern border of the Menominee Indian Reservation.[18]

Throughout these removals, the Mohicans prioritized record keeping and sharing tribal history, and unsurprisingly, this work began long before Euro-pean contact with a long line of what scholar Lisa Brooks calls "remember-ers" or "recorders."[19] Quoting nineteenth-century non-Native writer Electa Jones, Brooks notes that "the History, and perhaps we may say the entire lit-erature of the Muh-he-ka-ne-ok, was treasured in the minds of a succession of 'historians,' each of whom trained one or more to fill the office after his

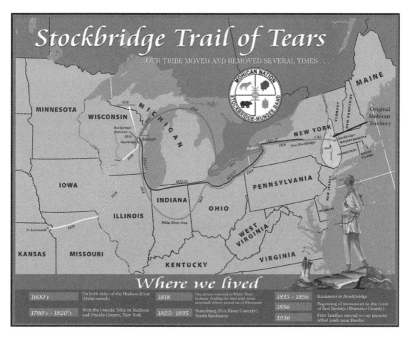

Figure 1. A tribally produced poster depicting the tribe's numerous removals between their ancestral homelands and current reservation in central Wisconsin. The bottom of the poster features a detailed timeline, identifying each move. Courtesy of the Stockbridge-Munsee Community, Cultural Affairs Department, Arvid E. Miller Library Museum.

death."[20] Established well before the arrival of white settlers, this practice was enacted through communal oral histories and recorded using tools like wampum for centuries.[21] Later, Mohican leaders like Hendrick Aupaumut and John Konkapot also used alphabetic writing to fulfill these recording roles in the eighteenth and early nineteenth centuries, a decision that enabled them to ensure the stability and survival of their traditional practice in the wake of colonization and present their histories to colonial audiences in order to address the erasure of Indigenous histories that was already underway.[22] In particular, Aupaumut's narrative "Extract from an Indian History," which was at some point collected by A. Holmes and published by the Massachusetts Historical Society in 1804, is identified by Jones and later Stockbridge-Munsee leader John Wannuaucon Quinney as the first of these written national narratives. Aupaumut's journal, which was later published as *Narratives of an Embassy to the Western Indians,* is also a vital source.[23]

By the mid-nineteenth century, John Quinney had taken up the rememberer role, and his written account of tribal history is preserved among his papers in the John C. Adams collection at the Wisconsin Historical Society.[24] He also mentioned this important tradition in an 1854 speech he gave in New York on the Fourth of July.[25] Reminding New Yorkers that they were "now standing upon the soil which once was, and now ought to be, the property of this tribe," Quinney recalled that councils "for the purpose of conveying from the old to the young men, a knowledge of the past" had always been held among the Muhheconeew tribe, and that these traditions were now preserved in writing.[26] He described the councils as being an event where "the stores of memory were dispensed; corrections and comparisons made, and the results committed to faithful breasts, to be committed again to succeeding posterity."[27] In the late nineteenth and early twentieth centuries, Stockbridge-Munsee children attended federal Indian boarding schools like Carlisle and Hampton, as well as in-state boarding schools such as Lac Du Flambeau and local mission schools such as the Emmanuel Lutheran Mission School in Red Springs.[28] In these institutions, they were forbidden from speaking their languages and taught that their histories and cultures were unimportant. In spite of this, leaders like Elmer Davids (Bernice Miller and Dorothy Davids's father), Carl Miller (Arvid Miller's father), Arvid Miller, and eventually members of the Historical Committee continued to record and provide "a record for future generations."[29] In other words, while it may be tempting to think of the archive as an entirely colonial tool, Stockbridge-Munsee Mohican leaders have been preserving and passing down the history of their people for hundreds of years.[30] Arvid and Bernice Miller and the Historical Committee are simply the most recent individuals to fill the long-held roles of Mohican recorders and rememberers. Still, these individuals all transformed this historical role in important ways.

The tribe's need for a centralized archive came in the 1930s with the formation of the Stockbridge-Munsee Business Committee, a group created to reorganize the Stockbridge-Munsee Community and regain land that had been lost as a result of logging and allotment. Carl Miller was elected chairman of the committee, and he and others began gathering materials and information that they would need to make their case. They were well prepared when Congress passed the IRA in 1934, ending allotment and supporting the creation of federally sanctioned tribal governments.[31] Almost immediately, they requested the establishment of a reservation that would reclaim Stockbridge-Munsee land.[32] As the Business Committee worked toward reorganization under the IRA, Arvid Miller and Bernice (married in 1935), became involved in the effort, particularly helping to organize committee meeting minutes and correspondence and collect and catalog historical records such as land and government documents that were needed for recognition.[33] The committee needed a place to house these materials, so the archive was formed. From 1935 to 1968 it remained in the Miller home, where many tribal members relied on it to study Mohican history and prepare for tribal government projects or affairs.[34] The IRA's success is widely debated by historians, and it is often framed as a moment in which tribes are forced to define themselves in relationship to the settler state, but the Mohican story does not end with submission to the federal government. Instead, the creation of the Business Committee prior to the act and their effort to regain Mohican land in this moment gives birth to the archive that would ultimately enable the tribe to tell their own story on their own terms and enact their sovereignty.

In 1941, Arvid Miller was elected tribal chairman of the Stockbridge-Munsee Mohican Nation. He served in this role for twenty-six years between 1941 and 1968 and was also a cofounder of two major American Indian coalitions, the Great Lakes Intertribal Council and the National Congress of American Indians.[35] In his various leadership roles, Miller frequently traveled throughout Wisconsin and the United States on tribal business and often made time to visit local, state, and national archives on his trips. Starting this work before photocopy machines were invented and made widely available, Miller transcribed most of these documents by hand. He also used archival materials to write new narratives, weaving different sources and his own experiences together to write new histories of the Stockbridge-Munsee Nation.[36] Bernice Miller organized and filed these handwritten accounts and notes in their home while also working on and filing her own writing in the collection. Eventually, she would go on to write several first-person narratives about her own life, as well as create the archive and search for records.

After the fire in 1968, Miller and the other women on the newly founded Historical Committee took up the remember/recorder role and made a plan for continuing Arvid's work of collecting. However, they reenvisioned how many people were involved by creating a committee to continue the work that had previously been done by individuals and shifted the motivations behind

Figure 2. Arvid and Bernice Miller sit with their son Alfred in 1936. Courtesy of the Stockbridge-Munsee Community, Cultural Affairs Department, Arvid E. Miller Library Museum.

recording and sharing history. While previous recorders focused on collecting materials to prepare for engagements with the state and recording history for tribal audiences, the newly formed committee expanded their focus outward and began to directly challenge existing narratives about Stockbridge-Munsee history in academic and public history spaces. Like the Indigenous leaders who adorned the walls of their homes and the Library-Museum (see Figures 3 and 4), they envisioned themselves as warriors, fighting for a better future where their history would be accurately represented by tribal members. During this time, the committee was composed entirely of women who supported their efforts through savvy fundraising, volunteer labor, and collecting aluminum cans that committee members traded in for money.[37] Miller's daughters, Leah and Sheila, were hired as the first librarians through grant funding in the 1970s, and Dorothy Davids, Miller's sister, also played a crucial role in organizing the committee and leading fundraising efforts in this formational period and beyond.[38] Coming from a background in teaching and activism, Davids was at the forefront of many of the educational efforts the Historical Committee developed and was key in their efforts to disrupt existing narratives of Mohican disappearance. Davids chaired the Historical Committee for many years, and her lifetime partner, Ruth Gudinas (who was also an educator, but not a tribal member), served as the Historical Committee's tribal secretary. Other members of the original Historical Committee included Miller's aunt Thelma Davids Putnam, Blanche Jacobs, Leila Bowman, Marceline Miller Sparks, Lucille Miller, Margaret Raasch, Lai Lonnie Kroening, Beryl Putnam Schwab, and Arminta Chicks Hebert.[39] Subsequent members have been mostly women and include two more of Miller's daughters, Tammy and Molly, as well as Arletta Davids, Mary Miller, Susan Davids, Cindy Jungenberg, Eunice Stick, Cassie Moede, Betty Groh, Jo Ann Schedler, Nathalee Kristiansen, Yvette Malone, Dr. Jolene Bowman, Dr. Nicole Bowman-Farrell, Heather Bruegl, Shawn Stevens, and Brent Michael Davids.[40]

At first glance, the women-led Historical Committee also seems like a departure from the traditional Mohican recorder and rememberer role, which secondary literature has recorded as being held by men. Yet, because of the frequency with which women were (and often still are) written out of historical narratives by colonial reporters, I want to leave room for the possibility that women have always been involved in the process of preserving and passing down Mohican history to future generations but were simply not

Figure 3. Longtime Historical Committee members Ruth Gudinas (*left*) and Dorothy "Dot" Davids (*right*) pose in front of a poster showing the famous Chiricahua Apache warrior, Geronimo. Courtesy of the Stockbridge-Munsee Community, Cultural Affairs Department, Arvid E. Miller Library Museum.

recognized as such. Other historical evidence also supports this theory. As historian Kallie Kosc has shown, Mohican women have always played an important role in community decision making and diplomacy, and they frequently served as leading advocates for the education of girls within the community.[41] Kosc has shown that Mohican women were instructed in these community roles by elder women and that among other roles related to education and medicinal knowledge, they also served as keepers of certain elements of tribal identity, such as language. She has also documented their attention to historical items and spaces with deep cultural meaning. For example, when the tribe was forced to leave New York in the eighteenth century as a result of increasing white settlement, Mary Peters, among other tribal leaders, stayed behind to ensure the care of sacred sites before joining her family in the southern Great Lakes.[42] This suggests that Stockbridge-Munsee women may have always been involved in the preservation of tribal history and that the women of the Historical Committee built out the traditional recorder/rememberer role to include other elements of their traditional roles as Mohican women, including education, the protection of sacred sites and knowledge, and language preservation.

The Historical Committee officially opened the Library-Museum in 1974 and moved their growing collection into a newly constructed building in 1976.[43] The building was constructed on a portion of Bernice Miller's land assignment, so many now joke that the Library-Museum sits where her asparagus patch used to be.[44] Throughout their early founding years and across the

Figure 4. Historical Committee members sort through archival records at their meeting in February 1974. As in the previous photograph, a poster of a famed Indigenous warrior, this time Hunkpapa Lakota leader Sitting Bull, adorns the wall. The committee members pictured are (*left to right*) Leila Bowman, Bernice Miller, Blanche Jacobs, Dorothy Davids, Lai Lonnie Kroening, Sheila (Miller) Moede, and Beryl Schwab. Courtesy of the Stockbridge-Munsee Community, Cultural Affairs Department, Arvid E. Miller Library Museum.

next several decades, the committee would produce a tribal newspaper and other publications, lead tribal members back to Munsee and Mohican homelands on educational tours, produce educational programming and curriculum, and work with museums and other public history venues to craft revised narratives of Stockbridge-Munsee history, all the while using the archive as an arsenal to support these projects. The constellation of their efforts is a testament to their immense work over the past five decades.

Throughout the 1970s, 1980s, and 1990s, the Historical Committee served in a more official role as advisers to the Stockbridge-Munsee Tribal Council and as the body that developed the policies and procedures for the Library-Museum.[45] During this time the Library-Museum had few or no full-time employees, since these positions were always dependent on grant funding. Instead, it employed Historical Committee members part-time when possible and relied on volunteer labor to still accomplish an incredible amount of work.[46] However, as this work was able to be more sustainably funded by

Figure 5. Bernice Miller stands in front of the first Library-Museum building, which opened in 1974. Courtesy of the Stockbridge-Munsee Community, Cultural Affairs Department, Arvid E. Miller Library Museum.

royalties from the Stockbridge-Munsee casino, which was opened in 1992, and other tribal operations, the Tribal Council appointed permanent staff in the Library-Museum, which became part of the Department of Education and Cultural Affairs.[47] The tribe also established an official Repatriation Office and Committee in 2001 and applied to the National Park Service to officially have this designated as the Tribal Historic Preservation Office in 2004.[48] These staff members took on some of the work Historical Committee members were completing on a volunteer basis and have continued to work with the Historical Committee throughout the first three decades of the 2000s. In the early 2000s the Language and Culture Committee was founded to focus on language and cultural revitalization. Again, this group worked closely with the Historical Committee, and the groups have had several overlapping members over the years. In 2018 the Tribal Council created the Department of Cultural Affairs to unite Library-Museum, Historic Preservation, and Language and Culture staff under one office, and today the relationship between the Historical Committee and the Department of Cultural Affairs is still a collaborative one. Each unit within the department has a committee composed of community members that provides input to staff. The Historical Committee serves as that committee for the Library-Museum, which still houses the Mohican tribal library, archive, and museum and also serves as a meeting space for the Historical Committee and the Language and Culture Committee, both of which continue to meet monthly as of this writing.[49]

This book primarily focuses on the actions of the Mohican Historical Committee. However, their work frequently overlaps with that of the Language and Culture Committee, the Library-Museum staff, the Tribal Historic Preservation Office, and the Department of Cultural Affairs, especially in the early 2000s. I aim to be as specific as possible when discussing who is involved in various initiatives but want to emphasize that these groups frequently work together and are all the result of the Historical Committee's founding and early actions. As the work has grown, more individuals have taken on these efforts, and the Tribal Council has appropriately expanded the number of paid positions to assist with the work of recovering, reclaiming, and representing the history and culture of the Stockbridge-Munsee Mohican Nation. Each of these groups plays an important role in Mohican archival activism, and they all have been, or are at present, the tribally designated representatives of the Stockbridge-Munsee Community on various matters of tribal historical and cultural importance. Their work highlights the importance of this (often invisible) labor and the role of tribal archives in larger movements for Native self-determination.

Archives, Nation-Building, and the Production of History

In his introduction to the important anthology *Tribal Libraries, Archives, and Museums: Preserving Our Language, Memory and Lifeways,* former Institute of Museum and Library Services director Robert Sidney Martin gives what he admits are simple definitions of libraries, museums, and archives. Libraries constitute purposefully selected collections of documents, most of which are one of several copies. Museums are distinct in their collection of material culture, and archives assemble documents that "bear an organic relationship to an organization and contain evidence of transactions carried out by that organization."[50] Starting in the last quarter of the twentieth century, however, "the archive" has come to represent something much larger because of theorists like Jacques Derrida, Michel Foucault, and Michel-Rolph Trouillot, who connected the collection and preservation of historical knowledge to politics, memory, and power.[51] Indeed, Martin also encourages readers to expand our conception of documents to consider both how they can be "read" as material culture and how repositories that are not books or texts might still hold knowledge.[52] Materials such as wampum, winter counts, awikhigans (symbols written on trees and birch bark), oral histories, and the land itself can also serve as archives of knowledge and history.[53] The Mohican tribal archive is both a library and an archive by these definitions, in that it both collects copies of documents and original materials that pertain to Mohican history and serves as the official repository for original records that detail Mohican Tribal Council minutes, Historical Committee and Language and Culture meeting minutes, and other unique materials that were created by the Mohican Nation and "bear an organic relationship" to it. It also holds original documents created or kept by tribal members. Likewise, its material culture collections can be read as archival materials that preserve historical knowledge. Therefore, I refer to the collection of recorded knowledge—print, aural, and material—in the Arvid E. Miller Library-Museum collectively as the "Mohican tribal archive" and use "Arvid E. Miller Memorial Library-Museum" to refer to the building that houses this collection and serves as a meeting place for the Mohican Historical Committee.

Archives play a critical role in the construction of historical narratives, all of which contain some silences. As Trouillot outlines, these silences enter historical narratives at four "moments" within the production of history: the creation of sources, the assemblage of those sources in archives, the retrieval of those sources to create narratives, and the interpretation of those narratives that shape our collective understandings of history.[54] Archives play a critical role in these moments, and the repositories created *by* or *in tandem with* nations are especially critical in the development of shared understandings of national history and identity. Positioned as storehouses of a nation's past, they help shape the narratives that are ultimately used to foster shared national identities and histories that bind individuals together, a process that Stuart Hall describes as the construction of heritage.[55]

Within this book, I group nontribal national archives and those created in tandem with nation-states together as "settler-colonial archives" and define them as repositories whose collection, cataloging, access, or publication policies prioritize, or have historically prioritized, the history and belonging of white settlers and settler-colonial nation-states while subsuming Indigenous peoples into settler-centered frameworks. Importantly, this does not characterize all non-Native archives. Settler-colonial archives are specific in their current *or* historical exploitation of Indigenous knowledge and the incorporation of that knowledge into settler frameworks that ultimately aim to eliminate Indigenous contexts and protocols and detach this knowledge from living Indigenous people.[56] The processes of narrative, and ultimately heritage construction, that Trouillot and Hall highlight is applicable in the context of settler-colonial collections. Both theorists have rightfully argued that archives enable nation-states to silence certain voices and create stories that can be used to bolster settler-colonial nationalism. However, this book turns that premise on its head to ask, How are these nation-building processes different when the nations and national archives in question are those of sovereign Indigenous nations?[57]

Tribal archives, the national archives of Indigenous nations, and the projects that stem from them are also nation-building projects: they serve the tangible needs of tribal nations to house records, act as arsenals of knowledge that can be used to defend and exercise Native self-determination in various contexts, and create the conditions for the production of new narratives that (re)build a common sense of tribal history and belonging within Native communities.[58] Yet they differ from settler-colonial archives and nation-building in distinct ways. To grapple with these differences, I turn to Native American and Indigenous studies scholars Daniel Heath Justice and Lisa Brooks, both of whom argue that contemporary Indigenous nation-building is characterized in part by its opposition to settler-colonial policies, histories, and narratives. In Justice's words, Indigenous nation-building is "a necessary ethical response to the assimilationist directive of imperialist nation-states."[59] Justice articulates Indigenous nationhood through his "peoplehood matrix," the intersection of language, sacred history, ceremonial cycle, and place/territory. It is the reclamation and preservation of these elements in spite of the nation-state's efforts to destroy them that characterize Indigenous nation-building.[60] This does not mean that Indigenous sovereignty and nationhood do not predate colonization, but that as federal policies like removal, assimilation, allotment, termination, and relocation all sought to deconstruct Indigenous nations in one way or another, Indigenous nations were forced to reconstruct and rebuild to survive.[61] Following Ngugi wa' Thiong'o, who asserts that colonialism is a form of dismemberment, Brooks frames this opposition as the reconstruction or "re-memberment" of a communal body.[62] For the Mohicans and other tribal nations, archives have come to play a key role in these reclamation and rebuilding processes. These tribal archives collapse what are typically framed as sharp distinctions between state-controlled and community archives, serving as the official repositories of Indigenous nations while also challenging dominant narratives of the U.S. nation-state.

When the Historical Committee was founded in the 1970s, the Stockbridge-Munsee Mohican Nation was facing many challenges. The tribe had been forced to leave their homelands in the Northeast and was subsequently pushed out of several other locations throughout the Midwest. These removals and the market for Indigenous objects and manuscript materials among collectors led to the records of their tribal history being scattered across dozens of repositories. The federal government's policy of assimilation led to several generations of Mohican children attending Indian boarding schools, and because of the practices of these abusive institutions, knowledge of Munsee and Mohican languages, lifeways, and history had been significantly damaged. The attempted destruction of these elements of community meant that a shared sense of history and belonging—of heritage and nationhood—had to be rebuilt. Externally, narratives like James Fenimore Cooper's *The Last of the Mohicans* (1826) had rendered the tribe invisible to many. Museums and public history sites in Mohican homelands reinforced false narratives of disappearance, and public schools' curricula in Wisconsin ignored Indigenous history and sovereignty altogether. In this context, "re-memberment" is a particularly apt term for describing Mohican archival activism. As the Historical Committee began its work, they were both *re-membering,* directly responding to the dismemberment inherent in settler colonialism by returning to Mohican homelands and gathering stories and records that were scattered through colonization, and *remembering,* making sense of those records to craft new historical narratives that would both cultivate a shared sense of Mohican nationhood and challenge the widespread erasure of Mohican survival.

The larger context of settler-colonial violence and persistent invisibility required that the Historical Committee not merely harness the power of archives to intervene in the production of historical narratives but also ground their work in traditional Mohican practices of record keeping and actively undermine the colonial power used in the production of historical narratives. The committee was cognizant of the fact that accepting existing historical documentation without rereading, relying only on existing sources, and organizing their collection by colonial standards would only reproduce colonial silences. Likewise, they were aware, and had likely experienced firsthand, the exploitative nature of research in Native communities that dominated the disciplines of anthropology and history up to that point. Primary sources, scholars, and public history have long depicted Indigenous peoples as savage and uncivilized and extracted Native knowledge and cultural traditions from the contexts in which they belong. In reclaiming and recovering their histories, the Historical Committee also performed a shift whereby they became the researchers rather than the researched, and they reimagined the production of Stockbridge-Munsee Mohican history so that this exploitation and misrepresentation would not continue unhindered.

To do so, they harnessed the very moments where Trouillot argues silences enter historical narratives—the creation of sources, their assemblage, the retrieval of those sources to create narratives, and the impact those narratives have on our shared understandings of history. We see this immediately during the committee's early years in the 1970s; a 1978 list of goals highlights how these efforts overlapped and were interwoven with each other:

1. Follow-up on research leads; write letters, make phone calls, travel to places where the research is needed at libraries, historical societies, courthouses, etc.

2. Obtain documents, photographs, books, and/or copies of such which are pertinent to [the] library collection.

3. Continue to work on papers in present collection. Sort, catalog, code, and file. Collect and catalog records of current events: news-clippings, photographs, newsletter, tribal and community news. Work on additional materials obtained.

4. Oral histories: identify and contact people to interview; develop lead questions.

5. Plan programs (Historical and cultural) for public and schools. Develop written programs (seminars, workshops, speakers, filmstrips) for availability to local community, schools, other interested groups.

6. Purchase supplies needed: for preparation of displays and preservation of materials.

7. Purchase simple furniture: for development of public conversation area.

8. Continue work in preparing proposals in seeking funding.[63]

This list shows that the Historical Committee thought strategically not just about creating the Mohican tribal archive but mobilizing it to fundamentally change how Stockbridge-Munsee Mohican history was produced. As part of the Stockbridge-Munsee Historical Project, the committee created new sources (goal 4: creating new oral histories), changed the way sources were assembled (goals 1, 2, and 6: centralizing previously scattered materials so that they could be accessed and represented on Mohican land), shifted how the materials were retrieved (goal 3: reorganizing the collection around Mohican, rather than settler colonial history), and intervened in the creation and distribution of historical narratives (goals 5 and 7: new programs and materials, plus space for community members to cultivate further discussions). By intervening in the same moments where silences enter historical narratives, the Mohican Historical Committee contested the silencing of their history and fundamentally shifted the production of Stockbridge-Munsee history.

This is not to say that Indigenous nations are immune to silencing or marginalizing the voices of individuals or groups of people within their own nations, or that the new narratives created by Indigenous nations do not contain silences of any kind. All historical narratives contain silences of some sort, and the Mohican Nation, like any community, is not a monolithic group without political differences. However, these silences are not the focus of this manuscript. My aim is to highlight how the Historical Committee has collected materials and used them to produce new narratives that highlight Mohican nationhood and survival. Moreover, I am uninterested in classifying the centering of Native voices and stories and the marginalization of white voices as silencing. When we silence, or at least quiet, the deafening histories that center settler voices and stories, we evoke these Indigenous narratives that reshape our understanding of U.S. history.

The processes of *re-membering* (bringing the scattered pieces back together) and *remembering* (creating new and intervening in existing narratives) illustrate that while both settler-colonial archives and tribal archives can support processes of nation-building, these types of repositories are distinct. While settler-colonial archives were constructed in tandem with the founding of settler-colonial nation-states, tribal archives have had to be fortified and reconstructed through a process of recovery. Settler-colonial archives center settler histories and thereby support settler-colonial nationalism, while tribal archives work in opposition to these dominant narratives. Framing these collective efforts as distinctly activist highlights the fact that the tribe's new collection and projects work directly against historical settler-colonial policies, as well as contemporary settler-colonial practices in public history. Mohican resistance to these policies and practices is embodied in a type of Indigenous nation-building that aims to rebuild and reinforce a shared sense of tribal history and belonging, assert the tribe's sovereignty in various contexts, and contest ongoing invisibility in public history contexts and beyond.

Archival Activism in the Fight to Recover and Reclaim Native History

The late twentieth and early twenty-first centuries have seen unprecedented debates about who owns and has the right to represent Native cultures and histories, particularly within the context of public history. These debates have been punctuated by several major events, including the passage of the Native American Graves Protection and Repatriation Act (NAGPRA) in 1990 and the publication of the "Protocols for Native American Archival Materials" in 2007, but the Mohican story shows that the fights to reclaim Native history began much earlier than these major milestones and demonstrates the role that grassroots activism played in the lead up to these major changes at the turn of the century.

In fact, when the Mohican Historical Committee was founded in the aftermath of the 1968 house fire, Native activists across the United States were in the midst of a much larger movement for self-determination. Earlier in the decade, Native leaders had gathered at the 1961 American Indian Chicago Conference, which supported the development of inter-tribal coordination and resulted in the publication of the Declaration of Indian Purpose. The document emphasized "the inherent right of all people to retain spiritual and cultural values" and the importance of preserving Indigenous heritage.[64] Arvid Miller, along with Dorothy Davids and her father, Elmer Davids, all attended the event, along with future Historical Committee members Blanche Jacobs and Margaret Raasch. Reflecting on the conference in 2022, Miller's daughter Molly said the conference was "everything. They came home with a new understanding of the future. It was a reawakening."[65] It was with this renewed enthusiasm that Mohican leaders returned to their reservation, and when Miller's house caught fire seven years later, they were ready to spring into action.

After the Historical Committee was founded, they were further energized by national events happening within the Red Power movement and saw their work as a part of larger efforts for self-determination. Their meeting minutes often referenced events within the larger movement, and indeed, much of what was happening nationally aligned with their local efforts. Though Red Power is more commonly remembered for occupations like those at Alcatraz (1969–71) and Wounded Knee (1973) and marches like the Trail of Broken Treaties (1972), it also included significant attempts to change the way Native history was taught and written. For example, when they occupied Alcatraz, Native activists set up a school and included a request for a Native-run university among their demands.[66] In the late 1960s, the founding of tribally controlled community colleges and the first American Indian studies departments at universities provided new, often Native-led, spaces to learn and teach Native history. The creation of research centers for Native studies, such as the Center for American Indian and Indigenous Studies founded by Métis writer and activist D'Arcy McNickle in 1972 at the Newberry Library, aimed to intervene in colonial institutions and carve out space for Native people and scholarship that was more informed by Native communities. The Trail of Broken Treaties march culminated with activists breaking into and trashing the Bureau of Indian Affairs archives, a clear challenge to the power of settler-colonial collections. In 1972, activists within the American Indian

Movement founded "survival schools" in the Twin Cities, creating alternative spaces for Native children to learn Native culture and be engaged in community.[67] Later in the 1970s, the group Indians of All Tribes took on additional historical reclamation work in Oakland, launching an oral history project and working with the Oakland Museum of California and Oakland Public Schools to develop better programming and training.[68] In other words, Native activism in the latter half of the twentieth century extended far beyond the marches and occupations for which this era is typically remembered, and by attempting to recover and reclaim the materials and representations of their history, the Mohicans were taking part in a much larger movement for Native self-determination, much of which centered on the production and representation of Native history.

Similar attempts to change the production and distribution of historical narratives were also underway within other activist movements of the same era, including the civil rights and Black Power movements, the women's movement, and the fight for gay and lesbian liberation. As historian Lara Leigh Kelland argues, it was the synthesis of these fights that ultimately led to the emergence of public history as a discipline. Activists within these groups and within more local grassroots movements like that of the Historical Committee harnessed the methods that would later be embraced as a way to share stories with public audiences, and their early adoption of these strategies made their interventions in museums, archives, and other public sites more effective. However, their efforts also triggered conservative backlash that led to the subsequent birth of the "culture wars," where white men clung to the authority that they had always had over how history was produced and how it was represented in history curricula and cultural institutions like museums.[69] Still, this period saw unprecedented conversations and changes about who had the right to collect and represent history, and for Native communities in particular, the combination of grassroots activism and larger self-determination initiatives within the Red Power movement led to significant advancements in reclaiming Native peoples' right to collect and represent their own histories, especially within public history spaces like museums and archives.

The majority of these advancements came in the last quarter of the twentieth century, beginning with the 1978 "Preconference on Indian Library and Information Services On or Near Reservations," held at the White House. Author and activist Vine Deloria Jr. produced his "Right to Know" report for

the occasion, calling for specific services that would support tribal archives
and libraries and transform how records were cataloged on a national level.
Though the federal government chose not to implement his suggestions,
the Preconference helped found the American Indian Libraries Association
in 1979, and the report laid the groundwork for a National Endowment for
the Humanities (NEH) grant in the 1980s that supported the production of
John Fleckner's *Native American Archives: An Introduction*. This document
became a valuable resource for tribal archives being created and expanded
during this time.[70] The late 1980s also saw increased calls for non-Native
museums to return the hundreds of thousands of human remains and sacred
items that were stolen from Native communities. Sparked by Northern Cheyenne representatives who discovered that the Smithsonian held nearly 18,500
human remains, increased dialogue and activism around this issue eventually led to the passage of NAGPRA in 1990.[71] This landmark legislation
requires that all institutions that receive federal funds repatriate Native American human remains, associated and unassociated funerary objects, sacred
objects, and objects of cultural patrimony in their collections to "culturally
affiliated" Indian tribes and Native Hawaiian organizations.[72] It also requires
these same institutions to work with Indian tribes and Native Hawaiian organizations if Native American human remains, associated or unassociated
funerary objects, sacred objects, or objects of cultural patrimony are found
and/or removed from federal or tribal lands.[73] The creation of tribal libraries, archives, and museums peaked shortly after the passage of this law, as
many tribal nations needed spaces to house and display their recovered
items as well as support to assemble historical documentation to provide
evidence for repatriation cases.[74] NAGPRA requires that tribal nations provide evidence of their cultural affiliation with items, proof that they were
taken from the tribe without permission, and that they show they are culturally significant. This tangible need for historical records was a major factor in
the growth of tribal archives, and similar needs also spurred the creation
of tribal archives that occurred before this period. For the Mohicans, this
need came when the tribe was reorganizing under the IRA in the 1930s and
needed to consult historical maps and papers. Then in 1968, the same year as
Arvid Miller's death and the unrelated fire, a successful land claim required the
tribe to develop an official tribal roll, spurring the early organization of the
Millers' collection.[75] Other tribal nations started their repositories as they were
collecting materials for legal cases, especially in the wake of the passage, in

1953, of House Concurrent Resolution 108, which sought to eliminate the federal recognition of several tribal nations.[76] Tribes seeking to restore their federal recognition are required to assemble significant evidence proving their historical existence and relationship with the federal government, prompting the need to have ample historical evidence available for consultation and research.

As more tribal nations have developed their own archival repositories, debates over the right to house and represent Indigenous historical materials have extended beyond museums and the human remains and cultural objects they hold to settler-colonial research libraries and archives and the texts and knowledge contained within their collections.[77] This started with the creation of the Aboriginal and Torres Strait Islander Protocols for Libraries, Archives, and Information Services, which were published in 1995 by the Australian Library and Information Association.[78] Those protocols served as a model for the U.S.-based "Protocols for Native American Archival Materials," which has become one of the most widely cited documents to advocate for increased collaboration between tribal nations and settler-colonial archives.[79] The latter protocols were published by the group First Archivist Circle in 2007, an organization formed to promote collaboration among tribal and nontribal archivists, and have since been endorsed by the Society of American Archivists (SAA) and the Association for College and Research Libraries (ACRL), if only recently and after much debate and resistance. SAA only endorsed the protocols in 2018, followed by the ACRL in 2019, and as of this writing, most archives are still determining how and to what extent they will implement the practices.[80]

Still, the protocols provide best practices for both settler-colonial and tribal archives to help increase Indigenous peoples' access to documents that pertain to their history and improve the way Native history is represented in archival spaces. These efforts were further taken up by the formation in 2010 of the Association for Tribal Archives, Libraries, and Museums and the twenty-first-century movement around "data sovereignty," which asserts that Indigenous nations have the right to control the collection, access to, and distribution of data collection about, with, or by individual tribal nations. While initially framed to protect medical data in particular, the principles of data sovereignty have since been extended to include human remains, cultural objects, and the Indigenous knowledge contained within print sources through policy briefs and resources published by the U.S. Indigenous Data

Sovereignty Network, which was founded in 2001 and is housed at the University of Arizona.

This book is a history of the grassroots activism that led to these monumental shifts in the way Native history is collected and represented, told through the story of one community. The Mohican tribal archive is one among dozens of tribal archives that were created and expanded during the last quarter of the twentieth century, and as the work of the Mohican Historical Committee and the Department of Cultural Affairs demonstrates, these new collections have been consistently leveraged to support large-scale interventions in how Native history has been collected, taught, and represented on a national level ever since.[81] Indeed, the Mohican Nation is not alone in its efforts to reclaim access to and sovereignty over its historical materials or create new, Native-centered historical narratives. In the first quarter of the twenty-first century, the Chickasaw Nation founded Chickasaw.tv, a repository to document Chickasaw culture and traditions for future generations; the Citizen Potawatomi Nation initiated efforts to recover and share their history with the public; eight tribal nations collaborated with the University of Washington to form the Plateau Peoples' Project, a website that allows tribal members to re-describe and restrict public digital access to materials held by non-Native museums; the Eastern Shawnee Nation of Oklahoma received funding from the Administration for Native Americans for a recovery and rewriting project that has already resulted in a new published history; the Myaamia Nation worked with Miami University of Ohio to found the Myaamia Center, a campus-based project focused especially on centralizing archival records and revitalizing the Myaamia language; the Catawba Indian Nation is creating a community resource center that will consolidate library, archival, and material culture collections that have been dispersed across several locations; the Wyandotte Nation is crafting a new digital database that will compile primary sources from public and private archives; and the Hopi Tribe worked with the University of Arizona to publish two new volumes on Hopi history that reread and reinterpret Spanish materials with Hopi oral traditions and worldviews in mind.[82] These are only a few of many community-based history projects that have sought to recover and reclaim Native history.

The story of Mohican archival activism is not meant to speak for all of these diverse projects. Each tribal community approaches these interventions in the production of history in a distinct way. Rather, a close examination of the growth and strategic use of the Mohican tribal archive exemplifies what

Indigenous archival activism *can* include in practice and highlights the essential place of tribal archives within the larger movement for the reclamation of Native history and culture. While settler-colonial archives are still in the process of transforming their collections and evaluating to what extent they will collaborate with tribal nations, tribal archives and activists like those on the Mohican Historical Committee have already begun the work of extracting the materials relevant to them from these institutions and reassembling these materials in new, Indigenous-led repositories.

Methodology

In the context of debates about who has the right to represent Native history, positioning myself within this story and explaining my relationship to the Stockbridge-Munsee Community is particularly important. As a non-Mohican, non-Native historian, I am cognizant of the tension between *positioning* myself in relation to this work and *centering* myself in this narrative. I aim to do the former; this story is not about me, but I believe it is important to be transparent about how I came to this work and what the collaborative process of constructing this narrative looked like. Doing so not only gives due credit to the women on the Stockbridge-Munsee Historical Committee and in the Department of Cultural Affairs who have deeply influenced and contributed to this work, but also emphasizes the necessity of community collaboration in Native studies and the way tribal archives can play a positive role in this process. Still, this relationship was formed in a specific context, and the decisions I made in conversation with community members are not meant to be a portable template that can be adapted to any tribal nation. Each Native community's priorities and protocols for collaboration and the production of new research are distinct. Instead, I hope to emphasize the necessity of ongoing, reciprocal relationships between non-Native researchers and institutions and Native nations in order to produce both ethical and accurate scholarship.

I came to this project knowing little about the Stockbridge-Munsee Mohican Nation, in spite of having grown up in northeastern Wisconsin. In March 2010, when I was completing my undergraduate thesis at the University of Minnesota, I was introduced to members of the Historical Committee through a video series produced by the Library-Museum. The series, titled "We Are Still Here," was one of many efforts the tribe had initiated to contest the pervasive myth of Mohican disappearance popularized by James Fenimore Cooper's well-known novel, *The Last of the Mohicans*. That spring break and the following winter of 2011, I drove the seventy miles from my parents' home to the Library-Museum every day to watch videos within the series. I got to know staff in the Library-Museum, who encouraged me to also explore the archival materials in their collection. I continued visiting and exploring the archives over subsequent spring, summer, and winter breaks and was eventually invited to attend Historical Committee meetings. I met with the committee frequently to share my findings and research interests and asked for feedback on what research the tribe was interested in pursuing. After completing my undergraduate thesis, I became interested in pursuing a PhD. I presented my interests to the committee and asked for their feedback and permission to pursue this project. We worked together to consider how documenting the history of the committee and the Library-Museum would be useful to the tribe and what elements of the story would be most important to tell an accurate story. The Historical Committee reviewed my dissertation and this book in its entirety and was generous enough to write a foreword to the manuscript.

Forming this type of reciprocal relationship with a tribal community and respecting the specialized knowledge that they possess on their own history has become an important research practice within the field of Native American and Indigenous studies.[83] As researchers within this field, we are entering into contexts that have historically been rife with exploitation and misrepresentation, and working against these settler-colonial histories requires additional action to ensure that we are not contributing to settler-colonial practices or doing more harm. Asking for feedback and permission before publishing material is about recognizing the specialized knowledge that community members hold. It helps to ensure that the story I am telling is accurate, confirms that I am not unwittingly sharing culturally sensitive knowledge, and checks that, as a non-Native person, I have not misinterpreted information represented in historical records on which Mohican people undoubtedly have more information. Though the tribe has not requested it, I have also made the personal decision not to publish information about community politics or interpersonal conflicts that I have learned about while reading tribal archival records or been privy to in private conversations and community meetings. This is not a form of whitewashing, an effort to serve as a protector to the community, or a suggestion that this is a utopian or monolithic group without conflict. Instead, these details do not advance the stories I aim to tell, and I am attentive to my responsibilities as someone who has been invited into these spaces as a guest. I have made decisions about what information to share based on the trust that has been extended to me.[84]

In addition to shaping decisions about what to include in this narrative, my community-engaged methodology has also extended to my research itself. I have sought to rely as often as possible on sources created by the Mohicans themselves in order to center their agency and their voices in this story. Since the bulk of the archival materials I have relied on for this project are housed in the tribal archive on the Mohican reservation, my physical presence in this space has also facilitated countless conversations with tribal archivists and other Historical Committee members about details beyond the written record. Talking with these individuals and with others who have worked in the Library-Museum or within the Department of Cultural Affairs over the years has allowed me to capture details and experiences that were not formally recorded and archived. Working with the committee to define mutual goals, such as recording more formal oral histories, has also been a major outcome of this project. Together, and with input from the tribe's Legal Department, we created a process for oral history collection whereby I conducted oral histories of committee members but waived my copyright and filled out preemptive deed of gift forms to ensure that these recordings are ultimately deposited into and administered by the tribal archive. My role as a non-Mohican researcher working in the tribal archive exemplifies the power the archive has to facilitate collaboration and to shift authority over Mohican history and historical materials to the Mohican Nation.

Reciprocal, mutually beneficial relationships also lie at the heart of collaboration and community engagement. Prior to research trips beyond Wisconsin, I consulted with committee members about additional archives I could visit in the regions where I was traveling, and we collectively determined what additional materials I could scan for and return to the tribal archive. At the request of the Historical Committee, I have also worked to share the history of the Mohican Nation in various tribal and nontribal spaces, often as a co-presenter with a tribal member. More than a decade of collaborative work, ongoing conversations, and friendships have fundamentally shaped the community-driven narrative of this book.[85]

This close collaboration and relationship with the Stockbridge-Munsee Mohican community has enabled me to tell such a community-focused story.

Doing so allows me to demonstrate exactly how Indigenous archival projects can fuel significant changes in historical representations and new national narratives. Yet, I do not mean this to say that community engagement should be sought after because it provides a sort of unfettered access to a community from which data can then be extracted. This sort of exploitative thinking was all too common in the history of colonial research practices. Instead, I mean that, because of collaboration, this narrative is more accurate and is less likely to do harm. This book is more meaningful and useful to the community, it is more likely to do good, because community members were significantly involved in shaping, revising, and contributing to it as firsthand participants in the events about which I write. Community engagement should not be performative or sought because of the access it can provide to knowledge. It is simply ethical and produces better scholarship.

With that in mind, I hope that this book contributes to the growing tide of scholarship that centers Indigenous voices and perspectives and recognizes Indigenous expertise on tribal histories. My goal is that both its tracing of Indigenous engagements with public history and scholars and its reflections on my own methodology as a non-Native scholar can make a strong case for consultation and collaboration with Native nations within the scope of research and public history. Its spotlight on tribal interventions in collaborative projects with public history institutions and its detail of my own collaboration emphasize that community-engaged research must consist of an ongoing, reciprocal relationship with a tribal nation that adheres to their research policies and practices: it cannot be an afterthought or be determined solely on the non-Native researcher's or non-Native institution's terms. With these ethics in mind, I return to the story of Mohican archival activism.

Tracing Mohican Archival Activism

In many ways, this book is what historian Antoinette Burton calls an "archive story," in that it collectively seeks to tell the story of an archive's "provenance, its histories, its effect on its users, and above all, its power to shape all the narratives which are to be 'found' there."[86] *Indigenous Archival Activism* tells the story of the Mohican tribal archive and the historical projects that have come from it. In doing so, I show how Native nations use archives to change the way both Native and non-Native audiences understand and encounter Indigenous history and tribal sovereignty.

Focusing on different elements of Mohican archival activism, the chapters of this manuscript are laid out thematically rather than chronologically. I encourage readers to return to the timeline at the beginning of the book and use this as a guide for understanding how Historical Committee actions played out over time and connect to each other. The first two chapters of the book focus on the creation and expansion of the tribal archive on the Mohican reservation in Wisconsin. In chapter 1, "Indigenizing the Archive," I outline the founding years of the Historical Committee and tribal archive and examine the archive's official creation in 1972, as well as subsequent organization, management, and access policies, to show how tribal archives can challenge settler-colonial collections and archival practices. Expanding the archive also includes Historical Committee efforts to produce new primary sources that center tribal perspectives and attend to gaps in the existing historical record. The Mohican tribal archive and its expansion is an embodiment of tribal sovereignty at work, showing how Indigenous nations use archival repositories to increase access of materials to their citizens, claim control over the distribution of their historical materials, and thus shape how future narratives of Native history are constructed.

In chapter 2, "Mohican Oral History Projects," I address the expansion of the Mohican tribal archive through a series of tribally initiated oral history projects throughout the 1970s and in 1998, 2006, and 2009. Unlike many oral history projects that outside researchers initiate and then deposit in off-reservation archives, these oral histories were created by and for the tribe. Therefore, I argue that they shift how power is typically mediated in Indigenous oral history projects and that the assemblage of these interviews in the tribal archive further establishes the conditions for new narratives of Mohican nationhood and survival. When Indigenous nations shift the types of sources created and the materials that future researchers will look to, they change the production of future narratives about Indigenous peoples.

The second half of the book moves beyond the tribal archive to examine the mobilization of this repository, highlighting its use as a tool to shift the collection, production, and representation of Mohican history more broadly. Chapter 3, "Archives as Arsenals for Community Needs," examines how the Historical Committee has used the tribal archive for local narrative creation and reclamation efforts that primarily benefit tribal audiences. The growth of the archive went hand in hand with the community's production of its own secondary historical narratives and expanded in accordance with community needs in everything from land reclamation efforts to repatriation cases. This chapter profiles several of these efforts, including the first tribal newspaper, Mohican language revitalization, the 1991 and 2006 repatriations of a stolen two-volume Bible and Communion set, and the reclamation of Mohican land within reservation borders. In these efforts, the tribal archive serves as a readily accessible arsenal for evidence and information that can be shared with or used to directly benefit Stockbridge-Munsee community members. Each of these efforts supports Mohican nation-building and self-determination in unique ways, and the archive is an essential tool in these initiatives.

In chapter 4, "The Mohican Historical Trips," I trace ongoing Mohican returns to their ancestral homelands through which the Historical Committee teaches tribal history to tribal members through place, challenges misrepresentations of Mohican history, and asserts ongoing tribal connections to these sacred and important historical places. Reuniting tribal members with these historical landscapes fosters the formation of new collective memories and a sense of belonging among tribal members. Moreover, the trips reestablish long-standing ties to these places, directly opposing removal efforts and positioning the tribe to more directly intervene in the representations of its history in the Northeast. The archive is critical to planning for these trips and the interventions they enable, and these returns exemplify the types of historical projects that can grow from tribal archives.

My final chapter, "New Narratives for Public Audiences," examines Mohican interventions in various types of public education beyond the Mohican reservation, from education curriculum in public schools to museum exhibits in the Northeast. It also extends to the production of new public history projects that are aimed at external, in addition to tribal, audiences such as public walking tours and signage. Again, the archive is foundational for these efforts, which I argue embody a politics of self-representation whereby the tribe asserts its right to represent its own history. Through actions like these, Indigenous nations undermine narratives that locate the tribe's importance in the past and instead demonstrate Mohican survival and nationhood.

The fifty-plus years of multifaceted efforts that span these five chapters define Indigenous archival activism. They are overlapping and methodical, and collectively they demonstrate how tribal archives enable larger interventions in both academic and public-facing narratives. Moreover, the constant movement, labor, and resiliency these efforts require demonstrate how Indigenous peoples are reimagining archives that have long been characterized as colonial tools and why these ongoing efforts embody important types of Indigenous activism and nation-building.

In the Conclusion, "Indigenous Archival Activism beyond Tribal Archives," I outline the outstanding challenges that many tribal archives still face and emphasize the work that settler-colonial archives and other non-Native public history institutions must do to support the ongoing efforts by tribes to recover and reclaim their histories. I frame this analysis around the tenets of Indigenous archival activism—access, sovereignty, and narratives—to think about how these pillars might extend beyond tribal archives to provide a framework for action. Settler-colonial institutions must prioritize and facilitate Indigenous access to their existing collections, prioritize Native data sovereignty in revisions of their policies and protocols, and recognize that these shifts will lead to the production of new, Native-centered narratives that counter the settler-colonial histories their collections have undoubtedly supported. Highlighting how a handful of organizations and archives have begun to shift the way Native history is collected, accessed, and represented shows us what is possible, but also emphasizes the important work that remains.

1

Indigenizing the Archive

Those who are interested in the Stockbridge-Munsee Tribal Historical Project want to make certain that accurate historical information and authentic materials are collected by tribal members themselves and preserved within the tribal community for the use of tribal members now and in the future. They believe that, if such materials are made available to the tribe, more Stockbridge-Munsee people will study their own history and increase their pride in and understanding of their own cultural and historical tradition.

—Stockbridge-Munsee Mohican Historical Committee, Proposal for the Stockbridge-Munsee Historical Project, 1974

After the 1968 house fire in Bernice Miller's home, several of her friends and relatives worked together to form the Stockbridge-Munsee Historical Committee and began formulating a plan to continue the Millers' work of collecting historical materials from other archives and bringing copies of the items back to the reservation. Miller led this effort, collecting so much over the next three decades that friends nicknamed her "the Gatherer."[1] She recalled that "our goal was to gather everything about our tribe in one place," "every little thing, even if it's a receipt with one of our people's signatures on it . . . we're bringing them back to life."[2] Her daughter Sheila recalled this process in detail:

> Our collecting fever had begun. People brought in articles from their personal collections and started traveling and finding and bringing things together. Dorothy [Davids] and Ruth Gudinas searched Madison and invited others of us to come down and do the same. The summer youth kids helped in typing hard to read copies. . . . The Green Bay Agency papers were found on microfilm and we purchased them and several people took their turn reading and indexing references to Stockbridge. . . . The process of learning how to catalogue the materials began.[3]

As they gathered, Historical Committee members cataloged, transcribed, and organized the Millers' papers along with their new collection. Though many of these recovered materials were created by U.S. government officials or with the interests of the state in mind, the tribal archive provided an Indigenous space where Mohican people could reclaim the knowledge contained in these sources by reorganizing and reinterpreting them. The reclamation of these materials allowed the committee and eventually others to use these sources for new books, legal repatriation cases, revised curricular materials, and other types of new narratives that exemplify Indigenous survival and nationhood. Their efforts to reunite and reorient these materials around Mohican history

Figure 6. Bernice Miller (*left*) and Dorothy Davids (*right*) sort through archival records. Courtesy of the Stockbridge-Munsee Community, Cultural Affairs Department, Arvid E. Miller Library Museum.

work directly against settler-colonial archives that marginalize Native histories and bolster settler-colonial nationalism. In contrast, the Mohican tribal
archive has allowed the Stockbridge-Munsee community to both increase
tribal members' access to Indigenous knowledge and exercise data sovereignty: their right as a sovereign nation to determine how their historical
materials—data about their community—are retrieved. Together, these elements allow them to reconstruct the process by which narratives of Mohican
history and knowledge are produced.

After they officially opened the Library-Museum in 1974 and it was designated as the repository for the Stockbridge-Munsee Mohican Nation, the
committee set their sights on not just collecting but also conducting research,
creating new sources, reorganizing their collections, and creating new narratives of Stockbridge-Munsee Mohican history for both Native and non-Native
audiences.[4] While the rest of this monograph traces these interconnected
goals and how they stem from the tribal archive, this first chapter begins
with an examination of the formation, organization, and access and use policies of the Mohican tribal archive, as well as the creation of new written primary sources for the repository. Anchoring my analysis around access and
sovereignty—the first two pillars of Indigenous archival activism—I show why
tribal archives are such powerful tools in shifting the production of Native
history and how they serve as the nucleus from which the other aspects of
Indigenous archival activism emerge. Each section of this chapter takes up
a problem with settler-colonial archives and shows how tribal archives defy
the colonial methods through which Native history and knowledge have been
collected and produced. These efforts constitute an important form of Indigenous nation-building through which tribes create new shared national histories and identities.

Countering Settler-Colonial Silences and Erasure

In settler-colonial archives, Native voices can at times be missing or difficult to locate. Common sources for Indigenous history, such as surveillance
reports of Indian agents, the journals and travel narratives of early white settlers, and records of state institutions like Indian boarding schools, include
content *about* Native people but less frequently include their first-person
narratives. Instead, non-Native authors often used these sources to assert a
sense of superiority by casting Native people as savage or strange and often

centered the actions of white actors.[5] For instance, early settlers and traders often made detailed observations of Native knowledge, spirituality, and lifeways, but still insisted that Indigenous people had no history, law, or religion. Likewise, bureaucratic documents such as annual reports were designed to demonstrate the astuteness of white Indian agents more than anything else. While one agent leaving a reservation post might report success among a tribe in terms of cultivating crops and children attending school, the next agent might write of the backwardness of the same reservation, bemoaning the mess he or she inherited.[6] The representations of Native life in these sources often require reinterpretation, and though often present, Native voices are not immediately apparent. Records that do center Native knowledge, such as the notes or publications of anthropologists, must also be treated with caution. Native people had varying levels of agency in the creation of these sources, and while in some cases they acted as informants who made strategic choices about cultural knowledge to reveal to and be preserved by anthropologists, in other cases this knowledge was taken out of context and misrepresented by white authors.[7] Publications and writings by Native people themselves are not unheard of either, but they were less commonly collected, and as we will see in the case of Mohican leader Hendrick Aupaumut's writings, often archived within the collections of white leaders. In other words, while Native voices are not absent from settler-colonial archives, they are often difficult to locate or must be filtered through the writing and representations of white individuals.

In response, the Mohicans have long recognized the need not just to recover existing sources but also to create new, primary sources that center the experiences and knowledge of Native people. This began with early writers like Mohican historian and diplomat Hendrick Aupaumut. Born in 1757, Aupaumut was a Mohican leader who sought to carve out a space for his people and their relatives in the wake of white settlement.[8] His writings, including the 1790 "History of the Muh-he-con-nuck Indians" (published in full in 1854 by Electa Jones and in part prior to that in 1804 by the Massachusetts Historical Society) and the 1792 "Narratives of an Embassy to the Western Indians" (published by the Historical Society of Pennsylvania in 1827), record important details about early tribal history and relations with other tribal nations.[9] Aupaumut's narratives archived Mohican history and emphasized the importance of Native kinship protocols and Mohican lifeways, offsetting settler narratives from the same period that sought to emphasize American dominance.[10]

When they started the Historical Committee in 1968, Miller, Davids, and others also recognized that copying colonial sources and making them more accessible in the tribal archive was not enough. An uncritical use of these sources would only reproduce the existing silences around Mohican histories that were rampant in existing historical narratives. So in addition to copying materials verbatim, they began recording their own experiences to create new primary sources for future generations. For Miller, this mostly materialized in recording stories about her own life, histories she heard from others, and stories about others like her father and husband. Her archival collection includes stories with titles such as "Story of my home," "Story about Pa—his life" and "Story of Red Springs." Miller was also intentional about documenting the Historical Committee's actions, writing narratives like her own account of the tribe's fight for a Bible and Communion set that was stolen and sold to a museum in the Northeast, as well as her memories of the processes of searching for family histories and descendants, with narratives titled "Story of Planning and Having Library-Museum Grand Opening" and "Story of search for descendants of Henry Davids."[11] Writing these stories was such a significant part of her life that she often listed stories to write in the future on pieces of paper like her grocery lists, adding reminders to herself to write the story of "AE [Arvid E. Miller] death & the fire" next to "cough drops and oven cleaner."[12] She archived all of her writing in what would become her own collection, which includes four different folders titled "Notes, Ideas, Plans," and other collections of her own narratives. In doing so, she ensured future readers would not only have information about family histories and traditions, but also firsthand accounts of the Mohicans' fight to recover and reclaim their history. Such a practice suggests that she considered these activist efforts a vital part of Mohican tribal history and nation-building. If, as Foucault argues, the archive is the means by which statements become events and things, Miller was recording what she thought should become an important part of tribal history, what was important enough to be remembered by future generations, and asserting her right to tell that story.[13] In her traditional role as a Mohican woman, she was also acting as a caretaker, gathering, recording, and rewriting the history of her people for future generations in coordination with the other women of the Mohican Historical Committee.

Miller's sister and Historical Committee cofounder, Dorothy Davids, also recorded her own memories and stories in new primary sources, but in a

much more public venue: a long-standing column in the Mohican tribal newspaper titled "Rambling through History with Dot Davids." Davids regularly
used the space to reflect on her own life, write stories of community members who were traveling or had passed on, and update readers on current
Historical Committee projects. She wrote about turning points in her own
life: when she first attended a National Congress of American Indians (NCAI)
meeting in Chicago; when she decided to quit her teaching job to work for
NCAI executive director Helen Peterson; when her father lost their family
land because the bank refused to let him make payments on his mortgage,
forcing him to sell his beautiful lake property instead.[14] As Davids remembered, the bank told her father "We don't want your money Elmer, we want
your land."[15]

She also recounted childhood memories of churning butter, tapping maple
trees for syrup and sugar, and attending the government school on the reservation, sharing these stories with the community and using the memories
to educate readers about tribal history. In these sources, Davids recorded
some of the same topics that anthropologists documented in the early twentieth century: plant medicines, cultural practices, and community stories.
But as we see in her story about tag alder bark tea in Figure 7, this information was woven together with other details about family, Native food-
ways, and comical personal memories. These details counter the extractive
nature through which non-Native researchers and authors have long presented Native people. For example, a 1933 entry about the same plant (also
known as speckled alder) in an ethnobotany of the nearby Forest Potawatomi community notes that juice from the inner bark is used to treat itchi-
ness and that tea brewed from the bark is also used to stop the discharge
of fluids. Noted as part of the birch family alongside its Latin name, *Alnus
incana*, it is listed as having emetic and astringent properties.[16] The entry is
straightforward but sterile. Unlike her story about the same plant, it is dis-
connected from living people and specific places. In contrast, Davids connects the collection of tag alder bark to specific places and people. Since she
was writing for a tribal audience, we can assume her reference to "the" rather
than "a" swale from which the bark was collected is a low, marshy place familiar to other community members. Her memory also notes a specific time of
year for collection (spring) and states that her father collected the bark while
her mother brewed the tea. She also ties the use of the plant to the larger
context of Big Lake, a place on the northeastern side of the reservation, and

WHAT'S SO FUNNY?

If laughter is the best medicine, how come I have so many pills to take every day? In my youth, we rarely took pills. We had medicine, though. Every spring Pa would go down to the swale and get tag alder bark which Ma would brew into a tea -- a spring tonic she said -- to clean all the winter sickness out of our systems. We kids had to drink a whole glass of this concoction which was so bitter it would drive the devil out of anything. Sometimes I wish we could find some tag alder trees again.

This brings back memories of life on Big Lake. Pa built a small raft for us kids who practically lived on the lake, skating in the winter time (the old clamp on skates), and swimming and fishing in the summer. I remember one time when Deedee (Marion) and I were fishing just a short distance off shore. We were about eight and ten years old. All of a sudden Deedee yelled, "I've got one; I've got one." I watched her struggling with her pole thinking she was probably just caught in the weeds. Then, peering over the edge of the raft, she said, "It's a big one." I leapt up and stepped to her side of the raft upsetting its balance. Into the water we both went, bait can and all with Deedee screaming so loud that Pa came rushing from the garden. He waded out to the raft and grabbed Marion and pulled her in. She had never let go of her fish pole on which was hooked a huge black bass, not quite as large as Pa's which filled the bottom of the dishpan but enough so that we had fish for supper. I rescued the raft and pulled it to shore. We still laugh at the catastrophic time when Deedee almost lost her fish.

After the Lutheran Indian Mission closed its boarding school, in 1933 I think, we attended Lakeside school. This meant about a mile and a half walk every morning –except, we cut through our cow pasture, across Aunt Wildie's field, through the barbed wire fence and across Koonz' cow pasture Thereby cutting off a half mile or so. Even so, I was tardy 143 times out of 180 days of the school year. I remember one day I came puffing into the building, hung my coat in the hall and stepped into the classroom. Everybody laughed and pointed. I looked down to discover that I had forgotten to put on my skirt. There I stood red-faced in my flour sack petticoat. Needless to say, I rushed home again.

Figure 7. An example of one of Davids's many "Rambling" columns. Courtesy of the Stockbridge-Munsee Community, Cultural Affairs Department, Arvid E. Miller Library Museum.

to other food sources like black bass that tribal members depended on. Told alongside another story about falling into the lake, followed by another about forgetting to put on her skirt for school, this alternative primary source counters more common ethnobotany sources in settler-colonial repositories by grounding plant medicines within specific tribal contexts and threading memories of family, joy, and laughter together.

Davids wrote about contemporary topics, too, indicating her excitement in doing historical research but also her frustrations. She explained how difficult it was for the Mohicans to be constantly in the process of recovering elements of their national tribal identity and how frustrating it was when white authors asked the Historical Committee for feedback but then failed to take their suggestions. She wrote about her relatives after they passed on, narrating the kinship webs they were connected to and the parts of the community they touched with their lives. She wrote about traveling to Mohican homelands, living through federal policies like relocation, and always shared her political opinions with readers, critiquing global capitalism as it was connected to development projects such as mining in northern Wisconsin in 2012.[17] As so many storytellers do, Davids used her column to "connect the past with the future, one generation with the other, the land with the people, and the people with the story."[18]

Both she and Miller created new primary accounts of their own memories, and the Historical Committee would continue this work by leading several tribal oral history projects over the next forty years. As Historical Committee member Jo Ann Schendler explained, the existence of the tribal archive has also made community members more comfortable contributing their own family history research and photographs they have in personal collections: "In the past, when you didn't have the computers and copy machines people were reluctant, I think, to leave things, but the Library-Museum, with having the ability to go to people's home or just make a copy for them and give them their pictures right away, I think there's more sharing."[19] Tribal member Jolene Bowman agreed, noting that "everyone relies on it [the Library-Museum], and the community has confidence that it's being secured in the correct manner."[20]

Recording the memories, stories, and voices of tribal members works directly against the erasure or appropriation of Indigenous voices that is typical in settler-colonial archives. Unlike materials that were created by white settlers or extracted from Native contexts by anthropologists, these new sources center the voices and experiences of tribal members. Within tribal archives, they are arranged in the context of tribal histories. In creating and depositing these materials, community members have flipped the common trajectory of outsiders coming into Native communities and extracting research, and they have fundamentally shifted the sources that are available to those researching Stockbridge-Munsee Mohican history in this space. These new sources and their organization in the tribal archive redefine the important moments, turning points, people, and places in Mohican history—they contribute to the reconstruction of a shared Stockbridge-Munsee Mohican heritage and nationhood.

Prioritizing Access: Recovering Mohican Sources

As the Mohicans began their process of recovering archival materials, one of the biggest barriers they faced was the geographic distance between their reservation and the materials related to them. In part, this is due to what Kimberly Christen calls the "colonial collecting project," whereby Indigenous materials and knowledge were removed from Indigenous nations, compiled by collectors, and scattered across the globe, where they are separated from the contexts from which they came.[21] This has worsened with the privatization and professionalization of modern archives, as materials are more commonly bought and sold, scattering them across the United States and beyond.[22] Removal of Indigenous nations from their homelands is also a major factor in this geographic scattering of records. Since the Mohicans were forced to leave their ancestral homelands in the Mahicannituck (Hudson) River Valley, most of the archives that hold and continue to collect records about their homelands and lives are more than a thousand miles away from their current Wisconsin location. Likewise, because the tribe was forced to move seven different times before arriving at their current reservation, archival records about these movements and the tribe in each of these places are in repositories in not only Massachusetts, Connecticut, New Hampshire, and New York but also Pennsylvania, Ohio, Indiana, Illinois, and Wisconsin. Others ended up in even more distant federal repositories in Virginia, Utah, and Oklahoma because of colonial collecting practices, as well as the removal of Mohican children to distant boarding schools. In total, I have identified fifty-five archives with Mohican materials across ten states (Map 1).

Map 1. A map of archives that contain materials related to Stockbridge-Munsee Mohican history.

Traveling to these vastly distant archival locations is not possible for most individual Mohicans. The trips are time-consuming and expensive, and they can be overwhelming for anyone without prior knowledge of these archival collections. Indeed, even with the collective efforts of the Historical Committee, the process of collecting these materials has taken an enormous amount of labor over nearly fifty years and is still underway. As a result, the Historical Committee, and Arvid and Bernice Miller before them, identified proximity to the Stockbridge-Munsee reservation in Wisconsin and to tribal members as a key factor in access when they started collecting. The committee often used this rationale in their grant writing, noting in one 1974 proposal that "until a safe place is provided and a coding system set up, the study and circulation of tribal materials cannot begin, and Stockbridge-Munsee history will continue to be scattered here and there—usually out of the reach of the Stockbridge-Munsee people themselves."[23]

However, it is worth noting that this is not the case for every tribe, especially as digital sharing and access has become more common. For example, the Miami Tribe of Oklahoma's collaborative Myaamia Center at Miami University in Ohio has become the main repository of Myaamia materials for the tribe. Though physically distant from most tribal members, the archive resides within tribal homelands, and the tribal nation sees the center as the "research arm" of its community.[24] Other tribal nations have prioritized digital collections and access to serve tribal citizens who do not live on the reservation and to expedite sharing among archives and tribes. Unlike when the Mohicans started collecting, digitization is now a standard part of most archives' and libraries' work. So, while many tribal members still travel to archives or work with archivists to photograph or scan materials manually, there are often large batches of materials that have already been professionally digitized and can easily be shared. The 2007 creation of the content management system Mukurtu, which allows tribes to arrange, add content about, and restrict digital access to archival records and material culture from several different repositories, has also supported increased interest in digital sharing.[25] The descriptions created by tribally designated representatives often challenge and correct settler-colonial assumptions about items and correct terminology and context for the materials, ultimately assisting community members with finding items related to their histories and ensuring that all researchers have access to accurate descriptions and terminology.[26]

The gathering of previously scattered records in one place is also a significant element of access. As Historical Committee members emphasized in one 1986 grant application, "Prior to the establishment of our facility, there was no one place that one could go to research and piece together this information."[27] The Mohican tribal archive offers a single, local repository for these historical materials, producing conditions where Mohican tribal members can "piece together" the relationships that have always been present between these documents, thereby strengthening tribal members' sense of identity and belonging within the nation and supporting the creation of new Mohican-centered narratives that challenge myths of disappearance. Reflecting on one of her own ancestor's letters, scholar Alice Te Punga Somerville writes: "The letter can be read by itself, on its own terms, but it is

richer—and indeed it is only visible—when considered within the world" of
other related photographs, letters, telegrams, institutional records, and family memories.[28] In the same way, every letter, photograph, treaty, map, or
journal the Mohicans recover from settler-colonial archives can be read on
its own, but these materials are much richer, and indeed only fully visible,
within the world of the other materials of the Stockbridge-Munsee Mohican
Nation in their own national archive. Somerville further emphasizes that
although archival materials may be physically scattered in various archival
locations, records of an Indigenous people's history are and have always
been connected by the fact that they document the nation's presence. It is
the Mohicans' mobility between these archival collections over the last century that calls attention to the intimacy among these historical sources that
has been there since their creation.[29] The connections Historical Committee
members recognize between these documents and the way they reorganized
the materials in a new archive on Indigenous land allow us to see these materials in new ways.

Once they overcome the physical difficulty of traveling to different archives,
the Mohicans and other tribal nations face additional hurdles to gain access
to, locate, and research materials related to their histories *within* collections.
This begins with basic access policies at some repositories regarding who
can enter archives, what credentials they may need, and the protocols they
must follow to do research. For example, Dorothy Davids recounted one
archival trip to the William Henry Smith Memorial Library at the Indiana
Historical Society in Indianapolis in the early 1990s, when committee members encountered "tight restrictions on the use of primary source materials."
Davids lamented that "the reproduction of most items was not allowed, forcing us to waste precious time taking lengthy notes in pencil."[30] In another
instance, Sheila Miller remembered that when she and another Historical
Committee member arrived at the Onondaga County Library in Syracuse,
New York, to look at a specific set of records, the archivist "found someone
to watch us, while she went up in the archives and came down with several storage boxes, put them on the table in front of us, and said we couldn't
look at them without making an appointment!" She and the other committee member had to make an appointment for the following afternoon and
then return to look at the materials. Again, they were not allowed to make
copies and had to copy everything by hand.[31] Miller and others encountered an even stranger regulation on a different trip to the Indiana Historical

Society, where at that time researchers were only allowed to copy one-third of any single document. She remembers that she and the others "discussed the possibility of each copying a different third and ending up with the entire article." This demonstrated, as she called it, "Indian ingenuity!"[32] Even at other institutions where making copies was allowed, Historical Committee members were usually required to pay for copies of many of the collections they were interested in, something they were not able to do consistently on a budget funded by aluminum can sales and grant funding.[33]

In reflecting on her experience working for the Pointe-au-Chien and Isle de Jean Charles Band of the Biloxi-Chitmacha Confederation of Muskogees in their battle for federal recognition, literary scholar Courtney Rivard describes similar barriers. She notes that her status as a doctoral student enabled her to secure research funding to travel to various archives across the country that others would not have access to, while her experience as a historical researcher enabled her to access and navigate immense collections. While these barriers are not insurmountable for researchers outside of the academy, others are. Rivard detailed the extensive paperwork process required at some archives, such as the Huntington Library, where she was required to complete an application detailing her reasons for research and prove she had advanced to doctoral candidacy by providing a letter of verification from her university and dissertation adviser. The Huntington application for independent scholars not affiliated with universities was even more extensive, requiring individuals to detail their previous research, published works, and other archives consulted, as well as provide two "letters of reference from scholars in good standing who are familiar with [their] research and can attest to [their] need for access to the Huntington collections."[34] Even less-obtrusive barriers like heightened security, sterile spaces designed for solitary work, and requirements to provide government-issued ID cards can make Indigenous researchers feel unwelcome in settler-colonial archives.[35] These measures can feel intimidating if one has not spent significant time in an archive, discouraging access to the collections and at times even entry into the space.

If they are able and feel comfortable gaining entry to and using an archival repository, tribal historians often face additional challenges in navigating the vast collections because of the way that settler-colonial collections have been organized and cataloged. In the vast majority of archives, the principle of *respect des fonds* dictates that collections of archival records are grouped by the entity from which they were received and kept in their original order. For Indigenous materials, this means that records are typically grouped with others that a particular collector assembled and embedded in subfolders of the white settlers they interacted with or the records of important places where they were observed (depending on how the collector organized the material). Likewise, Indigenous knowledge or stories that were extracted from communities are often attributed to their white collectors rather than the individuals or nations to whom the information belongs. Therefore, knowing who or what you are looking for in these archives is usually not enough unless you also know what other actors or significant events they interfaced with or where and how they would have been recorded.[36] While in some cases the summaries or subject headings of these collections mention tribes, others do not, making it difficult to determine where to start looking. As a result, research on the history of Indigenous nations typically means assembling what Shayne Del Cohen calls "a cast of characters" or a "chronology of given and place names of people who interacted with the tribe and/or the geographic sites involved in the tribe's evolution."[37] In many cases this goes even further, requiring tribal members to "operate within the colonialist, racist logic . . . to choose search terms that yield desirable documents."[38]

For example, the Historical Committee has mined the collections of John Sergeant Sr. at Harvard and Dartmouth Universities; Jonathan Edwards at Yale's Beinecke Library; Lawrence Lynch and Silas Whitney at the Stockbridge Library in Stockbridge, Massachusetts; Franz Boas and Frank Speck at the American Philosophical Society; and Timothy Pickering at the Massachusetts Historical Society, among many others. While many of the collection descriptions for these men's papers include mention of "Stockbridge Indians" in a keyword or subject heading, finding aids vary in their usefulness for pinpointing the location of relevant material. Historical Committee members still have to sort through the vast collections to find relevant materials, then scan those pages and bring them back to the Mohican tribal archive where they can be reorganized within the collections that center Mohican history.

In other cases, collection or item summaries fail to include anything about the Mohicans, so knowing that a collection or item may have relevant information requires specific knowledge and research about these historical figures. For example, the collection summary for Jonathan Edwards's papers does not include a reference to the Mohicans at Stockbridge, let alone Native people in general. The only clue that the collection houses relevant materials to the Mohicans is the Library of Congress subject heading "Indians of North America—Missions—Massachusetts." In research I completed for the Historical Committee I have also spent hours sifting through the collections of white men like Jasper Parrish, an Indian agent in upstate New York, journalist Elmo Scott Watson, and collector Edward E. Ayer.[39] While the committee had asked me to help locate information about the tribe's removal from their New York homelands in Parrish's collection, for example, I came up with only traces of tribal members by mention of their names among larger lists.

While for non-Indigenous researchers like me this process is merely difficult and mundane, for Indigenous researchers this process can be retraumatizing. Finding these records and expediting the research process often requires operating in a colonialist mind-set, whereby Indigenous researchers must imagine how and why their ancestors would have been surveilled or recorded in colonial records. Conducting this type of research requires not only reviewing thousands of irrelevant materials to find a few relevant ones but also reckoning with how one's ancestors were racialized, removed, and murdered in the interest of advancing white society, and confronting what are at times horrific pasts.[40] Settler-colonial archives are not typically equipped to support researchers who are responding to historical trauma. The spaces are typically solitary and sterile, and there are seldom places where researchers can go to decompress, use traditional medicine like burning sage, or be given resources for trauma support.[41] Much of what I have outlined above is difficult to change. Archives require security, cold temperatures, and clean spaces to protect materials, and collections are often organized by donors or primary authors according to principles within archival theory. Due to space limitations, fewer subject headings were applied to collection items when libraries still used physical card catalogs, and many institutions have not re-cataloged materials, even though digital catalogs do not present the same issue. I outline these issues not to label settler-colonial archives as irredeemable but rather to consider what might be reshaped in the future and, more important, to highlight the alternative spaces that tribal archives offer. Settler-colonial archives can do a great deal to make spaces more accessible for Indigenous researchers, but tribal archives offer necessary spaces that are created by and designed for Indigenous researchers and counter many of the challenges in settler-colonial institutions.

Reshaping Access in the Tribal Archive

Confronting the access barriers I have outlined and ensuring they were not replicated in the tribal archive was a major part of the Historical Committee's early work. Before their research could begin, the committee assembled their own "cast of characters." They made lists of important people and places, identified possible locations of materials, and wrote letters to countless archives asking for information, such as a 1973 letter from Bernice Miller explaining, "I am searching for information about the Stockbridge Indians . . . do you have census rolls or land transactions or birth dates or marriage or death records? Who should I contact to find this information? Are there other historical groups I could contact? Can you help me?"[42] Once they located relevant collections, they applied for countless grants, raised thousands of dollars by collecting aluminum cans, and used personal savings to fund their trips.[43] Likewise, they built long-term relationships with archivists who work within their ancestral homelands and could assist with the process of locating and copying materials within their own and nearby archives, as well as wrote to authors who had researched Mohican history and asked them to donate their papers to the tribal archive.[44] Once they arrived at various repositories, the Mohicans searched through thousands of documents that were largely created by white men, reading them completely and then extracting and copying what was relevant to their tribe and reassembling that material on the Mohican reservation, where it can readily be accessed by tribal members without appointments, letters of recommendations, or specific credentials.

Many of the materials the Mohicans have copied are in larger collections or items that group multiple tribes together. For example, the missionary journals of John Sergeant Jr., which are held by Dartmouth College, have been copied by the Historical Committee and made available for research in the tribal archive. John Sergeant Jr. was one of the missionaries who led the Christian mission at Stockbridge, which the Mohicans agreed to have established in their village Wnahktukuk in 1735. Sergeant Jr. followed his father, John Sergeant Sr., who founded the mission and kept a journal that recorded his activities for semiannual reports for the "Society in Scotland for propagating Christian knowledge."[45] The text contains vital records like baptisms and funerals that are useful for locating tribal names, as well as correspondence. However, because it covers the period when the Mohicans were forced to move farther north into New York with the Oneida Nation, not everything in its pages is relevant to Mohican history. This means that merely copying

Sergeant Jr.'s entire journal and making it available to community members on the reservation would still leave tribal researchers with much data mining to do. Much like other items created by early settlers, Sergeant Jr.'s journal also contains several speeches and letters of Mohican leaders like Hendrick Aupaumut. In its current location at Dartmouth College, the finding aid does not credit, let alone mention, Aupaumut or others, making it difficult for those interested in him to find this item. To address these issues in this and other similarly vast collections, the Historical Committee has created indexes to accompany certain items or collections, carefully noting the page numbers that point to significant moments in and information about Stockbridge-Munsee Mohican history. These indexes allow community members to skip to sections of an item that are most relevant to their history, as well as credit Indigenous leaders with the words they penned that have become embedded in other collections. In the archive's current form, which researchers access digitally on one of two public computers, indexes like these typically appear as a single document within a larger digital folder for the collection that contains other subfolders in addition to the index.

Prior to the digitization and migration of the collection into the archival softwares Laserfiche and PastPerfect, which began around 2005, Historical Committee members sorted materials by topic and cross referenced related files and topics on three-by-five index cards.[46] As Leah Miller remembered, "that was before computers, so everything was done on a typewriter or by hand and picking up catalog cards and putting them in a little drawer."[47] The committee was also intentional about involving the broader community in this sorting process. In 1980, when they created the library's first catalog with grant funding from the National Endowment for the Humanities, they provided community members with stipends to read and annotate historical items. The cataloging team met for monthly sessions to share their findings, and as Sheila Miller and Dorothy Davids wrote in the catalog's introduction, "patterns and pictures began to form from the fragments of history on our shelves and in our files."[48]

By locating these materials and reassembling the documents in their own Indigenous archive, the Mohicans and other tribal nations can also be purposeful about reorganizing materials in the context of their community knowledge, not only making them easier for tribal members to find but also ensuring they are most appropriately placed within the context of other, like materials. During this time, Historical Committee members took part in some

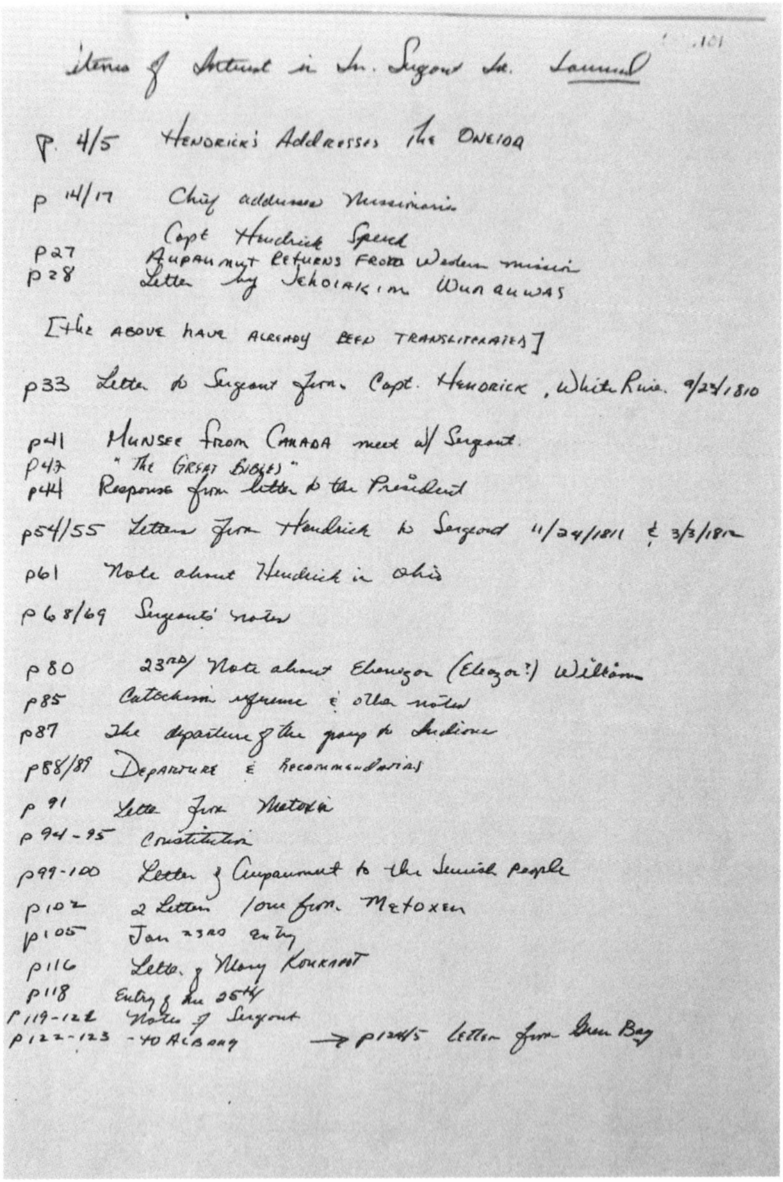

Figure 8. An index of "items of interest in John Sergeant Jr.'s journal," one of several guides created to help tribal members and other researchers readily locate information about Mohican history within larger primary sources. Courtesy of the Stockbridge-Munsee Community, Cultural Affairs Department, Arvid E. Miller Library Museum.

Figure 9. Historical Committee member Sheila Miller uses a microfilm reader to sort through archival papers and organize files. In the bottom-left corner, the three-by-five index filing system the committee initially used to organize and cross-reference each archival file is visible. Courtesy of the Stockbridge-Munsee Community, Cultural Affairs Department, Arvid E. Miller Library Museum.

cataloging and archival trainings, but they relied on their own instincts to determine what organizational methods would be most useful for their fellow community members.[49] Some tribes like the Mashantucket Pequot have even gone beyond purposeful organization tactics by taking aim at larger classification systems like the Library of Congress Subject Headings, which are at best not Native-centered and often erase Native histories and sovereignty, and are at worst outright offensive.[50] Through their Thesaurus of American Indian Terminology Project, the Mashantucket Pequot Nation has created a sourcebook of over twenty thousand terms, including an additional twelve thousand terms describing tribal names. The guide has been used to rewrite narratives in public history spaces like museums as well as to modify archival classification systems in order to better reflect Indigenous worldviews by using consistent vocabulary.[51]

Other Indigenous groups have created similar guides, such as the Maori Subject Headings Thesaurus, the Aboriginal and Torres Strait Islander Thesaurus, the National Indian Law Library Thesaurus, and the First Nations

House of Learning Thesaurus, which include Indigenous communities and are more reflective of Native worldviews. In the 1970s, librarian Brian Deer also created his own classification systems for two collections, one at the National Indian Brotherhood and the other for the Union of British Columbia Indian Chiefs. Though limited in scope to the geographies in which these two collections are situated, other archives with similar collection scope, such as the X̱wi7x̱wa Library at the University of British Columbia and the Cree Cultural Institute, have adopted this system.[52] While the Stockbridge-Munsee Mohicans have not yet created such a comprehensive guide or, to my knowledge, pushed specific archives to reclassify or rename collections pertinent to their history, they choose not to use Library of Congress Subject Headings, or any kind of subject headings for that matter, to classify their materials. Instead, archival materials are accessed through Laserfiche or PastPerfect software, and users can either search by keyword or sort through folders and subfolders that are listed within each collection. Searching by keyword is similar to how one might search for materials in a standard online library catalog but made much more effective by the fact that many of the materials have been transcribed, so search results are based on both these transcriptions and the names of individual files. Alternatively, users can search manually through folders, as one might in a typical archive. All of the folders and subfolders the archive contains are listed and appear like standard computer files within Laserfiche. Users can click through them and explore their content based on their interests.

The majority of these folders are sorted and named for people and families, elevating community voices and perspectives and reinforcing Native knowledge systems and kinship. Important tribal leaders such as Arvid E. Miller, Bernice Miller, and Dorothy Davids have their own collections, and an entire collection of "People Files" holds folders for dozens of other tribal members. Individuals' personal papers that they collected can often be found in these collections, as can the records of different tribal affairs they may have been involved in or things that are related to or about them. For example, if one was interested in learning about termination, they would need to know who the tribal leaders were during this time in order to know that most of the records about termination are held in the Arvid E. Miller Collection. In my own research, I have found that though there is a folder dedicated to the Historical Committee, the vast majority of materials about the formation of the Library-Museum and subsequent historical projects are filed in the Bernice Miller and Dorothy Davids Collections. In other words, knowledge of who was involved in certain aspects of tribal history is often necessary to navigate these collections, making clear that the collection centers Mohican history and is especially geared to tribal members.

This format is also especially relevant to tribal members who are interested in their own family histories. Since the digitization of the materials began in the early 2000s, more than a dozen other tribal members have been involved in the organization and accessioning of materials. As they sorted and labeled materials, tribal members like Jessica Boyd and Stephanie Bowman were able to identify materials related to their own families and share items with others. Boyd located photographs of her great-grandfather dancing, while Bowman was able to locate photos of family members she never had a chance to meet, like her grandmother, who died of scarlet fever when Bowman's mother was a child.[53] Reflecting on the experience, Bowman said, "It was amazing. I kinda teared up a little bit when I saw them [the photographs]. I couldn't believe that my great-grandmother, great-grandfather, great-aunt, great-uncle . . . I had always heard but I never knew. It put everything in perspective for that side of the family."[54] Carlton Stevens, whose wife is a tribal member, emphasized that sorting the materials allowed him to better understand "the closeness of people and the relationships of people together." He elaborated, "You see people whose grandparents are in photos talking to the grandparents of these other people you know in the community, and you know those families are still that close together."[55] These kinship webs are evident to those living in the community and make these materials a rich resource for tribal audiences.

Though organizing archival collections by individuals is not uncommon in non-Native archival processing systems, Native actors are rarely given their own collections in settler-colonial repositories, because their materials and writings are typically grouped by provenance or by the collector who assembled the materials. In contrast, the tribal archive privileges people over provenance by grouping materials collected by *and* about individuals under their collection or folder. This approach highlights the importance of Native leaders, and the notes about family connections throughout exemplify and annotate the webs of kinship within the community. Assembling these documents in a way that is rooted in relationships is an Indigenous type of archival activism because it connects materials and knowledge that have been separated due to settler colonialism and makes space for new Indigenous narratives. In turn, recognition of these kinship networks influences the histories both Mohicans and non-Mohicans read in and write using the tribal archive.

Beyond family connections, placing materials within the context of other, like items from an Indigenous perspective may also encourage researchers to better understand historical people and actions and work against the problem of attribution in colonial collections. For example, if we return to the records of Hendrick Aupaumut, we see that his writing and words appear in his own published work at the Historical Society of Pennsylvania, in the journals of missionaries John Sergeant Sr.'s (stored at Harvard University) and John Sergeant Jr. (stored at Dartmouth College), throughout the papers of U.S. emissary Timothy Pickering (at the Massachusetts Historical Society), within papers related to Mohawk leader Joseph Brant in the Lyman Copeland Draper Manuscript Collection (at the State Historical Society of Wisconsin), and within the writing of Electa Jones (published and available at several libraries, including the Newberry Library). Separated across these archives and mostly stored within the papers of others, Aupaumut's words and actions are difficult to find and piece together. While his name appears in the finding aids of some collections, such as Sergeant Sr.'s journal, it is absent from others, such as Electa Jones's narrative, the description of John Sergeant Jr.'s journal, and the guides to the Pickering and Draper papers. Searching by Aupaumut's name in the Massachusetts Historical Society's online catalog (where the Pickering papers are held) yields only two results, one of which is inaccurately labeled under the subject heading "*Mohegan* language texts," and neither of which is the Pickering papers or the *Collections of the Massachusetts Historical Society* volumes, which both include his writing.[56] This is a common challenge in most archives, as it is impossible to list every person and place that is mentioned in a collection. Yet best practices in archival processing do suggest noting significant historical figures, especially when they have authored something like a speech, narrative, or letter within a collection. Unfortunately, this practice is not always extended to Indigenous leaders like Aupaumut whose words and actions were so often archived within the papers of white leaders. Tribal archives allow Native nations to extract relevant information about their relatives from these larger collections, reorganize previously separated papers in a new space that centers Native actors, and credit these Native writers and orators for their words that have long been archived within the works of or attributed to white actors.

The new Hendrick Aupaumut collection in the Stockbridge-Munsee Mohican tribal archive includes copies of materials harvested from Harvard, the Massachusetts Historical Society, the Historical Society of Pennsylvania, and the State Historical Society of Wisconsin, as well as published letters to Aupaumut from Thomas Jefferson and Henry Knox. It places previously separated reports, letters, and narratives authored by and about Aupaumut together for the first time, allowing us to connect his actions as a tribal historian who was responsible for recording the history of the Stockbridge-Munsee Mohican people, and as a tribal leader who aimed to foster peace while still carving out independent Native space, even as he and the other Stockbridge-Munsee Mohicans were forced to move west.[57] The collection also includes new materials that provide further context for Aupaumut's actions, such as secondary sources that have been written about him, and information about how he is remembered today, such as photos of and articles related to a historical marker in Kaukauna, Wisconsin, near where Aupaumut is believed to be buried, and a letter regarding his recognition as a Revolutionary War hero. The copied documents from other archives are also accompanied by a handwritten family tree visually mapping Aupaumut's family and a biographical note presumably written by one of the tribal historians or archivists. This assemblage of materials could only have been gathered by Mohican tribal members who know Aupaumut as their own kin. The information they have gathered about him and the way they chose to organize, describe, and make this information accessible allows those who access the archive to understand Aupaumut in a new way that places him firmly within Stockbridge-Munsee Mohican history and identity—rather than on the margins of the white leaders' collections, where the original copies of many of his papers reside.

The recovery and intentional reorganization of historical papers like these also allows those accessing the archive to understand Mohican actions across time and to create new narratives that connect different Mohican leaders to each other. For example, how might the placement of Aupaumut's narratives in the Mohican tribal archive, among the writings of other Mohican writers, yield new histories about centuries of Mohican place-making and writing history? As a former record keeper of the Stockbridge-Munsee Mohican Nation, what does it mean to have his writing and recordings of Mohican history in the same space as those of more recent Historical Committee members who have carried on this tradition? How might Mohican leader John Quinney's speech about land theft and the U.S. federal government's dishonesty, which can be found within Historical Committee founder Dorothy "Dot" Davids's collection, elucidate a longer history of Mohican resistance when placed in the same collection that testifies to Davids's continued activist work? Positioned adjacent to each other in the archive as they are now, how might Arvid and Bernice Miller's new narratives about Mohican lives and histories reveal the beginnings of this archival activist movement?

Arranged within an Indigenous archive that exemplifies kinship ties and networks as important pieces of Indigenous histories, these documents, and thus tribal archives as new assemblages of knowledge, hold the potential to inform new narratives of Indigenous history. By assembling the tribal archive in a way that centers Indigenous voices and perspectives, Historical Committee members push back against the common reality of Indigenous materials being archived within larger collections that focus on white settlers. They change the process of constructing historical narratives about their nation by making these sources more accessible to tribal members and asserting control over how the records of their history are assembled; in doing so, they create a distinctly Mohican archive.

The recovery of these materials from settler-colonial archives and their assemblage in Mohican space is also an important part of Stockbridge-Munsee nation-building efforts. Much as in settler-colonial archives, the organization and assemblage of archival materials identifies the important people, places, and events that inform the production of historical narratives and collective memory. Yet again, these nation-building efforts are not equivalent. Tribal archives are created by gathering and reassembling stories, records, and pieces of Indigenous history that are scattered across multiple archives due to removal, assimilation, and other settler-colonial policies, a process that has never been necessary for settler-colonial archives. The construction of the Mohican tribal archive is a way of re-membering Mohican communal history and bringing pieces of Mohican identity back together, one that allows Mohican tribal members to enrich their identities as Mohican people and see themselves within the national story of the Mohican Nation.

Exercising Sovereignty over Access to and Use of Indigenous Knowledge

The extraction of Indigenous knowledge and its placement in settler-colonial archives has also made it difficult to protect sacred or sensitive knowledge that was recorded and removed from Native communities, often without permission from tribal members. Much of this is the result of intentional campaigns to collect Native culture that have been ongoing since the colonial era. For example, religious leader Roger Williams led efforts in the seventeenth century to collect and publish Indigenous languages, traditions, and spiritual practices, and Jonathan Edwards Jr., who spent time with the Mohicans as a child and later after they were forced to leave Stockbridge, engaged in what he called "acquisition" practices, researching and recording Indigenous linguistic data.[58] Thomas Jefferson continued this practice, encouraging others to join him.[59] In his 1785 *Notes on the State of Virginia,* Jefferson called on scholars to "collect their [Indigenous peoples'] traditions, laws, customs, languages, and other circumstances which might lead to a discovery of their relation with one another or descent from other nations."[60] With this directive, and other sections of the text, he propelled what was then considered "scientific inquiry" into racial difference between people in the Americas, and a long tradition of non-Native scholars studying Native people and collecting their languages, cultural items, and traditions, and even their bodies. Moreover, he named libraries as important places to engage with this information.

These extractive practices continued throughout the nineteenth century and peaked in the late nineteenth and early twentieth centuries, in the midst of larger projects of scientific racism like social Darwinism that aimed to order and control nonwhite bodies. At its height, anthropologists, archaeologists, and the academic institutions that supported their endeavors traveled to Native communities to record, collect, and at times outright steal Native knowledge, objects, and human remains.[61] Today these efforts are collectively known as "salvage anthropology," and we know that most of these collectors and academics were primarily motivated by their desire to "preserve" the Native cultures and languages they erroneously thought were disappearing. While these academics and collectors may have had what they considered admirable aims, as Shawnee Second Chief Benjamin J. Barnes argues, these individuals "were not interested in preserving the material for our [Native peoples'] latter generations; rather they published their research with very little context or input from the communities from which they reaped their information."[62] In doing so, they exposed sacred and sensitive information, such as that related to funerary or religious customs, that was never meant to be shared beyond tribal communities or outside the context of particular cultural protocols. Today this information is still held in settler-colonial archives, made available in academic libraries, and in some cases, widely published online. The content is rarely covered under traditional all-rights-reserved copyright or Creative Commons due to their failure to recognize third-party ownership and communal property. Moreover, as the copyright on many items expires in tandem with the increasing popularity of digitization, more and more of this content is in the public domain and readily available to the public.[63]

Many original archival materials related to Native people still remain in settler-colonial archives, and though many institutions are beginning to work directly with tribal nations to implement policies and protocols for these items, these changes are recent. In most non-Native repositories, tribal nations still have little control over how culturally sensitive materials are accessed or used, so tribal archives again provide an immediate alternative. In most cases original copies of items remain in settler-colonial collections, but Indigenous nations can assert some level of control over the access and use of *copies* of these materials and hope that as their collections grow, more researchers will travel to and prioritize conducting their research at tribally run repositories.

To address how these materials are used in their collections, many tribes, including the Mohicans, have also created policies to hinder the further production of inaccurate historical narratives or the unauthorized circulation of Native knowledge, as well as committees that can review new research and publications.[64] The Arvid E. Miller Library-Museum policy is not unlike standard policies found in many settler-colonial archives. It outlines the role of archivists in supervising the use and circulation of materials and explains the reciprocal responsibilities of the researcher, noting that the Library-Museum allows access to its collection only "with an understanding that researchers will seek permission to publish substantial portions of materials that they are permitted to use, whether copyright to those materials is owned by the Library-Museum or by someone else."[65] While consultation with the Historical Committee is not required as a part of this policy, I have found that it is usually a natural outcome of an outside researcher coming to the reservation and working in the archive.

When you enter the Library-Museum, you are immediately required to consult with an archivist. For one, the previously mentioned organizational emphasis on people and families requires some consultation with tribal archivists who can help direct you to what you are looking for. But also, the archive is only made available to non-staff researchers on one of two password-protected computers in the lobby of the building, a high-traffic area where anonymity is not possible for outside researchers like me. In my own experience working in this space, the days are filled with casual conversations with the tribal archivists as they go about their daily work, collective discussions about interesting materials I or they may find throughout the day, and the regular flow of people coming in and out of the Library-Museum, a communal space where people drop in to ask questions, share information, or just visit. As people enter the building, they often stop to visit with me as they walk past my usual spot at the computer. They ask me who I am, where I am from, and what I am doing research on during my visit.

Many of these individuals are members of the Historical Committee who are invested in the production of accurate tribal histories and want to build relationships with researchers to ensure that they produce accurate narratives. Therefore, committee members often inform researchers about Historical Committee meetings, which have long served as a place to connect Native and non-Native scholars with community members and ensure that research projects are being shaped by community knowledge and are not perpetuating common misrepresentations of Mohican history and life. This is how I was first invited to a meeting, and evidence of similar interactions is clear in Historical Committee meeting minutes and through conversations with other researchers I have met at Historical Committee meetings. In other words, conducting research in a tribal archive creates several opportunities for conversations and consultations with tribal members. These reciprocal relationships are an intentional product of a Native-run archival space. Many other tribal nations take a more formal approach by creating tribal IRB (institutional review board) protocols and/or different types of research review groups to protect their data sovereignty. Elder review boards, research councils, and cultural committees like the Historical Committee are often delegated by the Tribal Council to review research proposals and publications.[66]

But policies and review boards can only go so far. None of the policies or protocols outlined above are legally binding, and Indigenous data sovereignty is still an emerging concept in most fields. This is where collating archival materials from dozens of different repositories can play a significant role not just with access, but with sovereignty. By collecting historical items from vast archival locations and consolidating them into a single collection, the Mohican Nation has created "the most complete collection of information about the Mohican People that exists," and the collection also includes materials that are not available elsewhere, such as Tribal Council and Historical Committee meeting minutes and the personal collections of tribal members.[67] The unique assemblage of these and other sources makes the Arvid E. Miller Library-Museum an essential archival destination for those studying and writing Mohican history, and thus increases the chances that non-Mohican researchers will travel to the tribal archive to conduct their research *on* the reservation and *in consultation with* tribal archivists, rather than in multiple national, state, and private archives over which the tribe has no control.

Over the years, the Historical Committee has also used the impressive nature of the collection to rightfully position themselves as experts on their own tribal histories and encourage both researchers and institutions to work directly with them. For example, in 1981, Dorothy Davids wrote a letter to historian Patrick Frazier, informing him that "it has come to our attention that you have written a book about the Stockbridge-Munsee Indians. . . . We know that you have the vast resources of the Library of Congress at your disposal, but you may be interested to know that our Tribal Historical Library has books, booklets, tapes, microfilm, maps, personal journals, tribal documents, etc."[68] In doing so, Davids emphasized that Frazier's research was likely incomplete without the vast materials held in the Mohican tribal archive, as well as consultation with the Mohican peoples themselves, and invited him to form a relationship with the tribe.

The Historical Committee also published and circulated the NEH-funded catalog of the archive's holdings in 1980 through Muh-he-con-neew Press, the publishing arm of the Historical Committee. The catalog includes an overview of Mohican history that starts with a paragraph about the historians and record keepers in the tribe who had long "carried in their memories the traditions, the legends, the ceremonies, [and] the significant events in the lives of the People." It goes on to explain that while Hendrick Aupaumut committed these oral histories to writing, his words soon "passed from Indian hands," and the "fur traders, the missionaries, the schoolteachers, and Indian agents recorded their version of the history of the Mohicans." It continues by detailing how the Historical Committee was formed and how it had gone on to collect materials from several different archival repositories, establishing the Mohican people as the experts on their history since time immemorial.[69]

The remainder of the catalog is similar to those created by settler-colonial repositories in many respects. It includes a list of materials sorted by type of item (articles, audiotape, books, government documents, maps, microfilm, journals, periodicals, etc.), and each item has a complete bibliographic entry. Most also have a description of what kind of information readers will find in each source. The catalog differs in one very significant respect, however. In addition to the details already outlined, many catalog entries include commentary added by Historical Committee members about the validity of the sources and their merit. An 1845 account of the Stockbridge-Munsee by Thomas Allen is described as "slightly biased," while further down the page, Hendrick Aupaumut's "A Narrative of an Embassy to the Western Indians" is "recommended reading."[70] Some sources like John Quinney and Hendrick Aupaumut's *The Assembly's Shorter Catechism* have more specific guidance: "this rare book is an excellent primary source for those studying the Mahican language," while others include more detailed critiques: "reflects eighteenth century stereotypes of Indians."[71] In the catalog's introduction, the Historical Committee explained their choice to annotate these sources:

> We realized, however, that some of the materials present a balanced, positive, and authentic history of the Stockbridge-Munsee People, while others reflect limited or stereotyped perspectives. We decided therefore to include brief evaluative statements here and there to guide and/or challenge researchers. Our hope is that inquiring minds will pose their own theses, research thoroughly, and share their findings with the Stockbridge-Munsee Historical Committee.[72]

While less frequently used in today's digital world, this catalog was distributed to researchers visiting the Mohican tribal archive in person throughout the late twentieth century and is still available for consultation today. The Historical Committee also sent copies to researchers like Patrick Frazier to encourage them to travel to the reservation and to assert the committee's expertise on their own tribal history.

In many cases, this strategy worked. More and more researchers did start to travel to the reservation to conduct research, and using the archive to position the Historical Committee as experts worked especially well for relationships with public history institutions. Unfortunately, others were not convinced. In his response to Dorothy Davids, Frazier admitted that he had not communicated with the tribe since 1977 (four years prior) but that he "got the impression that the tribe at that time did not have any material relevant to the period I've covered in my manuscript." He wrote that he "felt unable to

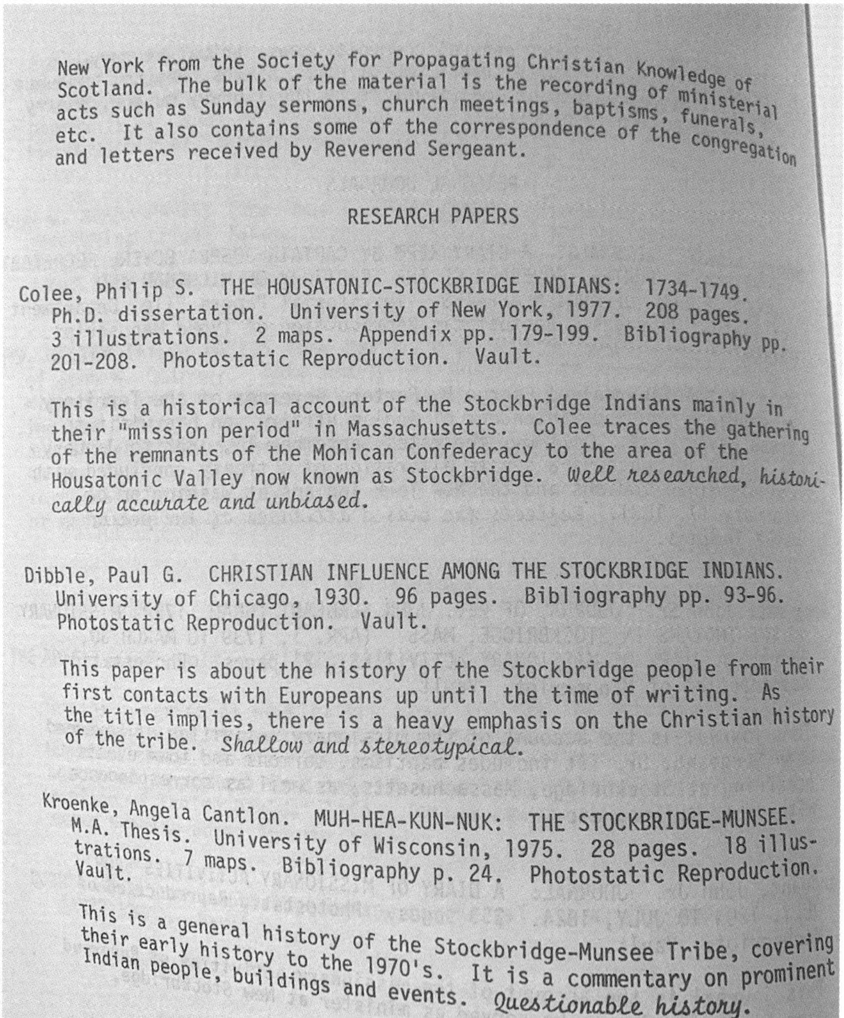

New York from the Society for Propagating Christian Knowledge of Scotland. The bulk of the material is the recording of ministerial acts such as Sunday sermons, church meetings, baptisms, funerals, etc. It also contains some of the correspondence of the congregation and letters received by Reverend Sergeant.

RESEARCH PAPERS

Colee, Philip S. THE HOUSATONIC-STOCKBRIDGE INDIANS: 1734-1749. Ph.D. dissertation. University of New York, 1977. 208 pages. 3 illustrations. 2 maps. Appendix pp. 179-199. Bibliography pp. 201-208. Photostatic Reproduction. Vault.

This is a historical account of the Stockbridge Indians mainly in their "mission period" in Massachusetts. Colee traces the gathering of the remnants of the Mohican Confederacy to the area of the Housatonic Valley now known as Stockbridge. *Well researched, historically accurate and unbiased.*

Dibble, Paul G. CHRISTIAN INFLUENCE AMONG THE STOCKBRIDGE INDIANS. University of Chicago, 1930. 96 pages. Bibliography pp. 93-96. Photostatic Reproduction. Vault.

This paper is about the history of the Stockbridge people from their first contacts with Europeans up until the time of writing. As the title implies, there is a heavy emphasis on the Christian history of the tribe. *Shallow and stereotypical.*

Kroenke, Angela Cantlon. MUH-HEA-KUN-NUK: THE STOCKBRIDGE-MUNSEE. M.A. Thesis. University of Wisconsin, 1975. 28 pages. 18 illustrations. 7 maps. Bibliography p. 24. Photostatic Reproduction. Vault.

This is a general history of the Stockbridge-Munsee Tribe, covering their early history to the 1970's. It is a commentary on prominent Indian people, buildings and events. *Questionable history.*

Figure 10. A page from the 1980 "Catalog of Materials" that the Historical Committee created for the Mohican tribal archive. Comments from catalogers appear in cursive directly after the item description. Courtesy of the Stockbridge-Munsee Historical Committee.

make a trip to Wisconsin" but that "the intense involvement with the research has given me a feeling of closeness to the tribe, even though I have never met any of its members." In spite of his refusal to consult with tribal members themselves, he did not hesitate to ask that the Historical Committee take the time to "Xerox and send to me any relevant pages from your new catalog."[73]

Certainly, research practices have changed since Frazier was writing in the 1980s, and we can hope that similar correspondence would be met differently today. Still, his response highlights how difficult it can still be for tribes to assert complete authority over their histories. Like Frazier, numerous non-Mohican scholars have written, and continue to write, Mohican histories without working directly with the Mohican Nation. As Dorothy Davids remarked, even those who do come to the reservation are often surprised to learn something from tribal members themselves. In one of her regular newspaper columns, she observed that often scholars "come to help and discover that we are the ones who can help them." Referring to one encounter specifically, she noted that "they didn't seem to be aware of our resources, but we shared a lot of history."[74]

These sorts of encounters and the frequent correspondence between Historical Committee members and non-Native authors shows that in addition to the labor of assembling the archive, the Mohicans have consistently had to publicize their collection and advocate for their role as authorities on their own history. For many researchers, tribal archives are still seen as being outside the realm of historical research or not worthy of their time. The Mohicans and other tribal nations continue to combat these assumptions, and as the collection of the Stockbridge-Munsee Library-Museum continues to grow, there is hope that more and more researchers will travel to the Mohican reservation, giving the Mohican Nation increased control over the production of historical narratives about Mohican people, history, and culture.

Digitization and web-based collections also have the potential to both help and hinder Indigenous data sovereignty. Given the large amount of Native culturally sensitive material and knowledge that is already available online, the Mohicans, like many other tribal nations, have strategically decided not to make the digitized archival materials within the scope of their tribal archive openly accessible on the internet.[75] Though it does not prevent other archival repositories from digitizing and sharing Mohican knowledge, it does encourage researchers who want to use the unique tribal collections to physically travel to the Mohican reservation to consult with Mohican tribal archivists, fulfilling one of the Historical Committee's long-held goals, that "people seeking information are referred to us [the tribe] more than we refer them to others."[76]

However, many tribal nations have begun to reconsider the rejection of web-based collections as archival content management systems that allow tribes to digitize but still restrict access or assign cultural protocols to materials become available. For example, Mukurtu, a content management system that enables tribal nations to rearrange and add their own descriptions to digitized materials, also allows tribal nations to restrict access to digital content based on certain protocols. Tribes can designate digitized items as only available to tribal members, or design specific restrictions around things like gender-based tribal protocols.[77] Other digital tools, like those within the Local Context project, allow Indigenous communities to add additional culturally specific agreements to materials they already hold the copyright for or traditional knowledge (TK) labels to materials that have already been digitized and for which tribal nations do not hold copyright.[78] While they are not legally binding, TK labels help Native communities communicate the context in which the digitized information should be used, such as only for noncommercial use, only during a certain season, or only within communities. They can be assigned in tribes' own digital collections or added to the catalogs and digital sites of settler-colonial archives in consultation with tribal nations. Though a label cannot physically prevent someone from viewing culturally sensitive or sacred information or images, it can warn tribal members before they view something that violates cultural protocols and encourage all others to reconsider viewing and/or further publishing something that is culturally sensitive.[79] These tools harness the power that digitization has to make geographically disparate materials more accessible to tribal nations without further exposing culturally sensitive materials to the broader public, and I expect we will only continue to see the increased use of digital tools in the wake of the Covid-19 pandemic. While the Mohicans have not yet created their own digital collection of materials, the pandemic did prompt them to utilize other digital tools to share their histories, such as Zoom and Facebook.

The creation of the tribal archive is at the core of Mohican archival activism. It is the space from which the Historical Committee and subsequent employees in the Library-Museum and Department of Cultural Affairs can increase access to information for tribal members and enact data sovereignty over how the materials are used by others to create narratives. As we will see in subsequent chapters, both moves have enabled and shaped the production of a wide array of new narratives. However, they also have the immediate impact of contributing to a shared sense of history, belonging, and identity among community members. Assembling a new collection that identified important people, places, and events in Mohican history contributes to a shared sense of heritage among community members that assimilation sought to destroy. Providing access to these materials and encouraging their use in tribal contexts is an important element of Mohican nation-building that aims to provide stories that define Mohican nationhood and bring the pieces of Mohican history back together to "re-member" the Mohican Nation. Moreover, the reorganization of the materials and increased engagement with non-Native scholars and institutions unearths Mohican voices and perspectives to combat erasure and resist settler-colonial ways of organizing, distributing, and representing Indigenous history and knowledge.

As we will see throughout the remainder of this book, the tribal archive serves as a repository from which new narratives can emerge and as an arsenal that tribal members can draw from as they work to regain land, recover items that were stolen and placed in museums, revitalize language and culture, and reclaim the authority to serve as experts on their own stories in public history spaces. It is the nucleus from which Mohican archival activism grows and spreads. And yet, as they collected, the Historical Committee recognized that the information recorded in the settler record could only take them so far—these colonial materials could never completely capture Native experiences, voices, and knowledge in the same way that sources created by Native people for future generations could. The Historical Committee recognized that the creation of new Mohican-centered narratives required the creation of new Mohican-centered sources, so in addition to new written primary sources, they turned to collecting new oral histories to expand the record base from which new narratives would be created. As we will see in the next chapter, these new oral histories are a vital part of the new Mohican tribal archive, and they play a critical role in the Historical Committee's larger efforts to change the production of their history.

2

Mohican Oral History Projects

Besides entertaining us, stories can instruct us, inspire us, and pass on our culture. I can think of no better way to demonstrate this than by telling a story.

—Theresa Puskarenko, former director of the Department of Education and Cultural Affairs, *Stories of Our Elders*, 1999

Settler-colonial archives have ample records that contain Indigenous subjects, but few that were produced by or adequately reflect the perspectives of Native people. This documentary record has served as the foundation for the production of historical narratives about the United States, and, unsurprisingly, has led to misrepresentations and outright erasure of Native peoples from dominant narratives. Oral history is uniquely suited to address this uneven coverage, and as a result, many tribal nations (along with other racialized and marginalized communities) have turned to oral history projects as a tool not only to preserve the knowledge of their citizens but also to counter the lack of Indigenous-centered sources within settler-colonial archives and enhance the sources that are present.[1] For these reasons, and because of the centrality of orality and storytelling within Indigenous cultures, its unsurprising that in addition to collecting existing archival sources and writing down personal experiences, the Mohican Historical Committee identified conducting oral histories as one of their first priorities after its founding and the initiation of the Stockbridge-Munsee Historical Project in the early 1970s. Recognizing that there was vital information that had never been recorded in the documents they were collecting from traditional archives, and that not everyone would be interested in recording their own memoirs by hand, they knew they had to create new oral sources before they or others could construct more accurate and complete narratives of Mohican history.

This identified need materialized in dozens of oral histories collected between the 1970s and early 2000s, all of which are now available in the Arvid E. Miller Library-Museum. The Historical Committee began conducting informal oral interviews with tribal elders in the 1970s, but the majority of interviews were collected in two formal projects, the first between 1998 and 2006 and the second between 2006 and 2009.[2] The first project, "Memoir-izing Our Mohican Lives: Elders Write Their Stories," was initially structured around a weeklong workshop in 1998 that was meant to record the histories of elders but also involve younger generations of students, who ultimately gathered stories using tape recorders, transcribed the materials, and constructed the final narratives. The tribe later printed these narratives as a series in *Mohican News,* the tribal newspaper, and in 1999 the collection was published by the Historical Committee's publishing company, Muh-he-con-neew Press, as *Stories of Our Elders,* in coordination with the tribe's Department of Education and Cultural Affairs. More interviews with elders were completed in 2006, and a second edition of the volume was created in 2010.[3]

The Historical Committee's most extensive oral history project is the *Hear Our Stories* video series, a compilation of thirty-eight interview videos, each between ninety minutes and two hours in length, recorded over three years and released in June 2009.[4] Unlike other projects meant to be transcribed and reproduced in writing, the video series was always intended to remain in its visual form so that audiences would not only read Mohican histories but see and hear them communicated by Mohican elders, a unique format that more effectively captures the affective elements of storytelling that are less visible in written and even aural documentation. The series as a whole contains nearly sixty hours of film and includes videos of forty-one elders discussing their lives as well as their views on tribal culture, history, and the future of the Mohican Nation.[5] When the series was released in 2009, the Historical Committee also used it as a way to cultivate community conversations and celebrations of elders' lives. The videos were screened weekly at the Arvid E. Miller Library-Museum, where we can imagine that community members likely not only watched the videos but also shared their own related stories and memories in a group setting. In their description of the series, the tribe stated, "the years that our Elders live hold stories of wisdom, experience, advice and humor. It is very important for our People that these stories will be carried on to the next generations."[6] Given the extensive nature of this project, this chapter primarily examines *Hear Our Stories* to reveal the potential that oral history projects such as these hold.

While these projects enlist elements of Western oral histories, such as scripted questions and planned taping sessions, they are distinct from most existing academic oral history projects with Native communities in three ways. First and foremost, they were created by and for community members within the Stockbridge-Munsee Mohican Nation. In standard academic projects, when a researcher is entering a community, the scholar who is conducting the interviews holds significant power regarding who will be interviewed, what the interview questions will be, and what information is being sought. After the interview, the scholar determines how the content of an interview is used to construct a historical narrative. As literary scholar Alessandro Portelli states, those being interviewed "speak *to* the historian, *with* the historian and, inasmuch as the material is published, *through* the historian."[7] Second, like the new written sources that Bernice Miller, Dorothy Davids, and others created for the archive, these new oral primary sources preserve knowledge and first-person narratives of Native people in the twentieth century that are not recorded elsewhere. Finally, unlike most academic oral histories that are extracted from communities and deposited elsewhere, these stories are preserved in the Mohican tribal archive, remaining in the community contexts from which they originated. This chapter considers how the standard power dynamics of oral history collection shift when Indigenous community members initiate or maintain control over their own oral history projects and how that shift affects access to and use of these new sources in the production of historical narratives.

The tribally led creation of new oral sources has played a critical role in all three pillars of Indigenous archival activism. In terms of access, the Historical Committee's oral history projects are fundamentally about preserving knowledge and making it accessible to future generations. The committee aimed to gather and preserve knowledge from dozens of tribal members, not just the tribal historians whose memories and stories are more readily represented in written archival materials, and was intentional about involving youth in the process of recording so that these histories would be more readily learned by future generations and support the cultivation of a shared sense of tribal identity and belonging. In the context of tribal sovereignty, the creation of new historical sources within a tribally led process aims to shift the very foundation of the production of Mohican historical narratives. The fact that these projects were produced by and for Mohican citizens ensures that the tribe can exercise data sovereignty over how these sources are accessed and used and enables the creation of sources that counter silences within settler-colonial archives and challenge narratives of disappearance. Finally, having more available sources that center Mohican perspectives ultimately increases the chances that those constructing new narratives about Stockbridge-Munsee history will rely on these instead of (or at least in addition to) sources created by non-Native authors. Focusing on both the methodology and content of the Historical Committee's two major oral history projects, this chapter outlines why the preservation of oral histories is ultimately about providing greater community access to tribal knowledge, how a tribally controlled process can yield sources that respond to gaps and erasures in the settler-colonial record, and how the projects positioned the Historical Committee, and by extension the tribe, to assert greater control over the preservation and production of their histories. The chapter concludes by highlighting how this control was mediated in the few oral history projects that have either been attempted or completed by nontribal members, including the oral histories I conducted for this book project.[8]

Sharing and Preserving Cultural Knowledge: A Process Grounded in Indigenous Futures

Preservation of knowledge, stories, culture, and customs has long been the aim of most oral history projects, including those led by the Mohican Historical Committee. But throughout much of the nineteenth and twentieth centuries, this goal of preservation was primarily dictated by non-Native historians and anthropologists and approached with the purpose of extracting knowledge from Indigenous communities to share with the general public. Tribal interests, priorities, and protocols were rarely honored, if even considered, and once the oral histories were recorded, the interviewer typically held the copyright for the material, giving the individual and the tribe little to no control over how the data were circulated and used. The goals of these non-Native researchers also shaped what knowledge was preserved in the interview, as nontribal members controlled the questions, and their reactions and interests shaped the content of the testimony given. Native researchers have also conducted oral interviews with their fellow community members. Some of these dynamics between interviewer and interviewee still hold true—interviewers will undoubtedly carry their own interests and experiences into a conversation, and those elements shape the content of any interview. However, when tribal members interview tribal members, they do so with a different sense of and relationship to many of the topics at hand. When the interviewers react to the testimonies of other tribal members, they come from a familiar place, and these fluencies ultimately shape the content of an interview.[9]

Likewise, because these projects were all tribally initiated and shaped by tribal goals, the information Historical Committee members sought to record was *for the benefit of the tribe,* rather than to fulfill the goals of an external research project that may or may not be relevant to tribal interests. When tribal members were asked to reflect on cultural traditions and ways of knowing practiced in their homes as a part of the *Hear Our Stories* series, the intent was not to share this information with a broad audience beyond the tribe for an anthropological project about Mohican culture, but to record this information so that it could be made accessible to future generations of tribal members—a vital part of the Historical Committee's larger efforts to gather records of Mohican history and build the Mohican tribal archive.

This was evident in tribal elder Dave Besaw's *Hear Our Stories* interview, where Besaw explained the importance of responsible hunting and gathering practices in a way that was clearly directed at other tribal members rather than an outside audience.[10] Besaw was the tribe's first Community Health representative and eventually directed the Community Health Clinic for nearly twenty years, so his knowledge of tribal food and wellness practices would have been especially meaningful for future generations.[11] Besaw and other tribal members, such as Robert Little and Eleanor Martin, instructed their audiences about the importance of laying tobacco when taking from the land, and that Mohican hunters should only hunt when they need to and use whatever resources they take.[12] Each elder was also honored with tobacco at the beginning of their interview, so that this cultural practice was not only discussed but modeled for future generations.[13]

When recording the *Hear Our Stories* series, Historical Committee members were purposeful about crafting interview questions that prompted elders to share what they considered important cultural knowledge. More than a third of the elders interviewed shared herbal remedies their parents used, and Robert Jacobs used time in his video to explain the practice of smudging and demonstrate this practice for those listening.[14] Historical Committee cofounder Dorothy Davids shared the cultural tradition of hanging a kettle outside one's home to welcome guests, and elders Doug and Chenda Miller (who were interviewed together) and Vaughn LaBelle related memories of gathering maple syrup in the spring.[15] Besaw and others, like Dorothy Davids and her brother Bruce, related other oral histories and traditions passed down by their families in their interviews, ensuring that they would be passed on to future generations.[16] Relatedly, elders Aught Coyhis, Bruce Davids, Doreen Metzger, Patricia Miller, Averil Jayne Pecore, and Sheila (Miller) Powless shared bits and pieces of the Mohican language they had learned as children.[17] Even if they were only a few words, their memories were recorded so that future generations could learn from them by watching the videos.

Historical Committee members, who arranged many of the interviews in people's homes, also encouraged the elders who were interviewed to share photographs, historical items of personal importance, or any other relevant objects that would help the interviewees pass on cultural ways of knowing.[18] For example, Patricia Miller held and explained the medallion she wears in her video. Tracing the beading with her thumb and forefinger, she explained the significance of the star pattern and used the item to signify her pride in being Mohican.[19] Other elders, like Ruth Peters, showed photographs of their families, while Robert Jacobs showed examples of his wood carving.[20] Sheila (Miller) Powless also included photographs in her video, lining up the images side by side and using her finger to point out different landmarks and places. She used the images to narrate changes in the reservation, explaining where buildings in the photographs were previously located and where each photograph was taken.[21] Other elders, like Roger Cuish, took this even further—his video ends with a tour of his yard complete with an explanation of a historical building on his property, a view of an antique sled that he mentioned in an earlier story, and a casual conversation about the need to mow his lawn. Fae Church and Ruth Peters, who were both accomplished musicians, ended their videos by playing the piano, an embodied practice that we would have been unable to see or hear in printed archival sources.[22] In this way, the videos become archives in and of themselves, assembling not just stories but also objects, music, photographs, and in some cases even writing. Robert Jacobs's DVD, for example, includes a note that informs viewers that they will be able to view his poems on the DVD when inserted into a computer.[23]

The video format of the series is ideal for the Historical Committee's preservation goals, and also allows us to see the body language elders use while they are telling stories, effectively capturing an element of storytelling that is expected when you listen to someone tell a story in person, but often lost in written documentation or aural sources. The videos show elders' gestures that help illustrate their stories—such as Opal Erb's hand motions that show how she carried water from the river to her family's garden, and Sheila (Miller) Powless's illustration of how her grandfather used his hands to show the size of a trout he caught.[24] Many of the elders also used their hands to point to places, situating themselves in a particular place and in relationality to other places and people. Roger Cuish, who is seated outside his home in his video, pointed to his right when referencing tribal member Robert Chicks to demonstrate that Chicks lived in that direction.[25] Sheila (Miller) Powless does this too. Her video was filmed in the parking lot of the Library-Museum, so she pointed to the house where she grew up (behind her) and in the direction of places where different events she describes took place, telling us that we (those at the filming and those in the Library-Museum) are sitting in her mom's old garden and that she raised her own children "right across the road here."[26] The videos capture these images, gestures, and moments, ensuring that materials, photographs, and places that elders consider important to their life stories were also recorded. As Timothy Powell argues in his work about digital stories, recordings not only preserve details that are often erased from written documentation but also more effectively represent Indigenous practices of oral history and storytelling that have been ongoing since time immemorial. Digital recordings "animate qualities of traditional knowledge" in a way that print culture simply cannot.[27]

These cultural practices, stories, items, and knowledge were likely more readily shared with tribal interviewers. Likewise, interviewees who did choose to share this kind of knowledge with outside researchers would likely have framed their responses differently if they knew the primary audience for their interviews would not be future generations of the Stockbridge-Munsee Mohican Nation. But these elders knew that their stories would become important records for younger tribal members, and indeed almost every one of them emphasized the importance of having future generations learn about tribal history and culture. Former tribal chairman Aught Coyhis did so by explaining what he does not know about his grandparents, using his lack of knowledge to make a case for his own grandchildren and the grandchildren of others to learn more about their heritage.[28] In a similar manner, Elaine Jacobi stressed that she had to do a lot of research later in life to learn about her culture and heritage. She argued that children need to understand where they come from much earlier than she did and hoped that the *Hear Our Stories* project accomplished this.[29] Nearly half of the elders interviewed expressed similar sentiments, communicating the importance of Mohican history and the urgency of passing their knowledge to the next generation.[30]

Many of the elders in *Hear Our Stories* also made a point to include advice for future generations. Many of them covered community politics. Elders like Aught Coyhis and others specifically addressed the need to reform the Mohican Constitution, which, like most tribal constitutions written as part of the Indian Reorganization Act, has not been revised since the 1930s. Coyhis and others urged the next generations of Mohicans to think about enrollment beyond blood quantum so that more Mohican descendants could officially become tribal members.[31] Many of these elders had undoubtedly already started passing this knowledge and advice on to their children and grandchildren orally, but recording their stories within the oral history project was another way of ensuring their histories and their knowledge were preserved and passed on.

Within both the "Memoir-izing Our Mohican Lives" project and the *Hear Our Stories* series, the Historical Committee also prioritized passing knowledge on to younger generations by making younger members of the tribe responsible for gathering as well as transcribing the interviews from elders. This method of teaching history resonates with the traditional role that women on the Historical Committee have taken up, which includes educating the next generations. Working with youth in this way allowed Historical Committee members to teach history in action, while also training them to be the next generation of recorders and rememberers of the Mohican Nation. Committee members helped younger tribal members practice interviewing and modeled listening and learning from elders by including youth in both the taping and the production of the recordings.[32] For the "Memoir-izing Our Mohican Lives" project, youth also set the project objectives, which were published in *Stories of Our Elders,* the booklet that was published after the project's completion. The objectives separated goals into three categories:

FOR THE MOHICAN NATION
- To have stories of the past
- To know our history so that we know ourselves

FOR THE ELDERS
- To be remembered long after they are gone
- To be recognized and honored
- To help them know that people still care for them

FOR THE YOUTH
- To get to know the elders
- To learn about past mistakes so they are not repeated
- To be inspired by elders
- To have a new learning experience[33]

These goals range from broad, high-scale objectives like gathering stories of the past for the nation, to the level of the individual, like helping elders to know that people still care for them. This demonstrates the extensive reach that projects such as these can have and the extent to which they can have an impact on several facets of the community. The goals also highlight the connections between stories and identities, naming "knowing ourselves" as one of the primary goals at the level of the nation. Collectively, the objectives

Figure 11. Sterling Schreiber Jr. (*left*) and Donavan Malone (*right*) interview Leonard Welch as a part of the "Memoir-izing Our Mohican Lives" project. Courtesy of the Stockbridge-Munsee Historical Committee.

highlight the care for community well-being that went into the project and the multigenerational nature of this work. Including youth in these projects and actively involving them in all stages—from setting objectives, to recording, to transcribing—is an important part of ensuring that they become the next generation of Mohican rememberers.

In that sense, Mohican oral history projects not only served as key vehicles for collecting history and preserving it for future generations; they have also operated as tangible ways to teach younger tribal members oral history skills, cultural knowledge, and tribal history. Their success was evident. As youth transcribed, they also recorded their own reactions and interpretations of the interviews, writing that talking with elders was an experience that "left us in awe" and made evident "how much our elders mean to the community."[34] As the published booklet of their reflections and stories notes, these new narratives, which illustrate both the lives of elders and the impacts on youth, are "a bridge constructed across the generations" that show the potential these new histories hold.[35] In the reflections, we see plainly that this project sparked a renewed sense of shared history and belonging for many, and by extension, contributed to the Historical Committee's goal to cultivate a shared sense of Mohican nationhood as part of their larger Mohican historical recovery and tribal archive projects.

New Sources, New Narratives

In many of the tribally led historical recovery projects that have emerged in the late twentieth and early twenty-first centuries, community leaders have used the language of gaps or missing pieces in the historical narratives to explain the need for new sources and research within their communities. Oral history projects often serve as a promising way to meet this goal. New oral histories can shed light on Indigenous movement, labor, and day-to-day experiences that have been much less frequently recorded. For example, the Blackfeet Tribe of the Blackfeet Indian reservation received an Institute of Museum and Library Services (IMLS) grant in 2020 to use oral history to "fill in gaps in the reservation's history, specifically the land and places on the reservation."[36] In a similar vein, the Eastern Shawnee Nation recently pursued "a search for Shawnee history" that included conducting new oral histories, particularly focusing on the period from 1812 to World War II—a period that has received less attention from historians.[37] Other oral history

Figure 12. Front page of the 1999 booklet *Stories of Our Elders,* published after the "Memoir-izing Our Mohican Lives" project. Courtesy of the Stockbridge-Munsee Historical Committee.

projects aim to deepen tribal understandings of particular subjects. For example, historian William Bauer has conducted oral histories in his own community, the Round Valley Indian Tribe, in order to understand Indigenous labor in a way that surpasses what government documents recorded, while the Chickaloon Native Village's 2020 oral history project aims to record the experiences of Native veterans. In their description of the project, the Village explicitly states their interest in using the oral interviews in coordination with existing archival collections of photographs and documents to create new stories that will be accessible on the tribe's digital archive platform and in the Library of Congress's Veterans History Project.[38]

Similarly, the Mohican oral history projects have created new sources that address historical periods with little documentation or focus on subjects that existing records fail to adequately capture. The "Memoir-izing Our Mohican Lives" project explicitly listed one of its purposes as "provid[ing] readers a glimpse into the lives of American Indians in the early to mid-1900s," and in the *Hear Our Stories* video series, many of the elders discussed the discrimination they experienced throughout the twentieth century, a topic that is more likely to be captured in first-person sources like these.[39] For example, while veteran Robert Jacobs explained how identifying as Native in the military landed him on latrine duty, Aught Coyhis remembered that everyone in his military unit called him "Chief."[40] Alfred Miller remembered restaurants in town he could not enter because he was Native, while Bruce and Dorothy Davids explained how their family lost their land—the bank refused to take their father's money to pay his taxes, demanding that he give up his land instead.[41] These experiences have been overwhelmingly excluded from official government records of Native people in the twentieth century and therefore have received less coverage from historians.

Many elders also discussed federal policies explicitly, creating new first-hand testimonies of historical periods that will undoubtedly influence future narratives. For example, while much literature exists on the American Indian relocation policy, few documentary sources cover the Mohican Nation during this period or provide rich personal stories.[42] In the *Hear Our Stories* series, many of the elders discussed their experience with this policy in detail. Leona Bowman recalled how she cleaned homes in Green Bay, a city sixty miles southeast of the reservation, while Clarence Chicks described his move to Milwaukee to find a job.[43] Though Milwaukee is 175 miles southeast of the reservation, Clarence and others, including Doug Miller, also narrated their regular trips back to the reservation, "since that was home."[44] Like so many others, Dorothy Davids described her family's move to Sturgeon Bay so they could all work in the shipyards, one hundred miles east of the reservation.[45] Fae Church, who was forced to move away from the reservation to attend a school that could meet her needs as a visually impaired child, also communicated a history of labor, describing how her mother did beadwork for white clientele to earn money in their new home.[46]

While to some these stories may seem to narrate mundane details of daily life, each is a new source that testifies to Indigenous work, movement, and continued ties to place in the mid-twentieth century.[47] As historian Aroha Harris argues, life histories such as these "provide illuminating sources that can be read with and against the conventional archives and manuscripts." As she notes in the context of her work on Māori communities, those who write Māori history typically depend on these existing archives and manuscripts that do not include or prioritize the voices of individual Māori. Harris asserts that her interview with her grandmother

> shed[s] important light on historical understandings of Māori during a period of unprecedented change. It [her interview] shows the ongoing relevance of the home community even as its population moved away, and pitches Māori as engaging intellectually with the policies and circumstances of the time in ways that gave weight to Māori ways of being.[48]

In the same way, these Mohican oral history projects record life memories of work and labor that can be read with and against existing sources. Together, they contribute to new understandings of Indigenous labor and have the potential to inspire new narratives of Mohican survival and resiliency in the twentieth century.[49]

The oral history projects created by the Mohican Historical Committee are also ideal mediums for conveying the felt experiences of individuals—an illustrative element of storytelling that becomes especially crucial when dealing with histories of loss and trauma.[50] While many have criticized oral history projects for being subjective or unfinished, this is precisely what makes them such powerful methods for recording stories.[51] As scholars Kevin P. Murphy, Jennifer L. Pierce, and Jason Ruiz have argued, the strength of oral history projects lies not in their ability to examine *historical truth* but rather in their capacity to "reveal how narrators make meaning out of their lives, memories, and stories."[52] The recordings of Mohican elders reflecting on their memories of relocation, labor, and discrimination not only give us new details about specific time periods or subjects where there are fewer sources that center Indigenous voices, but also tell us how these experiences have continued to affect the lives of these individuals across time. The recordings capture the feelings and emotions of narrators, which scholar Dian Million argues should be framed as "culturally mediated knowledges" for Indigenous peoples.[53]

In addition to histories of movement and labor, one topic that nearly every elder discussed was their parents' experiences in boarding schools, the time they themselves spent in local mission schools, or their experiences in the public school systems, where they were often one of few Native children. While some had positive experiences in these education systems, many communicated trauma, discrimination, and sadness. For example, in her testimony, Fae Church described the prejudice she experienced from teachers in a school far away from the reservation, as well as the bullying and jeering she endured from other children, who routinely "told her to go back where she belonged."[54] For former tribal chairman Virgil Murphy, the schools near the reservation were not any better; he was routinely ridiculed and called a "dirty Indian." The prejudice he experienced was so severe that he was forced to withdraw from grade school and move to South Dakota to complete his education there.[55] Robert Jacobs and Verna Johnson-Miller noted that while they often asked their parents questions about their heritage, their parents refused to tell them anything, because they had been forbidden to talk about their culture and learn about their Native heritage when they were in boarding school.[56] Elders like Robert Little discussed their memories of the nearby mission school, where they spent their recesses killing the bats in the attic.[57]

Elders also reflected on parts of Stockbridge-Munsee history that they themselves did not experience; recording these reflections and relationships to historical events is equally important in order to understand how history continues to influence shared senses of Mohican identity and nationhood throughout the community. For example, in her interview, Fae Church narrates much of tribal history from the perspective of her own family. Her story begins in 1677 with the birth of her Mohican ancestor, sachem King Benjamin Kokhkewaunaunt. She narrates early events in Mohican history from his perspective, then moves to the wars and removals that temporarily separated different parts of the tribe through the eighteenth and nineteenth centuries.

In her narration, Church describes the events themselves as well as how she knows these facts, explaining how her mother showed her the removal route of her ancestors. Church then describes her grandfather's experience in the mid-nineteenth century when the U.S. government momentarily made Stockbridge-Munsee people U.S. citizens and simultaneously opened their land for public sale in 1843. Debates over citizenship and land loss caused major disagreements among tribal citizens and eventually led to a split in the tribe. Moving on to her mother's experiences in a mission school, Church seamlessly transitions to her own life and reflections. Her story illustrates how deeply the last three centuries of Stockbridge-Munsee history have affected her life, and her reflections on how her ancestors processed major changes in their lives provides critical framing and perspective that has the potential to shape new narratives of these earlier periods. Other elders, such as Vaughn LaBelle and Earl Plass, also reflected on the removal of their ancestors from present-day New York and several reflected on their own trips back to Mohican ancestral homelands.[58]

Unlike written documentation, oral history captures the changes in interviewees' tone and the pauses they take before discussing a memory that has affected their emotions. While some of these emotions translate when oral histories are written down, others do not. Listening to these oral histories communicates felt histories in a way that other sources cannot. This is even more effective in the *Hear Our Stories* video series, where viewers encounter not only the words of the elders but also their mannerisms, the objects some of them chose to share, and their facial expressions. The video format allows us to see Fae Church's expression when she pauses and hesitates while talking about the prejudice she experienced in her Janesville school and her father's difficulty to get a job during the Great Depression.[59] It is evident that racism has affected Patricia Miller too, as we see her get choked up when talking about the first time she learned about racial prejudice.[60] The videos allow us to visibly see the trauma that many of these elders experienced, but importantly, they also allow us to see their joy when reflecting on their lives. For instance, Opal Erb can't help but smile when she mentions meeting her husband. It takes some coaxing from her child (offscreen), who can be heard saying "It's a good story, Mom!," but she eventually shares the story of how they met, laughing and smiling all the way through.[61] Watching the videos becomes a very affective experience in that instead of reading about joy, trauma, and sadness throughout the lives of these elders, the audiences watch these narratives unfold on a screen. It is this affective portraiture, in conjunction with the powerful narratives the elders relate in their interviews, that makes these videos so moving for both tribal and nontribal members.

These types of sources—those that center Mohican emotional responses to federal policies past and present—are crucial for reframing existing and creating new narratives of Stockbridge-Munsee Mohican history. An overreliance on federal records like surveillance reports written by Indian agents and propaganda materials produced by boarding schools and relocation programs has resulted in only partial understandings of Indigenous lives in the late nineteenth and early twentieth centuries. By sharing these narratives of work, education, and daily life, the oral histories provide new sources that center Mohican felt experiences and, as scholar Ann Cvetkovich puts it in the context of LGBTQ stories, "stand alongside the documents of the dominant culture in order to offer alternative modes of knowledge."[62] Ultimately, these new sources support Mohican data sovereignty by further enabling the tribe's right to tell their own stories and shape the narratives that are produced about them.

These oral histories shift the foundation of how Mohican historical narratives are produced. However, in addition to providing new, more accurate perspectives, the Historical Committee also wanted to ensure that these new sources directly countered existing erasure narratives and instead highlighted Mohican survival and nationhood. The *Hear Our Stories* video series especially exemplifies these aims. Examining the title of the series alone, we immediately understand that the project is a clear assertion of the importance (and overwhelming absence) of Native voices in dominant narratives. The series demands that Mohican stories are taken seriously and that they are heard. Moreover, the video series ends with a final installment that features a compilation of numerous elders speaking around a single theme: "We Are Still Here." In this video, elders take direct aim at the common myth of Native disappearance, a myth that affects tribal nations across the United States but has especially affected the Mohicans because of the popular novel-turned-blockbuster film *The Last of the Mohicans*. The final compilation refutes this myth not only by pointing to living elders who chose to participate in the video series but also by asking them to respond to this common misrepresentation of their nation.

Longtime Historical Committee member Sheila (Miller) Powless expressed this sentiment succinctly, stating that for her, "it's most important that people know that we are not the last of the Mohicans."[63] Doreen Metzger and Robert Little concurred, Metzger adding that she wants more information available to people about the Mohicans, as she feels the general public should have more knowledge about the tribe.[64] Others, like Elaine Jacobi, expressed their pride that "the Mohicans are still here" and "will continue to strive to survive."[65] This project, then, as an important act of both historical preservation and self-representation, enables the Mohicans to demonstrate that they have not only defied the predictions and assertions of their demise but are a resilient nation that will continue to survive. The final video itself is a new narrative of endurance, strength, and survival. With all the elders sharing their memories and relating their life stories, these projects create new sources that lay the foundation for future narratives, in particular narratives that will center Mohican voices, survival, and nationhood. The projects make a powerful claim for inclusion in narratives of their history, taking direct action to ensure that new histories written will no longer fail to include tribal perspectives and perpetuate false myths about their nation.

An Archive of Memories

After these oral history projects were completed, the Historical Committee archived them in the Arvid E. Miller Library-Museum, a seemingly commonsense decision that actually challenges best practices in oral history and gives the tribe unprecedented control over the dissemination and use of their historical sources. Typically, oral historians are encouraged to deposit their recordings in a large public library, archive, or historical society that is easily accessible to the public, and especially to researchers who may use the recordings in their work.[66] These large, public archives are often significant distances from reservations, where academic researchers with funding and travel expense reimbursement might have easier access, but tribal researchers, many of whom live on reservations and may not have access to such funds, do not. This is not always the case, and many nontribal historians do work closely with tribes to determine where they would like records deposited. However, by conducting the oral interviews themselves and choosing to keep the recordings of the interviews on the reservation, the Mohicans prioritized the needs of tribal members and researchers who live on or often return to the reservation, rather than those of outside researchers. Moreover, as Jo Ann Schedler articulated, "keeping the stories of our elders here [the Library-Museum] and . . . keeping the audio at the library is really important" because "the youth come here to the Library and they tour," often as a part of their school projects.[67] This move is ultimately about access; it facilitates the transmission of cultural knowledge to future generations that so many of the elders prioritized in their *Hear Our Stories* interviews. Archived in the community contexts in which they were created, these interviews can then be used to "promote or celebrate a common identity—that is to say, a sense of community—within a particular social group," which, as Paula Hamilton and Linda Shopes argue, especially occurs "when a group or community has been silenced, threatened, or destroyed." In these moments, "interviews, often invoking loss, thus become acts of survival," and for the Mohicans, a critical practice of nation-building.[68]

Placing these recorded memories within the Mohican tribal archive also enriches the potential they hold for producing new narratives. As opposed to depositing them in an archive where they are some of the few Mohican sources, archiving these interviews in a repository where they are surrounded by centuries of other Mohican narratives makes them even more meaningful. They contribute to an existing tapestry of Mohican memories, felt experiences, and knowledge. For example, the interviews of elders like Clarence Chicks, Aught Coyhis, and others who served in World War II could indeed stand alone as new sources for Native participation in the twentieth-century U.S. military. When placed within the Mohican tribal archive, where they are surrounded by the records of other Mohican veterans throughout history however, they contribute to a different, more expansive narrative that stretches across centuries and attests to Mohican participation in the U.S. military as far back as the Revolutionary War. In a similar manner, Sheila (Miller) Powless used her interview to recall some of the first Tribal Council meetings that were held in her parents' home after the Indian Reorganization Act was passed. She narrated how she took notes at each of these meetings, intentionally keeping two sets of minutes so that one could be archived on the reservation while the other had to be sent to the Bureau of Indian Affairs. Alone, (Miller) Powless's memories attest to early archiving efforts; when archived with the actual minutes she took and the rest of her father and mother's records from this time period, they enrich and bring new life to a much larger story about survival, activism, and Mohican nation-building. These and other historical sources recorded in these oral history projects constitute powerful testimonies in themselves, but placing them in the midst of a much larger archive that testifies to years of Mohican survival is an intentional political action. In the Mohican tribal archive they are richer, and indeed, they are contributing to new narratives of Mohican nationhood.

Archiving these records on the reservation also contributes to the larger Historical Committee goal to create the largest collection of Mohican materials available and thus make the Mohican reservation a place that is difficult for researchers of Mohican history to ignore. By building this collection and preventing these oral histories from being available online, the Mohican Nation asserts data sovereignty over their materials in the hope that researchers intending to use the content of the interviews must come to the reservation and build a relationship with community members. This pushes those who intend to use the interviews for research purposes to communicate with the tribe.

This was exemplified in 2009 when Charles Hornett, an instructor at Northeast Technical College in Wisconsin, asked to interview elders of the Stockbridge-Munsee Mohican Nation. This decision was delegated to the Historical Committee, which decided that "it will be best if Mr. Hornett comes here to view our completed video tapes rather than be involved in this project."[69] Hornett seems to have had no prior relationship with the tribe, and the committee had little indication of what his interviews would be about, where they would be placed, or their purpose. While this demonstrates the Mohicans' ability to deny requests for projects they feel do not serve their interests, it is important to note that instead of simply sending Hornett away, they invited him to submit questions that the Historical Committee could vet and then choose to include or not include in their own oral history projects, before coming to the reservation to view the tapes once the *Hear Our Stories* project was finished. Hornett ultimately did submit questions, some of which were included in the *Hear Our Stories* project.[70] This demonstrates the tribe's resolve not only to assert control over their own historical sources but also to build relationships with those conducting research about their nation. Likewise, it shows their ability, given the existence of the numerous oral history projects they had already initiated, to change the way non-Mohican scholars produce Mohican history.

Does this mean then that historians who do not belong to the communities they work with cannot and should not conduct oral interviews? Yes and no. When I first began working with the Stockbridge-Munsee Mohican Nation in 2010, I thought I would never, nor should I ever, conduct oral interviews. As a non-Mohican and non-Native person, I believed it was not my place to collect these testimonies. Instead, I set out to watch the *Hear Our Stories* series in its entirety and read the ample firsthand testimonies and interviews from existing oral history projects the Historical Committee had already completed that were filed within the archive.

However, in 2016, I was attending a Historical Committee meeting and a committee member asked me if I was going to conduct interviews. I responded that I was not planning on it. She looked at me and said, "You know, I think writing about this archive and this committee without talking to the people who created it is like watching and writing about ants on an anthill."[71] I took her point and asked the other committee members present how they would feel about a new oral history project, one that documented the labor and history of collecting Mohican historical materials and building the archive and museum. They agreed with her and made suggestions for who among the committee should be interviewed. Those who were interested gave me their contact information. We then discussed what best practices around these interviews might be. In standard oral history projects, interviewers hold the copyright on the interviews they conduct, another "best practice" that often leaves tribal communities without control over their own histories. Instead, we agreed that I would sign a copyright transfer and deed of gift form for the interviews upon the completion of the project, and I worked with the tribe's Legal Department to draft the appropriate paperwork. The consent form we created clearly lays out these terms and reminds interviewees that "Dr. Miron and other researchers must adhere to all aspects of the most current Stockbridge-Munsee Community Arvid E. Miller Library Museum Policies and Procedures Manual and receive permission from the Tribe before publishing any of this material."[72]

The interviews I conducted are not equivalent to the previous projects where tribal members controlled the interview questions and shaped the progression of the interviews based on their positions and reactions as tribal members. The Historical Committee members I interviewed still spoke, as Portelli argues, "*to* the historian, *with* the historian and, inasmuch as the material is published, *through* the historian."[73] And yet they are distinct from an oral history project where a non-Native researcher maintains complete control over the recording, questions, and dissemination of interviews. Conducted with support and guidance from the tribe's Historical Committee and Legal Department, these interviews are still powerful new sources that attest

to the activist elements of assembling a tribal archive, and their diminish-
ment of Mohican control over their own histories is minimal. The contents
of my interviews with Leah Miller, Jo Ann Schedler, and Heather Bruegl
are woven throughout this book. Placed alongside the actions of the Historical Committee, these testimonies form a portrait of the labor required
to build a community archive. In their reflections on the emotional toll of
going through documents that concurrently show loss as well as survival,
these memories communicate the felt experiences of Indigenous archival
activism.[74] By narrating the role these Historical Committee members have
played in trips to Mohican ancestral homelands, reclaiming stolen items
from non-Native museums, creating new museum exhibits, and numerous
other projects, these interviews catalog the methods of the Mohican Historical Committee and produce a picture of just how many initiatives they
have undertaken.

   If non-Native scholars recognize the power dynamics within oral history,
they can potentially create projects that relegate some of that power to the
communities being interviewed. In these projects, the shape and content of
interviews are shaped by tribal interests, needs, and priorities. Testimonies
are not extracted from communities and made available to wider audiences
without tribal input; rather, they are controlled by and remain accessible to
tribal nations themselves. Placed within the Mohican tribal archive, I hope
this new oral history project will testify to the years of Mohican archival
activism, lay the foundation for new narratives that center these voices, and
inspire future generations of Mohicans, just as the existing Mohican oral history projects have undoubtedly already done.

Oral histories hold the potential to develop new narratives regardless of who
conducts the interviews and who maintains the records. They are affective,
documenting the felt experiences of history in a way that few other forms
of recorded history can, and they provide new sources that lay the foundations for new narratives. In both tribally initiated oral history projects and
projects where tribes have very little control, there are numerous examples where Native peoples have exercised self-agency to dictate the terms of
interviews or narrated histories that challenge existing sources.[75] However,
creating new sources that have the potential to inform new narratives of
Indigenous nationhood and survival is significantly more likely when Indigenous nations maintain control over the shape and content of the interviews,

or when at the very least these projects are conducted in consultation with Native nations with their interests and priorities in mind.

The collection of Mohican oral histories by the Mohican Historical Committee is a purposeful move that allows the Mohicans to not only expand their archive and prioritize the testimonies of their community members, but also assert data sovereignty over where the recorded knowledge is archived and who has access to this information. In these projects, the Mohicans undermine many of the standard power dynamics in most oral history projects conducted within the scope of a larger research project, and instead, record the testimonies of tribal members with tribal intentions in mind. As one of the elders who participated in the "Memoir-izing Our Mohican Lives" project emphasized, "to know our history is to know ourselves."[76] These oral histories preserve the memories and histories of tribal elders in the Mohican tribal archive and in doing so, produce the conditions for tribal members on the reservation to enrich their cultural identity and sense of belonging, as well as create new narratives that emphasize Mohican survival.

These oral histories have an immediate impact on those who view and listen to them on the reservation. Moreover, the Historical Committee has also used them to reach broader audiences by incorporating the recordings into other public history projects like museum exhibits. The committee also continued to prioritize new first-person testimonies in other forms, expanding the primary sources from which historians could draw. The next three chapters of the book focus on how the committee put the sources they collected and created to use in various types of public history projects and narratives, but as we will see, their interest in expanding the archive by collecting existing sources or creating new ones was never out of mind. These processes are inextricably linked, and all contribute to Mohican archival activism: the committee's efforts to intervene in the production of Stockbridge-Munsee history.

3

Archives as Arsenals for Community Needs

The Library-Museum serves as the heart of the community. Without the
heart, you don't have life, and without life, you don't have a community.

— Jolene Bowman, former director of the Department of Education and
Cultural Affairs, personal communication with author, 2022

In October 2001, the Stockbridge-Munsee Mohican Nation hosted a history conference called "Many Trails of the Mohican Nation: A Conference on Mohican History and Culture."[1] Held on the Stockbridge-Munsee
reservation over the course of three days, the conference was attended by
243 people and was organized by the Mohican Historical Committee. A
little over half of the attendees were tribal members, while others were non-
Mohican local residents or non-Mohican academic scholars who had written about the tribe.[2] The participants gave and heard presentations on topics
ranging from archaeology in Mohican homelands, the Mohican language,
and the place of Christianity in Mohican history to Mohican leaders, treaties,
and the experiences of Mohican women.[3] They had lively discussions about
how Mohican history should be represented, and notes from the conference
include observations of tribal members "getting to microphones" to voice
their critiques about some of the presentations.[4] In addition to the sessions,
Historical Committee members carved out time to highlight the Library-
Museum's collections. Attendees who were tribal members were encouraged
to explore their family histories in the archive, and the committee also orches-
trated a tour of the Library-Museum during the event so that attendees could
become more familiar with the archive's resources and the committee could
emphasize "the importance of Native people's writing their own accounts of
their history and culture."[5] Overall, the conference aimed to "build in Mohican people a deep pride in their heritage," "demonstrate that the Mohicans
are still here and that the 'Last of the Mohicans' is a nineteenth-century myth,"

and "share with others the stories of how contemporary Mohican people began to explore their identity, culture, and their history."[6] These goals came together that October, yielding a three-day event where tribal members led the teaching of Mohican history on Mohican land.

The conference is one of dozens of historical projects that the creation of the Mohican tribal archive and the reorganization of materials therein has fostered. With expanded access to their historical materials by the mid-1970s, Historical Committee members and tribal members alike began to use the newly accessible primary sources to craft new narratives of Mohican survival and nationhood. Their time spent in the archive allowed them to expand and illuminate their expertise on their own history and present themselves as experts in a variety of settings. The conference was a collection of these new "narratives" through which tribal members led the teaching of Mohican history and sought to prepare future generations of Mohicans to do the same. It created a space where multiple generations could learn about Mohican history, and in doing so the conference sought to cultivate a sense of shared national history among Mohican conference participants and thus a shared national identity. Tribal members reflecting on the conference wrote that the event was "very empowering—filled me with a deep sense of PRIDE" (emphasis in original). Another echoed, "I have always been proud to be a Mohican but after this conference I have a[n] even higher quality of proudness."[7]

The goals of sharing history, building a sense of shared belonging and nationhood, and contesting false narratives are consistent throughout the Historical Committee's work. In the first two chapters of the book we saw these goals play out in the collection of existing and the creation of new sources. The creation and expansion of the tribal archive accounts for a significant amount of the Historical Committee's work in their early founding years. While these efforts fundamentally changed the production of Mohican history by increasing the availability of sources to tribal members and shifting how they were assembled and organized, the committee also understood that not everyone was interested in archival research, and they knew that not everyone would come to the archive to seek out these new sources. They were faced with a different problem of access and needed to create new programs, narratives, and ways of teaching Mohican history and culture that would rely on the sources they collected but target a much broader audience. This audience includes both tribal and nontribal members, and, while

I discuss the latter group further in chapters 4 and 5, this chapter focuses on local narrative creation and reclamation efforts that were primarily aimed at tribal audiences on the Stockbridge-Munsee reservation.

This chapter profiles several of these efforts, including new narratives produced or facilitated by the Historical Committee, such as the tribe's first newspaper and publishing company; events like the Mohican History Conference, which aimed to teach tribal histories, languages, and culture; and legal reclamation efforts that used archival records as an essential tool in the repatriation of land and sacred items. As we will see, the archive has played an important role in each of these efforts. Returning to the three pillars of archival activism, this chapter highlights how the new, readily accessible archive served as an arsenal to protect Mohican sovereignty in activist fights and reclamation efforts, as well as supported the production of new narratives that primarily aimed to teach Mohican history in new ways that would strengthen a shared sense of tribal identity and nationhood. These, like the other public history projects and initiatives discussed throughout this book, are critical efforts in Mohican nation-building that defy attempts to assimilate and erase Mohican people.

New Historical Narratives

When the Millers started collecting in the 1930s, they were aware that while copying colonial sources and making them accessible on the reservation was an essential task, an uncritical use of these sources would only reproduce existing silences. So, in addition to copying sources verbatim and recording their own memories as new primary sources, they also began to, as Dorothy Davids put it in one interview, "read between the lines of the white man's history books."[8] Historical Committee members read and reframed colonial documents to create new secondary sources that not only challenged existing records but also weaved their own memories and knowledge together with colonial observations. For Arvid Miller, this mostly occurred as he traveled to different archives and copied sections of colonial materials. While he continued to copy most materials verbatim, he also carefully combined some of the new sources he was reading with his own memories to create new narratives, thus reconstituting, rather than outright rejecting, these colonial materials.

For example, in a narrative titled "On Christianity in Our History," Miller carefully stitched together fragments from different documents, creating a

cohesive account that challenges common narratives focused on assimilation and instead narrates change as well as resilience in Mohican homelands.
His narrative begins and is peppered with a recognition and documentation
of his sources: "I will start with a letter which King James issued in April 10,
1606 . . ." But he quickly moves beyond these colonial records to a story of
Mohican survival. Rejecting a portrayal of Mohicans as easily assimilated,
Miller wrote, "Our people did not at first enter into a church estate but rather
into a civil covenant to be the Lord's people which was in keeping to a great
extent to their belief in the Great Spirit, and we had what the white man
believed a Christianized community." The document is relatively short (just
two pages) and concludes with Arvid's own memories of missionaries in Red
Springs.[9]

Dorothy Davids similarly used colonial sources in her regular column for
the Mohican tribal newspaper, "Rambling through History with Dot Davids."
Sometimes she used them to shed additional light on a particular point, while
in other cases she held them up as examples of why colonial sources must
be examined with a critical eye. Sometimes she did both. For example, in
recounting her memories of tapping maple trees for syrup, Davids incorporated firsthand accounts from white settlers about Mohican seasonal rounds,
the regular migrations that tribal members made in response to seasonal
changes in their food sources. She used the sources to show that "making
maple syrup was not new to the Stockbridge-Munsee Mohicans," but also
used the settlers' words to show how ignorant they really were of Native
practices and land use. In the document that Davids draws from, missionary John Sergeant described seasonal rounds as "wandering" and bemoaned
that Stockbridge-Munsee people "moved, whole families together, with every
season. . . . We had to follow them out into the woods and live there with
them in deep snow for six weeks while they made sugar from the maple sap."
Davids reframed these sources in the context of her own memories about
maple sugaring to show how little these settlers understood about the value
of seasonal rounds, while still highlighting the survival of maple sugar and
syrup making across generations.[10]

These narratives are what literary scholar Kelly Wisecup calls Indigenous
compilations—texts made by assembling, but often rejecting, repurposing,
and rearranging colonial materials to take on new meaning.[11] In these new
texts, Miller and Davids compiled and rearranged the sources they were reading. They reread them with their own knowledge of Mohican culture and

lifeways in mind and rearranged them in a way that would resonate with fellow community members. Both authors use the pronouns "our" and "us" throughout, and Miller's "On Christianity" ends with a conversational phase, "you no doubt are aware of the following men who served in Red Springs and Morgan Siding."[12] Both writers' intended audience for the narrative is clear. Miller's narrative depends on a level of familiarity with places like Red Springs and Morgan Siding, and the call out to tribal members' own memories of these religious histories invites readers directly into the processes of recording and remembering tribal history. It is as if to say, "You too are aware of these histories, and thus your memories are meaningful and important." Davids's narratives were published in the tribal newspaper, which is primarily read by tribal members. "On Christianity in Our History" is one of hundreds of compilations, first-person narratives, and transcriptions in Miller's collection, which today includes fifteen different folders titled "Writings." Each contains transcriptions, along with new narratives in which Miller recorded his own memories alone or in conversation with colonial records. Likewise, Davids's column was a mainstay in the tribal newspaper for years, and the archive holds six folders of these publications. These new sources centered Mohican motivations and actors, creating new historical accounts that countered myths of Mohican disappearance and narrated Mohican nationhood and survival.

While the Historical Committee produced less compilations as a group, they did share the priority of producing and sharing new narratives and histories with community members as they were collecting materials from archives, and they often challenged or reframed the colonial sources they encountered. Their first medium for doing so was *Quin'a Month'a,* the tribe's first community newspaper, whose title means "Are you well?" and was first published in April 1972, the same year the Tribal Council officially granted space for the committee's growing archival materials.[13] By 1980 they had published fifty-five issues.[14] The publication had a Fact Finder section to share Historical Committee archival findings, distributed community news and Tribal Council meeting minutes, and shared historical narratives that Historical Committee members reconstructed based on new documents they acquired from other archives.[15] Similar to Miller's and Davids's new narratives, *Quin'a Month'a* aimed to provide community members with new interpretations of Mohican histories from Mohican perspectives for a broader Stockbridge-Munsee Mohican public. These new narratives articulated Mohican survival and nationhood, explicitly countering dominant narratives about

Mohican history that had largely been written by non-Mohican people without collaboration with tribal members. The committee used this as a way to distribute historical and other community information for more than twenty years, and when the tribe's full newspaper, *Mohican News,* was launched in 1993, the Historical Committee continued to contribute content. Historical Committee meetings included a review and discussion of historical items or articles identified by committee members, and together they selected what information they would send to both Tribal Council members and *Mohican News.*[16] More recently, the Department of Cultural Affairs has used Facebook to disseminate similar research findings and information. During the Covid-19 pandemic in 2020–21, department staff created a series called "Magnificent Mohicans" in which they created social media posts that honored and educated community members about important tribal leaders. Staff used the tribal archive to research each individual, put together the posts, and used them as a way to share information with tribal members while the Library-Museum had to be closed to the public for safety reasons.[17]

Perhaps the most comprehensive new narrative produced by the Historical Committee is *A Brief History of the Mohican Nation: Stockbridge-Munsee Band,* a short, printed booklet. Written primarily by Dorothy Davids in 2001, the same year as the Many Trails History Conference, the publication was revised by the Historical Committee in 2004, and recently updated again in 2017 with the help of funds from NATOW (Native American Tourism of Wisconsin).[18] The work begins prior to the arrival of European settlers and emphasizes the important relationships Mohican people have always had with the land and the environment in which they lived. When describing the arrival and impact of European settlers, Davids does not mince words. She details how "civilizing" policies disrupted Mohican economic patterns and hindered the production of traditional items and explains how Mohican lands were taken through "fraudulent means."[19] Still, while outlining these colonial policies and impact, she is clear about emphasizing Mohican survival, noting that many practiced traditional ceremonies secretly during the missionization period. The narrative continues to trace Stockbridge-Munsee history through several more removals and the eventual creation of the Mohican reservation. It also outlines the devastating impacts of more-contemporary policies like allotment, while again always coming back to survival and resilience. Emphasizing ongoing Mohican connections to land, the narrative notes that the forests on their reservation, which were once clear-cut by pine loggers, have returned, as have wildlife and other plants. Davids outlines the new housing developments created by the tribe as well as the expansion of the Pine Hills golf course and North Star Casino, which are major income drivers and employers for the tribe and the surrounding area. She ends by explaining the Historical Committee's work and the creation and expansion of the Arvid E. Miller Library-Museum.[20] Overall, the narrative provides an accessible yet comprehensive picture of Stockbridge-Munsee Mohican history from the perspective of Stockbridge-Munsee people themselves. It serves as an excellent starting point for those who are unfamiliar with Stockbridge-Munsee history and as an important counternarrative to the many colonial narratives that have been published about Mohican history, making it an ideal source for tribal members who are interested in learning about their nation's history. The booklet remains available in the Library-Museum today, and the fact that the Historical Committee continues to update it is a testament to their continued research and commitment to telling the most accurate version of their history possible.

The Historical Committee's and Library-Museum staff's most recent publication is a pictorial history book titled *People of the Waters That Are Never Still: Pictorial History of the Stockbridge-Munsee Band of Mohicans,* which focuses on the history of the Mohican Nation and specifically highlights the history of different Mohican families. Building off of the shorter *Brief History of the Mohican Nation,* the new pictorial book is more than six hundred pages in length and is heavily based in research conducted in the tribal archive.[21] As Leah Miller, one of the book's authors, noted, "Unless somebody devoted their life to being the one to go out there and research, it [writing the book and other new narratives] would be very difficult."[22] The book begins with the Mohican creation story and is followed by a historical overview of the tribe. It includes specific chapters about traditional Mohican labor practices like harvesting cherries, along with histories of places that are important within tribal history. Many of these chapters feature firsthand accounts from tribal members, which, like the new primary sources discussed in chapter 1, provide additional new sources that work against the absence of Mohican voices in archives and published sources. The bulk of the book, however, is dedicated to the history of twenty-four different Mohican families.[23] Each family has a printed family tree outlining their heritage, and short histories of select family members. Throughout, the Historical Committee uses photographs as well as scans of archival materials to create a

visual history that is easily accessible to those who are less interested in sorting through the archive itself but still want to learn the histories of their
families. The audience for this book is tribal members; as Miller noted, "we
want our own people to be the focus. . . . We want them to know about our
history, and we are proud of our history. . . . We look at this project as a way
of bringing more families together."[24] This is evident in the way the book is
used today. Copies are available in the Library-Museum, and tribal members
regularly access and rely on it for family research. When I was on the reservation in July 2021, a family came in with their young daughter and needed
help with a school project which required she research her family history.
The three sat and looked at the pictorial book together, using the mother's
and father's families and their respective chapters to construct a new family
tree for their daughter. The publications and narratives produced by the Historical Committee use the archival records collected to circulate information
among tribal members and are critical in strengthening the community's
sense of shared cultural knowledge and history. Ultimately, these works support the nation's ability to self-govern, facilitate local decision making, and
enable Mohican sovereignty in many contexts.[25]

   Beyond producing new narratives themselves, the Historical Committee
was also committed to facilitating new narratives created by individual tribal
members. As they wrote in a 1982 grant proposal, "Many important primary
sources remain to be researched by tribal members."[26] To assist with the
production and circulation of more new histories, longtime Historical Committee members Dorothy Davids and Ruth Gudinas created Muh-he-con-
neew Press, which became the publishing arm of the Historical Committee.
Muh-he-con-neew Press operated between 1980 and 2007, publishing eight
works during these years.[27] Two of the publications have appeared in previous chapters: the catalog of materials for the Arvid E. Miller Library-
Museum (1980) and the compilation of oral histories, *Stories of Our Elders*
(1999). The single curriculum published by the press, *The Mohican People:
Their Lives and Their Lands* (2007), is covered in chapter 5. The five other
works published by the press and written by tribal members include *Christian Religion among the Stockbridge-Munsee Band of Mohicans,* by original
Historical Committee members Thelma Putnam and Blanche Jacobs (1980);
Mama's Little One, a children's book by Kristina Heath (1998); *Chief Ninham:
Forgotten Hero,* a historical story for younger audiences by Eva Bowman
(1999); *School Days: Memories of Life in Morgan Siding, 1925–1933,* by Harry

Bauman, edited by Jeri Bauman (2006); and *Inner Dreams and Outer Circles,* by Dorothy Davids, edited by Beatrice Ganley (2007).[28]

Several of these books required archival research conducted in the tribal archive. For example, Bowman's *Chief Ninham* relied heavily on the "Ninham Files," a folder within the People Files Collection that the Historical Committee had assembled about tribal leader Daniel Ninham.[29] Ninham was Wappinger, a community that was related to and eventually became part of the Mohican Nation, and he is one of four tribal leaders who traveled to London in the eighteenth century in an effort to protect Mohican and Wappinger land. He was ultimately killed while fighting for the colonists in the Revolutionary War. The Historical Committee's previous gathering of materials related to Ninham from archives and libraries across the country made this information immediately accessible to Bowman and enabled her to craft a new narrative that educates audiences about an important leader who has been "forgotten" or perhaps erased from histories of early America and the Revolutionary War. Her work also positions Ninham within the larger context of Mohican kinship relations. Like many of the other projects within Mohican archival activism, Bowman's book is attentive to involving future generations in the writing process, so children from the local Bowler School District did all the illustrations for the piece. By providing an avenue for these new narratives to be published and circulated, the Historical Committee intervened in the production of Mohican historical narratives and worked to ensure that more secondary sources were created by Mohican writers.

Outside of the press, other tribal members like Historical Committee member Jo Ann Schedler and former director of the Department of Education and Cultural Affairs Jolene Bowman have also used the tribal archive to create other types of Mohican history projects. Bowman has conducted extensive research on the Lutheran Indian Mission School in Red Springs, the mission school that most tribal members attended in the early twentieth century, and has given several public presentations on her work. Reflecting on her research, she noted that without access to the materials in the tribal archive "I don't think I would have been able to get any information ... it was roadblock after roadblock." Within the tribal archive, she was able to access ample materials like letters and stories written by those who attended the school, as well as those who were in charge. These sources helped her tell this important story, so much so that she "felt like my ancestors were talking to me—people I didn't get to meet on earth. I felt like I could hear their voices."[30]

Schedler also considered the tribal archive essential to her research projects. Since 2008, she and her husband have been using the Library-Museum to locate Mohican Civil War veterans. Schedler noted that she and her husband "just really got into it. So we started doing even more, like pulling the military records of the people we found, looking for stories of who was in our tribe, looking at treaties during the 1850s–60s to see what people were there, and then started going deeply into their history and searching military records." In the process, they discovered that many of these veterans, locally and nationally, do not have headstones at their burial sites. They have worked on doing the research to locate the resting places of these veterans and have headstones installed. As Schedler noted, some of these resting places are local and especially important for community members because, as she put it, "Some people didn't even know they had relatives buried there, like me, I didn't know that. So to bring that information and history and [those] stories for the community to me was just wonderful." Schedler and her husband have located resting places for Mohican veterans across the United States and have also recorded the location information of each burial site in order to "basically write a book for the community so they can learn more. . . . We want to be able to share that history with our tribal members and then that way people can go back [to where their ancestors are buried]." Schedler narrated their process, noting that upon locating and arriving at a resting place of a Mohican veteran, "we put tobacco down, we thank them for their service, take a picture, do the GPS, get the address and information. And so those are going to be the things that we're going to try to share for [the] community."[31] Schedler ultimately wrote a chapter on American Indians from Wisconsin who served in the Civil War for a National Park Service publication.[32]

Schedler and others have also participated in a Mohican writers group, an initiative founded by Historical Committee members to get more tribal members writing and publishing their own work. As Schedler put it, "We know people were writing . . . and the tribe has a goal of educating their own people. . . . So that was the goal, to get these people who had been doing these writings to focus on our history."[33] Many of these individuals contributed to the 2015 volume *Reflections on the Waters That Are Never Still*, a collection of contemporary literature by Mohican writers. In the effort to produce more stories and histories by Native writers, tribal archives, and Indigenous archival activism more broadly, can play a critical role. For individuals like Jo Ann Schedler, Jolene Bowman, and Eva Bowman, whose new works required extensive historical research, the archive can, as John Fleckner argues, place previously scattered resources "in Indian hands, and thus encourage[s] interpretation[s] of tribal history from an Indian perspective."[34] But even for those who are recording their own memories, original stories, or knowledge that has been passed to them, the archive provides a repository where these materials can be accessed in perpetuity, and the Historical Committee's work over all these years to shift the production of Mohican history to primarily Mohican hands means that there is a solid precedent of Mohican writers paving the way for contemporary authors. These new primary and secondary sources are important pieces in the larger reconstruction and expansion of a shared sense of Stockbridge-Munsee history and culture. If nationhood is, as Daniel Heath Justice argues, "woven in large part from the lives, dreams, and challenges of the people who compose the body politic," then a recording of these elements is a critical part of creating a shared national story.[35]

History, Language, and Cultural Programming

Since its official opening in 1974, the Mohican tribal archive has enabled many types of programs that provide opportunities for tribal members to learn about Stockbridge-Munsee history and culture outside of the physical archive while simultaneously building a sense of community through shared experiences with other tribal members. The 2001 conference is a large-scale example of this, but other, smaller projects created by the Historical Committee and individual tribal members have had similar effects. For example, starting in 1992 the Historical Committee initiated the yearly celebration of W'Chindin, a New Year's community gathering that, as Dorothy Davids put it, is "loosely based" on anthropologist Frank Speck's observations and recording of the Munsee-Mohican "Bear Sacrifice Ceremony" outlined in *The Celestial Bear Comes Down to Earth*.[36] W'Chindin is held over the course of twelve days and is meant to be a community celebration of "feasting, playing, and healing." It includes time for storytelling, discussion among community members, history lessons led by Historical Committee members, and common winter activities like ice skating and drinking hot cocoa.[37]

Speck's source is a colonial one—the information for the book was collected between 1932 and 1938, a period when anthropologists were traveling
to Native communities, extracting and recording knowledge, and publishing
information about Indigenous ceremonies, traditional life, and languages,
all under the guise of "saving" a culture that was allegedly disappearing.
Many of the sources published by Speck and his colleagues in anthropology included information that was never meant to be recorded, and the
books were ultimately published against the wishes of tribal communities.
While this is not the case with *Celestial Bear*, which the Historical Committee has deemed appropriate for public consumption, the knowledge was still
extracted from communities and placed in publications and libraries that
were much less accessible to the people whose traditions they recorded.
When Historical Committee members were using the book to craft their
own W'Chindin ceremony in 1992, there was no Google Books that would
have enabled them to quickly locate and review the book for their own purposes. Instead, their access to this text relied on previous Historical Committee work to travel to various libraries and archives and make copies of these
materials. Had Historical Committee members not copied this text in years
prior, the closest location of *Celestial Bear* in 1992 would have been the University of Wisconsin–Madison library, 160 miles south of the reservation.

Dorothy Davids's notes related to W'Chindin make it clear that she and the
event's coordinator, Molly Miller, studied Speck's text closely.[38] Davids's collection in the tribal archive includes twelve pages of handwritten notes about the
text, including diagrams, observations, and notes for the Stockbridge-Munsee
version of the gathering.[39] However, the fact that she frames W'Chindin as
"loosely" based on the Speck's version of the Bear Sacrifice Ceremony is significant. Did Davids doubt Speck's interpretation and decide, in coordination with Miller, to reframe the ceremony based on their own knowledge?
Did the community simply have different needs than when Speck took his
notes, and did Davids and Miller decide to structure the ceremony based
on what their community needed most at the time? Was it a little of both?
Either way, the source's availability to Davids and Miller is significant. The
Historical Committee's work to copy the text and make it accessible for
research made it easier for Davids and Miller to study it, reread it, and take
from it what was most useful to them and their community in that moment.
Beyond W'Chindin, Historical Committee members have also coordinated
other types of historical and cultural programming to make community

knowledge more accessible. They led several history courses on the reservation for tribal members, and in 1995 they created Wea Tauk, a living Mohican village, to further engage both tribal members and visitors to the Library-Museum beyond the traditional archive.[40] Each of these programs uses the tribal archive as a vital resource but aims to create new narratives and forms of engagement that will reach beyond those interested in conducting research at the tribal archive. These programs work to undo assimilationist efforts that prevented tribal members from learning and practicing their own traditional lifeways and are critical forms of nation-building that attempt to cultivate a shared sense of tribal history and culture among community members.

In addition to historical and cultural programming, the Historical Committee also prioritized language revitalization and programming and considered it a critical part of their early efforts. Like other tribal nations across the United States and Canada, the use of Indigenous languages within the Stockbridge-Munsee community decreased significantly in the wake of children attending Indian boarding and Christian mission schools, where they were forbidden to speak—and often punished for speaking—their Native languages. By the 1970s, when the committee was starting its work, there were no living speakers of Mohican or Munsee living on the reservation. In fact, the last living speaker had passed away in the 1930s.[41] There *were* Munsee speakers living in Canada that the committee began working with, but for Mohican they turned to documents.

Working with living Munsee speakers began in 1982 and was led by Molly Miller, who traveled to Moraviantown, Canada, to attend a summer language camp for the Munsee dialect of the Delaware language as a part of her degree at the University of Wisconsin–Stevens Point. When she returned to the reservation she initiated language classes and pushed for the creation of a committee to continue this work, but there was no significant support for her efforts until the early 2000s, when the Language and Culture Committee was officially formed. Miller and other members of the newly formed committee, including Joe Pecore, Nicole Pecore, and Monique Tyndall, continued attending language classes in Canada. By 2007, Miller and other Historical Committee members had started putting on an annual Language and Culture Camp for youth in the community based on what they were learning.[42]

For many years, learning Mohican was limited to collecting and reviewing the records of anthropologists who had documented the Mohican language in various forms. Historical Committee members scanned and saved dictionaries, field notes, letters, and books from several different archival locations, and even corresponded with linguists like Carl Masthay, who published the most recent version of a Mahican/English dictionary in 1991. In fact, it was Dorothy Davids and Bernice Miller who were able to point Masthay to some of the sources that were critical in his work.[43] Historical Committee members collected, and individuals like tribal members Shawn Stevens, Jeremy Mohawk, Dorothy Davids, Molly Miller, Larry Madden, Sheila Miller, and Brock Schreiber invested, "hundreds of hours researching the language" so that they could begin to teach it to tribal members.[44] Like the Speck source used for the W'Chindin ceremony, many of the materials tribal members studied were colonial documents that had been extracted from the community primarily by European missionaries or non-Native anthropologists with the intention of preserving these texts for non-Native researchers. They were never meant for Native audiences, yet they are being reread and used by Native people today. In reflecting on the nature of these materials, Stevens emphasized that while the texts certainly are colonial, he views them more as records that his ancestors left behind for him to find: "We have found the seeds our ancestor left for us; we have to find fertile grounds and the right season to plant. The season is here, it is our spring. There is plenty of fertile ground to sow these gifts from our ancestors."[45] Today, these records are available in the tribal archive for study. The Dorothy "Dot" Davids Collection II has three folders on language materials that were collected in the Historical Committee's early years, and the History Records Collection has several more folders with anthropological publications about language, accompanied by notes from elders like Miller and Davids.[46]

However, these written records alone were not enough to revitalize the Mohican language. Questions remained about pronunciation, pacing, and where the emphasis in certain words should be. Those questions remained unanswered until 2006, when tribal member Larry Madden and Molly Miller met linguist Christopher Harvey at a conference and began to work with him to interpret these archival materials and speak Mohican for the first time in nearly seventy-five years.[47] Harvey worked informally with Madden, Miller, and other tribal members for two years before returning to graduate school to pursue his PhD in 2008 and focusing his work on learning and researching the Mohican language using these archival materials.[48] In 2017 the Arvid E. Miller Library-Museum received a grant to formally support this work, hiring Harvey as the community linguist.[49] In the same year, the tribe created a paid Language Manager position that would focus on language and culture. Larry Madden, Shawn Stevens, Molly Miller, and Joe Pecore have served in this role, working directly with Harvey to create and coordinate online language and teaching processes and to transmit information about teaching the language to tribal members like Madden, Miller, and Brock Schreiber, who serve as teachers in the community. Harvey sees himself as the "bridge between written documentation and linguistics and the people in the community who are going to be the main drivers behind whatever language revitalization they want to do."[50] This work continues today. Schreiber has begun creating original teaching videos that are shared on the Arvid E. Miller Facebook page and website, and Schreiber and Madden started teaching Mohican over Zoom during the Covid-19 pandemic. Tribal member Nicole Pecore has also started teaching Munsee over Zoom.[51]

Beyond the Mohican Nation, archival records have become a common tool for teaching history and revitalizing Indigenous languages and cultures. Native American and Indigenous studies scholar Cutcha Risling Baldy describes the process of her mother "por[ing] over anthropological records and sit[ting] with elders to remember stories and songs that have been passed on for generations" in her efforts to revitalize Hupa coming-of-age ceremonies, while other tribal nations like the Passamaquoddy and Wampanoag Nations are using wax cylinders, Bibles, and other archival materials for language revitalization in similar ways to the Mohican Nation.[52] These types of language, cultural, and historical programming are a critical part of building a shared sense of culture and heritage among those in the Stockbridge-Munsee community. As Jolene Bowman put it, "it offers the community a sense of place. Many times children don't know where they come from or who they are, and they really need that—a sense of home, a place to find themselves—that builds security and self-esteem."[53] The strategic use of the Mohican tribal archive has shifted how Stockbridge-Munsee history, culture, and language are taught to tribal members and has enabled the revitalization of knowledge that had long been erased or silenced. These activities work to recultivate a shared sense of national identity and belonging among tribal members and are thus a critical component of Mohican nation-building.

Archives as Arsenals in Legal Reclamation Efforts

As tribal nations face increased threats to their cultural and political sovereignty through environmental extractivism, repatriation battles, and other fights over reservation boundaries, archival records and historical sources have become critical tools. Having these materials locally available to tribal government and cultural heritage staff can empower Indigenous nations to defend their sovereignty within these contexts.[54] This has proven true for the Mohican Nation, which has used the tribal archive primarily within the context of repatriation efforts but to some extent in battles over reservation boundaries as well. In both cases, access to archival records increases the speed at which the Mohican Nation can respond to identified issues or legal challenges as well as the likelihood that they will be able to succeed.

In the context of repatriation, the Historical Committee, the Historic Preservation Office, and now the broader Department of Cultural Affairs have primarily used archival records in the context of cases that fall under the Native American Graves Protection and Repatriation Act, where historical evidence is typically required to prove tribal affiliation with items and human remains to be reclaimed from museums. However, in one case prior to the passage of the law, they also used archival records to fuel an ultimately successful publicity campaign that ended with the repatriation of a two-volume Bible set that had been stolen from the reservation in the 1930s. Again, in each of these cases, the proximity of the tribal archive and the research conducted by Historical Committee members and those within the Historic Preservation Office and the Department of Cultural Affairs staff was ultimately critical in the success of these cases.

To highlight the use of records for repatriation, I begin with an abbreviated version of the Stockbridge-Munsee Bible set story.[55] In 1745 the chaplain to the Prince of Wales gifted a two-volume, gold-lettered Bible set to the Stockbridge Mohicans, who had agreed to be part of the mission in their village Wnahktukuk (Stockbridge).[56] The Mohicans cherished this Bible as a sacred religious item and as a treasured gift connecting them to a particular historical moment.[57] When they were forced to leave Stockbridge shortly after the Revolutionary War, they traveled to upstate New York before ultimately being removed farther west. In New York, they also acquired a pewter Communion set that they kept with the Bible set and carried with them on their journey to Wisconsin.[58] The Mohicans guarded these items throughout their removal, and according to tribal member Elaine M. Jacobi, the items were "preserved, and always placed on the altar wherever they [the Mohicans] settled in a new home and a new church."[59] In the early twentieth century, numerous non-Native churches and museums began to inquire

Figure 13. The two-volume Bible and four-piece pewter Communion set. Courtesy of the Stockbridge-Munsee Community, Cultural Affairs Department, Arvid E. Miller Library Museum.

about how they could acquire the items, but the Stockbridge-Munsee people remained resolute—the items were not for sale.[60]

Throughout their history, the Bible and Communion set were kept in the homes of tribal leaders for safekeeping. However, as interest for the items grew, tribal members increasingly discussed whether they would be safer in a nearby bank vault. Before they could decide, the last leader charged with caring for the Bible, Jamison Quinney, passed away in 1929. After his death, local religious leader Rev. Frederick G. Westfall illegally entered the Quinney home while Quinney's widow, Ella, was away, and stole the Bible and Communion set, paternalistically assuming that the safest and most logical place for the items was his own congregation. However, Westfall had additional motivation for stealing the items than safekeeping. In the same year as his theft, Westfall began corresponding with Mabel Choate, a white resident of Stockbridge, Massachusetts, who was assembling a museum about the town's history, and several of her associates.[61] Choate worked with Westfall to acquire several historical items for both her museum and the Museum of the American Indian in New York, ultimately convincing him to sell her the Bible and Communion set, even though he admitted that he was not sure "if such an exchange is legal."[62] In the aftermath of Quinney's death, most tribal members thought that the items had been moved to a bank vault in the nearby city of Shawano. It was not until 1951, when tribal member Jim Davids traveled with his family to Stockbridge, that they discovered the Bible and Communion set were no longer in their possession. Instead, the items were being displayed in what had become the Mission House Museum—a re-creation of the eighteenth-century mission settlement led by Rev. John Sergeant.[63] Once they discovered the truth, tribal members were determined to retrieve the items, but they wanted to be strategic about their request. They knew the museum would be hard-pressed to part with the items, so they waited until their Library-Museum was officially open in 1974 to show they had a place to display the items for community members.[64] The tribe, led by the Historical Committee, made requests for the return of the Bible and Communion set in 1975 and 1981, both of which were denied by the organization that owned and operated the Mission House Museum, the Trustees of Reservations.[65]

At that point, the Historical Committee decided to initiate a public campaign, using archival documents from their own collection as a key tool over the next decade to solicit letters of support from across the country. Their efforts started locally in 1981, with the committee using their newsletter *Quin'a Month'a* to circulate a brief history of the Bible and Communion set to fellow community members and other contacts. The four-page account, written by Dorothy Davids and titled "Brief History of the Stockbridge Bibles," includes nearly as many pages of bibliographic notes and includes quotations and resources from a variety of sources, including published works about the Stockbridge-Munsee Mohicans dating back to the late nineteenth century; land grant documentation copied from the Berkshire Historical and Scientific Society in Pittsfield, Massachusetts; letters gathered from tribal members who were alive when the Bible and Communion set were still on the reservation; copies of Mabel Choate's side of the correspondence between her and Westfall; and minutes from church meetings that Westfall kept, presumably secured by tribal members after Westfall's congregation ceased to exist. On the first page of the account, a note clearly states, "all documentation for this paper was taken from materials which may be found in the Stockbridge-Munsee Historical Library Museum."[66]

By 1982 the Historical Committee had compiled and begun to circulate an additional booklet titled "The Stockbridge Bible: Documents Relating to Its Recovery by the Stockbridge Indians."[67] While this booklet primarily contained copies of primary and secondary source evidence that outlines Mohican ownership of the Bible and Communion set and the importance of returning these items to the tribe, it also includes a brief introduction that provides a description of the Library-Museum and a brief overview of its "over 4000 historical research items." The booklet includes firsthand accounts from 1836 and 1911 that describe the community's care for the Bible upon the tribe's arrival in and throughout their removals within Wisconsin; letters between tribal officials, their lawyers, and the Trustees of Reservations; and the deed of sale for the items from 1930. Like the "Brief History," this pamphlet urged readers to write to the Trustees of Reservations directly and urge them to return the Bible and Communion set to the Stockbridge-Munsee Community.[68] The availability of these archival materials to Historical Committee members was critical to their ability to research the history of these items, put together a public media campaign that outlined their findings, and ultimately to raise national awareness and support for the return of the tribe's Bible and Communion set.

The letter-writing campaign continued throughout the Mohicans' fight for the items. Hundreds of individuals from across the United States sent letters to the trustees, demanding that they return both the Bible and Communion set to the Mohican people.[69] Letters were sent from near and far, and even notable individuals like anthropologist Nancy Oestrich Lurie, Wisconsin governor Lee Sherman Dreyfus, and American folk singer Pete Seeger wrote to the trustees.[70] Newspapers and TV stations began calling the Mohican Historical Committee for more information, and the tribe continued to contact countless media sources to raise awareness for their cause. As a whole, a massive public campaign drew national attention to this important issue. As Dorothy Davids noted, the Mohicans "hope[d] the Trustees of Reservations [would] 'get the message' and agree to negotiate directly with the Stockbridge Indian representatives."[71]

In spite of this, the trustees mostly remained publicly silent for much of the 1980s. They ignored repeated requests from the tribe to meet in person and made no public statements about the issue.[72] Internally, however, their records show extensive strategic planning and discussion about how to keep the items. Trustee meeting minutes include racist assumptions about the Mohicans' genuine interest in the items and their ability to care for them, with one member of the organization asking "How straight is this Indian group—will we ever see the Bibles again?" and noting that "I'm not convinced

[the] Indians have good faith in their interest in the Bible and don't even want to sell it."[73] Another remarked that "co-ownership makes me shiver. Until somebody's been out there [the Mohican reservation] and seen their operation, we don't know where things stand or who they are."[74] Trustee leadership also carefully considered the impact their decision might have on other national conversations about the repatriation of Indigenous items that were happening in the late 1980s, and the poor publicity this issue might bring (or was already bringing) them.[75] Eventually, the final two topics proved to be key in turning the tide of this debate. The trustees were cognizant of the national discussion occurring about American Indian human remains and sacred items held by non-Native institutions, which was sparked when representatives from the Northern Cheyenne Nation discovered that the Smithsonian had possession of nearly 18,500 human remains in 1986 and continued over the next several years with legislative debates and national conversations.[76] Eventually, these debates and conversations culminated in the passage of the Native American Graves Protection and Repatriation Act (NAGPRA) in 1990, but in the late 1980s the trustees archived newspaper articles about the topic and wrote to other non-Native institutions to inquire about how they were handling similar issues. Ultimately, they realized that they would likely be pressured to return the Bible and Communion set if these debates continued, and they were very worried about a "media blitz" or "bad publicity" around the issue in the meantime.[77] As more letters from supporters who read the Historical Committee's research and newsletters poured in, this pressure continued to increase.[78]

In 1989 the trustees finally agreed to meet with tribal representatives in person, first in Stockbridge, Massachusetts, and then on the reservation in Wisconsin.[79] Again, archival records proved critical in these meetings. Stanley Piatczyc, one of the trustees who attended both meetings, referenced letters between Mabel Choate and Reverend Westfall that suggested the Stockbridge-Munsee Mohicans had approved of the sale. He noted: "I have been opposed to the return of the Bibles all these years because I have been going on documentation that we have at hand, letters written by Rev. Westfall and Mabel Choate primarily. Westfall writes of a 'happy consummation' in the sale, approved by both the Indians and himself."[80] After hearing evidence from the Mohican tribal archive presented by Dorothy Davids to the contrary, noting that the church was in need of money at the time and Westfall placed the items in the church under questionable means, Piatczyc said:

"We want to find a solution to this dilemma. Our sense of urgency has been greatly heightened by this meeting with you."[81] In August 1989 the trustees officially voted to return the items to the Stockbridge-Munsee Nation, and the Bible set was returned in March 1991.[82]

The Historical Committee was thrilled to have the Bible back in Wisconsin with them, but their retrieval work had only begun. After the passage of NAGPRA in November 1990, tribal nations like the Mohicans were inundated with inventory lists of human remains, funerary objects, and sacred items from non-Native institutions, all of which required extensive research before anything could be returned. In the most basic terms, NAGPRA requires that all institutions that receive federal funds[83] repatriate Native American human remains, associated and unassociated funerary objects, sacred objects, and objects of cultural patrimony in their collections to "culturally affiliated"[84] Indian tribes and Native Hawaiian organizations.[85] It also requires that these same institutions work with Indian tribes and Native Hawaiian organizations if Native American human remains, associated or unassociated funerary objects, sacred objects, or objects of cultural patrimony are found and/or removed from federal or tribal lands.[86]

Yet these requirements are, to some extent, overstated. They do not require institutions to immediately begin returning objects and human remains; instead, they require them to complete inventories of human remains and objects in their collections and send a copy of these assessments to the federally recognized tribes and Native Hawaiian organizations that they determine might be "culturally affiliated" with the items. From there, the burden of conducting significant historical research to establish and prove this "cultural affiliation" falls almost entirely on Indigenous nations themselves.[87] Human remains and associated funerary objects are typically returned upon receiving a request from a lineal descendant, Indian tribe, or Native Hawaiian organization that can show that they are "more likely than not" "culturally affiliated" with the remains or objects. However, the process for the repatriation of unassociated funerary objects, sacred objects, and objects of cultural patrimony is significantly more complicated and arduous. For these items to be repatriated, the claimant (tribes/Native Hawaiian organizations) must (1) show that the item is an unassociated funerary object, sacred object, or object of cultural patrimony; (2) demonstrate that the object was previously owned by the tribe or Native Hawaiian organization; and (3) present evidence to show that the federal institution in possession of the object did not have the "right of possession" when it obtained the object, meaning it did not secure the item with "voluntary consent" of the party who had authority over the item previously.[88] After tribal nations compile all of this research, holding institutions retain the authority to make decisions about whether tribes are "culturally affiliated" with the objects and human remains that they claim, as well as whether the items constitute sacred objects or objects of cultural patrimony.[89]

In response to this new legislation, many tribes established Historic Preservation offices. As Historical Committee member Leah Miller noted, though the Historical Committee led the effort to retrieve the Bible, the labor required to reclaim other objects grew to be too much for the volunteer-based group, leading the tribe to first create a Repatriation Committee and then, in 2004, to establish a separate office and hire staff to take on the time-consuming process of receiving inventories, gathering evidence, and establishing consistent communication between tribes and federal institutions.[90] Dorothy Davids was one of the first members of the Repatriation Committee after the passage of NAGPRA, and she noted that the tribe received more than 150 letters or inventories from different museums within the first seven years after NAGPRA was passed, writing that the committee

> studied each inventory and determined who had, who possibly had, and who probably did not have Mohican remains and/or funerary objects. To make these determinations, we had to intensely study our own history, especially the boundaries of our eastern homelands and subsequent sites to which we had been removed. Then we had to study maps to determine if the museums were within those areas or if the remains/funerary objects originated in those areas.[91]

Once Sherry White assumed the official role as tribal historic preservation officer, she also depended on archival materials for NAGPRA cases. The bulk of White's work was about verifying cultural affiliation for the items on inventories and conducting research to prove that the items met the requirements of NAGPRA, such as that they qualify as items of cultural patrimony or are sacred in nature.[92] Reflecting on her role, she noted that cultural affiliation was probably the most common way that museums attempted to oppose repatriation claims. In one case, staff at Brown University's Haffenreffer Museum of Anthropology attempted to contest cultural affiliation for several pipes in their collection. Though the pipes were labeled in museum records as "Stockbridge-Munsee," the museum repeatedly contested this affiliation and required White to provide additional evidence to prove the pipes were culturally affiliated with the Stockbridge-Munsee Community. It was not until 2022 that the tribe's current historic preservation manager, Bonney Hartley, was finally able to repatriate the pipes. While White was able to do much of her research in the tribal archive, she had to rely on other repositories as the archive was being expanded. She recalled the frustration of searching for relevant materials under the "many names we're known by. . . . I'd search 'praying Indians,' 'Housatonic Indians.' I'd look at things labeled Mohegan and wonder, 'is this the Connecticut tribe or did someone just misspell our name?'"[93]

In addition to the summaries they received, Davids noted that the Repatriation Committee also *sent* inventory requests to several museums that they thought might have Mohican remains or items based on their own research. They also visited museums that had yet to complete their inventories, like the Peabody Museum at Harvard University, which had completed inventories of only 2,000 of the 11,000 ancestors, or human remains, that they held by 1999, nine years after NAGPRA was passed. Reflecting on the visit, Davids wrote: "After a dozen drawers, I could feel a wave of depression wash over me. I thought about the thousands of people who wer[e] removed from their eastern homelands, yet one could view materials [*sic*] evidence of their presence preserved here in [the] museum. I thought about how difficult it is for us to recover items for our own museum."[94]

Davids's and White's summaries of these tasks shows the significant emotional and physical labor required not only to prove that items are "culturally affiliated" to the Mohicans but also to determine which items are actually Mohican and should be prioritized among the massive inventories given to the tribe following NAGPRA. Each object or set of remains that tribes attempt to reclaim requires individual research, and since scholars estimate that institutions that receive federal funding held between 300,000 and 2.5 million American Indian remains, funerary objects, and items of cultural patrimony when NAGPRA was passed in 1990, the inventories that museums created and tribes combed through were undoubtedly extensive.[95]

The significant research required for each of the items listed in these inventories speaks to how crucial tribal archives are for tribes working to prove cultural affiliation. The research Davids and White describe here is time-consuming in its own right, but it would have been much more difficult if they had been required to consistently travel to multiple different archives across the country to retrieve the required documentation. Since the passage of NAGPRA, the tribe, led by the Tribal Historic Preservation Office, has successfully retrieved several more items through repatriation, including the Communion set that was stolen by Westfall at the same time as the Bible set, a powder horn from the Oshkosh Public Museum, and moccasins and a wampum belt from the Berkshire Museum. As of this writing, they are in the process of reclaiming all the remaining items in the Mission House collection, which range from pottery to clothing.[96] They are also trying to recover several items from the Smithsonian.

In 2021, when I talked with Bonney Hartley about these most recent efforts, she noted that archival records can be particularly helpful in proving that items qualify as "cultural patrimony" under NAGPRA or the National Museum of the American Indian Act (which applies specifically to the Smithsonian but has similar regulations to NAGPRA).[97] Hartley typically looks for ways to say that an item is precious and would have been passed down through multiple generations and thus belongs to the community rather than a deceased individual, or that items were used by multiple community members. In the case of one item they are currently trying to retrieve, a coat owned by tribal leader John W. Quinney, the item records already show that the coat was passed through multiple generations, but Hartley is working to reinforce that claim by showing that Quinney likely retrieved the coat at an important diplomatic meeting. To do so, she is using a sketch of Quinney in the coat that was done by artist Frank B. Mayer at Fort Snelling in Minnesota Territory, leading up to the 1851 treaty negotiations at Traverse des Sioux and Mendota.[98] Hartley emphasized that in order to convince the holding institution that an item is sacred or an item of cultural patrimony, you have to be able to point to its historical importance in documents. This perceived requirement is troubling, particularly because NAGPRA lists "oral traditional information" as acceptable evidence for institutions to consider when making their decisions. We know from both Hartley's statement here and cases that have ruled against Native tribes that in practice this is not always the case.[99] In an ideal world, non-Native institutions would regard tribal members as experts on their own cultures and take tribal nations at their word when they say an item is significant and should be returned to a community.

Until that time, archival records continue to serve as critical evidence in repatriation efforts.

Like archival documents, items returned from museums can serve, as Bernice and Lucille Miller put it in one application, as "clues ... that [aid] us in our search for the truth about our culture and history."[100] The return of these items often relies on the existing archival collection, but they also add to the collection and the broader effort of the Mohican Historical Committee to recover their tribal history and rebuild a common sense of identity among tribal members that is based in shared heritage. As Historical Committee member Jo Ann Schedler put it in my interview with her, "It helps with our young people to look and see ... where did it come from? Why did it come? What happened?" She further emphasized that it is "so important for young people to see some of these [items] and then hear the stories about our tribe because so much was lost."[101] Tribal member Stephanie Bowman agreed. Reflecting on a pipe that was repatriated, she said:

Figure 14. Frank Blackwell Mayer's 1851 sketch of John W. Quinney, who is wearing the coat that the Stockbridge-Munsee Community is attempting to retrieve from the Smithsonian. Edward E. Ayer Art Collection, Newberry Library.

It's helping people to realize that we can bring a pipe back, because our ancestors had that. So we understand that we are just like other Native people: that
we did have a belief, that we did have a culture. It's putting the pieces back
together again, what we thought was lost. It's picking up things that were put
down so that we could survive. That's what I think the Library-Museum is
helping us to do.[102]

Placed within and made accessible at the Arvid E. Miller Library-Museum, the
Bible and Communion set, as well as other items the Mohicans have retrieved
from non-Native institutions, provide a vital link to the Mohican past that is
incredibly important to contemporary Mohican nation-building.

Land Reclamations

While repatriation is the most common legal issue for which the tribal archive
has been used, it has also proved to be a vital resource in several court cases
over reservation boundaries and remains a valuable repository for issues
that may arise in the future. As the central repository for records of the tribal
government, the archive serves as an important arsenal for evidence commonly required in land cases, such as maps, land deeds or transfer records,
treaties, and government correspondence, as well as research reports and documentation amassed in cases that the tribe has taken up in the past. These
kinds of records are compiled in several places within the archive, including a "Boundary Issues" folder within its History Records Collection, which
holds more than seven hundred pages of allotment records, treaties, summary
reports of reservation boundaries, correspondence, and newspaper articles
ranging from the 1890s to the 1990s. These records have been used as evidence in various land cases over the years. This same collection holds several
folders for land deeds, bills of sale, and depositions regarding land sales dating as far back as the 1630s.[103] This collection enables the Mohican Nation to
assert its sovereignty in court cases as needed, and having these records readily available on the reservation increases the chances that tribes can quickly
gather evidence that will be accepted in settler-colonial courts. It significantly
reduces the time and energy needed to track down relevant documents and
sort through unfamiliar archival collections.

    This use of the archive especially makes sense given its founding in the
midst of the Indian Reorganization Act. As outlined in the introduction, one
of Arvid and Bernice Miller's initial motivations for collecting was having

maps, land records, and other sources of tribal history on hand so that they could successfully reorganize their tribal government and help the newly elected Tribal Council write the community's new constitution. This use of the collection continues today, and representatives from Tribal Council and the tribe's Department of Cultural Affairs, which includes the Historic Preservation Office, frequently use the materials that have been amassed. As Leah Miller put it in 2016, "We have tribal officials over here researching our archives whenever a certain issue comes up."[104]

Readily available archival resources can play a significant role in preparing tribal nations to defend their sovereignty. However, no matter how prepared a nation is, cases over land boundaries are not frequently ruled in favor of tribal nations. We should not read this as a failure on the tribe's part, but instead as a reflection of ongoing settler colonialism. Since the Stockbridge-Munsee Mohican Nation was removed to north-central Wisconsin in the Treaty of 1856, which granted the tribe 46,000 acres on the southern border of the Menominee Reservation in the townships of Red Springs and Bartelme, they have faced significant challenges to their reservation boundaries.[105] Much of this acreage was lost through an 1871 congressional act, which sold fifty-four sections of pine-forested reservation lands to loggers, and the 1887 General Allotment Act, which allotted remaining land to individual tribal members, many of whom sold their parcels to feed their families or were forced to sell their land over mortgage payments and grocery bills. Another congressional act in 1906 further diminished reservation land, leaving the Stockbridge-Munsee people with almost no land remaining. Through the IRA the Mohican Nation regained about 15,000 acres of their land, but only 2,500 were officially placed in trust for the tribe.[106] The tribe continues to view their reservation boundaries as those set by the 1856 treaty and has continually worked to officially place in trust the original 46,000 acres that was granted to them by the U.S. federal government. But they have faced many challenges.

The most successful effort to officially restore reservation boundaries occurred in 1972, when the Historical Committee successfully used materials gathered in the tribal archive to support the Tribal Council in placing 13,000 acres back in trust for the tribe.[107] However, subsequent cases aimed at defending the 1856 reservation boundaries have not been as successful. In May 1991, tribal member Bert Davids was ticketed for fishing on Upper Gresham Lake without a license. Davids insisted that the lake was within the boundaries established in the 1856 treaty and that he therefore had a right to fish on tribal land as an enrolled tribal member. Davids was initially convicted and fined, but an appeals court overturned the decision in 1994, reasoning that because Congress had not explicitly stated in the congressional acts of 1871 and 1906 that it was changing Stockbridge-Munsee reservation boundaries, the reservation was still intact.[108] Unfortunately, this decision was overturned by the Wisconsin Supreme Court just one year later.[109] In 1998 the tribe faced a similar dispute. They had recently purchased the Pine Hills Golf Course and Supper Club, which was situated within the original Treaty of 1856 boundaries. Under its gambling contract with the state, which allows the tribe to operate certain types of gambling on tribal land, the tribe began operating slot machines at the golf course. They were ordered to cease operating the machines due to the state's belief that the golf course was not within current tribal lands. The tribe appealed the decision several times, but ultimately, 2004 and 2009 decisions ruled in the state's favor, asserting that even though it was not explicitly stated, Congress's intent in the acts of 1871 and 1906 was to eliminate the reservation.[110]

Though these latter two battles were ultimately unsuccessful, the tribal archive still played a crucial role in helping the tribe build its cases. A newspaper article covering the slot machine dispute notes that the tribe produced annual records from the Keshena Indian Agency from 1906 to 1925, specific correspondence from the Bureau of Indian Affairs (BIA) showing their recognition of the original reservation boundaries, and at least one map that ultimately served as "a key piece of evidence" in the case.[111] Government records like these are not readily accessible, even now in the days of digitization. The records from the Keshena Agency and other government-produced documents are still held by the National Archives and Records Administration at Chicago, which means that in order for these records to be readily accessible to tribal members in each of these court cases, Historical Committee members must have copied them in Chicago and brought the copies back to the reservation.[112] Other correspondence with the BIA was likely preserved by the Millers as the tribe was reorganizing, when they were filing all tribal records in their home. Yet cases like these often come down to each judge's interpretations of Congress's intentions. Though the Stockbridge-Munsee tribe was unsuccessful in these suits, in 2020 the U.S. Supreme Court ruled in *McGirt v. Oklahoma* that a significant portion of the state of Oklahoma remained Indian land belonging to the Cherokee, Choctaw, Chickasaw, Creek, and Seminole Nations because Congress had never formally disestablished the reservations.[113] As similar court cases across the country are brought forth in the wake of this precedent-setting decision, we will undoubtedly see similar uses of tribal archives in attempts to restore reservation boundaries.

In the context of Indigenous nation-building, it is important to remember that in addition to history, language, and culture, land is a critical element of shared political and cultural identity.[114] In that sense, the efforts to restore reservation boundaries are not just about reclaiming land so that the tribe can own more acreage; rather, land is intimately connected to Indigenous culture, and control over a specific land base is a critical component of Indigenous sovereignty. Ultimately, the fights to reclaim this land and the more successful efforts to repatriate Mohican material culture are both about rebuilding the community: its political status as a sovereign nation that controls specific territory, and the fact that its members share a culturally rich heritage. Together, these components define Mohican nationhood and make these legal efforts supported by archival records a critical component of Mohican archival activism.

Though these projects—tribal newsletters, repatriation, history conferences, boundary battles, and language revitalization—may seem disparate, the thread that connects them is their goal of preserving the future of the Stockbridge-Munsee Mohican Nation. Each of these projects or initiatives works to make tribal history more accessible to community members, support tribal sovereignty, and ultimately create new narratives that foster a shared sense of national heritage, identity, and nationhood among members of the Stockbridge-Munsee Mohican community. As Leah Miller emphasized, settler-colonial policies were "created by white people to divide us and to use that division to get what they wanted, such as our land. So knowing our history and knowing what we went through, I think, is a way of protecting our people."[115] As we have seen, archival records can play a critical role in these efforts.

These projects are critical components of Mohican nation-building, and they highlight the fact that the number one priority of Historical Committee members has always been caring for their own community members. And yet, these women also understood that caring for their communities also required changes in public opinion. As long as non-Native people thought the "Last of the Mohicans" were the individuals in Cooper's novel, the Mohican Nation was no closer to being recognized as a contemporary sovereign nation with unique rights. In other words, they were no closer to winning those court cases, reclaiming the items that had been stolen from their community, or being recognized as the best resource on their own history. As a result, Mohican archival activism was always a two-pronged fight that included a Mohican public and a non-Native public. The final two chapters move beyond the reservation to address the non-Native public more directly. While many of the initiatives discussed are still primarily aimed at Mohican community members, the Historical Committee's actions beyond the Mohican reservation demonstrate their understanding that broader shifts in Mohican historical narratives were critical to advancing the interests of their own community.

4

The Mohican Historical Trips

It seemed to me that those who were making the trip for the first time were discovering that we are a people with roots, people with a history. Though we have been uprooted and moved many times, we know who we are. We are the people-of-the-waters-that-are-never-still and the people of the Many Trails.

—Dorothy Davids, Historical Committee cofounder, report of the 1989 historical trip

The Stockbridge-Munsee Mohican reservation is more than a thousand miles from the tribe's ancestral homelands in the Mahicannituck (Hudson) River Valley, which the tribe was forced to leave in 1783. Yet in spite of this physical distance and the passing of more than two centuries, tribal members have never stopped returning to or relinquished their connections with these lands.[1] In particular, the Historical Committee has been teaching Mohican history in and continuing to care for their ancestral homelands since they began coordinating trips for tribal members in 1968, the same year the committee was founded. The Tribal Historic Preservation Office (THPO Office) also took up this work with its founding in 2001, as has the more recently founded Department of Cultural Affairs, which was created in 2018 to unite staff within the Library-Museum, the THPO Office, and the Language Department. Together, these tribal entities have made an enormous impact on the collection of, care for, and representation of Mohican histories in their ancestral homelands. In 1996 the tribe prevented Wal-Mart from opening a new store in Catskill, New York, after human remains were uncovered on the construction site. In 2005 they signed a Memorandum of Understanding with the West Point Military Academy, dictating procedure for human remains or sacred items uncovered in construction projects. And in 2015 they opened a satellite Historic Preservation Office in upstate New York (now based in Williamstown, Massachusetts), facilitating increased collaboration on land development and historical projects in their home-lands. These efforts are all important types of activism that exemplify how the Historical Committee has mobilized the Mohican tribal archive to restore connections between tribal members and their homelands and to challenge broader perceptions that the tribe no longer exists. This chapter examines how these interventions stem from and contribute to the creation and expansion of the Mohican tribal archive.

Since this first delegation in 1968, the Mohican Historical Committee and later the THPO Office have led more than a dozen journeys to their ancestral homelands. The trips have been funded in part by either the Stockbridge-Munsee Tribal Council or the Stockbridge-Munsee Historical Committee, and have been mostly limited to enrolled members of the Stockbridge-Munsee Mohican Nation.[2] They have varied in size from fewer than five people to more than forty, and have typically included a wide age range of travelers, including those as young as two and as old as eighty-four.[3] Tribal members typically spend significant time at historic village sites like Schodack, Peebles, and Papscanee Islands in present-day New York, and the area surrounding Stockbridge, Massachusetts—another site of an important Mohican village and the location of the mission that served as a major turning point in the tribe's history. On the way to or from the Northeast, the tribe has also retraced the route their ancestors traveled as they were forced to move west, stopping in Bethlehem, Pennsylvania; Loudonville and Gnadenhutten, Ohio; and White River, Indiana—places the tribe either lived in or passed through briefly during the process of removal. On several trips they also stopped to visit Munsee relatives in Ontario.[4] They have also visited the Carlisle Indian School, where several tribal members were sent in the late nineteenth century.[5] In each of these places, tribal members reorient and reground themselves, creating connected geographies that help tribal members forge new collective memories.[6]

When the Mohicans began coordinating the trips in 1968, they were one of many groups engaged in the post–civil rights phenomenon of "heritage tourism," trips motivated by an interest in the tourist's *own* history.[7] Especially influenced by Alex Haley's *Roots,* which traced the family history of an African American man sold into slavery in the United States, Americans from numerous racial groups began to see themselves as "whole, traceable across oceans and centuries to the remotest ancestral village."[8] Yet the stakes were different among these groups. While heritage tourism provided white

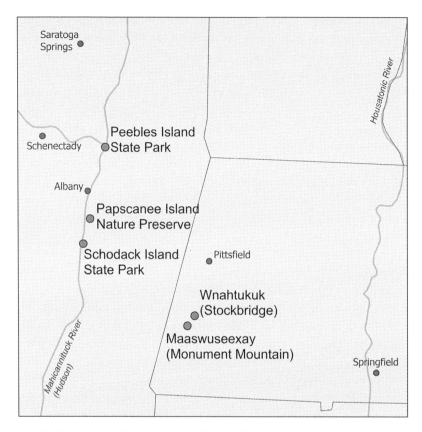

Map 2. Common stopping points on the Mohican historical trips, located throughout the Mahicannituck (Hudson) River Valley.

Americans with the opportunity to erase their own complicity in white-supremacist structures by making claims such as "I'm not white, I'm Italian," nonwhite Americans interested in their heritage had to conduct significant research to trace their histories as a direct result of these same structures.[9] For white tourists, traveling to their European countries of origin was an opportunity to return to a land their ancestors likely chose to leave, while African Americans and Native people returned to lands from which their ancestors were forcibly removed.[10] I set up these comparisons between different types of heritage tourism not to demean individual experiences but to show that the stakes are different. Mohican returns to their ancestral homelands work in direct opposition to settler colonialism and are thus an important type of Native resistance. They aim to reunite tribal members with lands their ancestors were forced to leave, reteach tribal histories that generations of Mohican children were prevented from learning, and challenge external perceptions that they do not maintain important connections to these lands. In reality, Stockbridge-Munsee people sustain a connection to both their ancestral homelands and their current land in Wisconsin, and they maintain that attachment through ongoing relationships, memories, and stories.[11] The Historical Committee supports these ongoing relationships by facilitating group experiences that rely on storytelling and memory making to rebuild a shared sense of heritage, belonging, and national identity among tribal members. Together, these efforts shift how both Mohicans and non-Mohicans access and learn Mohican history and are important types of Indigenous nation-building.

Among projects within the landscape of Mohican archival activism, the historical trips are notable in the sense that they touch almost every element of creating, expanding, and using a tribal archive. Moreover, while community archives are most often recognized for their local impacts, the Mohican historical trips show just how extensive a reach tribal archives can have.[12] This chapter sketches out the multifaceted aspects of these returns and their connections to the archive. To do so, I begin with the use of the trips to conduct research in archival collections and scan additional materials for the Mohican tribal archive. This was the primary motivation for early trips, but it continued to be an important aspect as they expanded and Historical Committee members sought to expose younger tribal members to historical research directly. I then move to what I consider the primary purpose of the trips: reconnecting tribal members with the homelands their ancestors were removed from and teaching tribal histories in this context. Historical Committee members used their newly collected materials to select locations for future trips and conduct research in preparation for sharing historical knowledge with other tribal members. The act of reteaching tribal histories in these spaces has a particular impact, and even joy, for those learning, but it can also trigger considerable trauma as tribal members learn how and why their ancestors were forced to leave these lands. The middle section of the chapter examines these outcomes that are seemingly at odds, grappling with the ways that both joy and sadness contribute to the formation of shared tribal identity. It also considers how the Historical Committee captured these responses by asking tribal members to keep journals of their experiences that were later deposited into the tribal archive. The final section examines how the trips have enabled the tribe to challenge erasure narratives and assert an ongoing presence in their homelands. These efforts ultimately led to the creation of a satellite Historic Preservation Office in tribal homelands. The office gives the tribe increased control over how their history is collected, primarily in land development projects that often unearth human remains or other important historical sites, and lays an essential foundation for even more direct, off-reservation interventions in public history and public education.

The pillars of archival activism are evident in the historical trips, which enable the Historical Committee, and by extension the Stockbridge-Munsee Mohican Nation, to shift the way tribal members access history (both through archival documents and place-based teaching), exercise sovereignty over the way their histories are collected by others, challenge the way that non-Native settlers create and circulate narratives about the Stockbridge-Munsee Community, and generate new narratives of their own history to both Native and non-Native publics. The trips show us how tribal archives are foundational to larger historical projects and activist efforts, and they demonstrate one of the many ways Indigenous nations use public history and public memory spaces to reclaim authority over their national histories.

Expanding the Archive

Bernice Miller described the first historical trip in 1968 as "successful in every way."[13] The group, which included Bernice's sister Dorothy Davids, their father Elmer Davids, their aunt Wildy Putnam, and Dorothy Davids's longtime partner Ruth Gudinas, traveled through Canada and New York to reach their destination of Stockbridge, Massachusetts. Stockbridge was the English name given to the town in 1735, but to the Mohicans this place was Wnahktukuk, an important meeting place and village for their ancestors. They explored Stockbridge, visited the Mission House Museum where the Bible and Communion set discussed in chapter 3 were kept, and walked through the old town cemetery looking for familiar names. Davids and Miller, who had recently resolved to build the tribal archive, were also on a mission to make copies of documents they could bring back to the Mohican reservation.

As the Historical Committee continued their work in subsequent years, Davids, Miller, and other members of the committee continued to travel to the Northeast in an attempt to learn everything they could about Mohican

Figure 15. Arminta Chicks Hebert (*left*) and Ernestine Quinney Murphy examine documents in the Stockbridge Library in Stockbridge, Massachusetts, as a part of the research component of their historical trip in 1989. Courtesy of the Stockbridge-Munsee Community, Cultural Affairs Department, Arvid E. Miller Library Museum.

Figure 16. Dorothy Davids (*front left*), Blanche Jacobs (*front right*), and two other tribal members examine library materials in an unknown location, probably either New York or Massachusetts, as part of the research component of a trip in the 1970s. Courtesy of the Stockbridge-Munsee Community, Cultural Affairs Department, Arvid E. Miller Library Museum.

history and gather information that had been scattered across countless archives. As the trips grew in size, the elders on the committee also taught others, especially younger tribal members, how to participate in the research process, including "how to identify one topic they would pursue, how to use the card catalogs, how to use the indexes, how to take notes, and how to keep a journal."[14]

Historical Committee members also used these trips as a way to build connections and collaborative relationships with local residents. To publicize their work in local newspapers, the committee regularly issued press releases in the hope that local residents might read about the Mohican goal of recovering and gathering history and be aware of additional resources that could be useful to the tribe.[15] Through their extensive research in various archives, committee members also built relationships with archivists, many of whom agreed to share new materials they received with the Arvid E. Miller Library-Museum. For the Stockbridge Library in Massachusetts, working together on this research facilitated collaborative relationships between tribal and nontribal archivists and a continuous exchange of documents. In particular, Grace Wilcox and Polly Pierce (both previous archivists at the Stockbridge Library) built long-term relationships with the tribe and advocated for the tribe on a number of occasions. Grace's grandson Rick Wilcox, who is also Stockbridge's former chief of police, has continued much of this work.[16]

Rick Wilcox regularly does extensive archival research in both Stockbridge and the surrounding area and transcribes eighteenth- and nineteenth-century materials in support of projects within the THPO Office. He has also served as an advocate for the tribe on several issues, including a current campaign to repatriate a series of documents that were previously held by the Stockbridge Town Offices and another to return the Indian Burial Ground in Stockbridge to the tribe. Though the Mohicans have worked with several generations of archivists to make copies of local records, they still, as of this writing, do not own a single original document from their time in the town between 1737 and 1790.[17] That could change with what is as of this writing a potential repatriation of the Indian Proprietorship Records—a series of documents that outline Indigenous land ownership and negotiations in Stockbridge in the mid-eighteenth century. Wilcox has supported this effort by transcribing the records in full for immediate tribal access and convincing fellow Stockbridge residents to vote on the return of this material through an op-ed he penned. As of this writing, the town has voted to return the materials to the tribe and is awaiting official permission from the state to do so.[18] Relationships with Wilcox, his grandmother, and other archivists have been fostered over years of ongoing Mohican returns to and presence in their ancestral homelands. In that sense, the returns are important for not only collecting and copying historical materials but also for the relationships tribal members have forged that have allowed them to further expand their archival collection.

It is significant that the trips began with the goal of expanding the archive. By gathering these materials, the Mohicans improved access for tribal members while simultaneously undermining the colonial way in which Mohican history has been archived across multiple non-Native institutions. This work laid the foundation for what was to come. As the trips continued and expanded beyond the purpose of collecting material, so too would their use in the larger sphere of Mohican archival activism.

Cultivating Shared Heritage and Belonging through Place

After the first few trips in the late 1960s and 1970s, which focused primarily on archival collection, the Historical Committee responded to a growing interest in returning to Mohican ancestral homelands by leading buses of tribal members east. While document collection still occurred on these later trips, the focus shifted to a type of commemorative travel in which committee members taught Stockbridge-Munsee history to tribal members as they traveled and aimed to forge common Mohican identities and a shared sense of heritage grounded in specific places. As Vine Deloria Jr. has asserted, this connection between history and place is significant because "every location within their [a tribe's] original homeland has a multitude of stories that recount migrations, revelations, and particularly historical incidents."[19] Places serve as important repositories of stories and memories that act as tools for reconstructing tribal histories and identities, which many tribal members were discouraged from taking pride in during the assimilation era.[20] Describing her boarding school experience in the late 1920s and early 1930s to the Wisconsin-based *Shawano Evening Leader,* Bernice Miller recalled that "nothing of Indian culture was ever allowed in the school, so while the staff chatted in German, students were punished for using Indian words."[21] Historical Committee member Leah Miller similarly noted that because of the legacy of these policies, "A lot of our history has been lost and there are gaps in the oral telling of our ways, making it difficult to trace the past."[22] Filling these gaps and recovering what has been lost are important types of Indigenous nation-building that work directly against colonial policies. As geographer Laura Harjo notes, "finding and returning to our places enables us to specu-late with our relatives, to gather information based on all our senses, and to be in a place that shapes a felt knowledge that we can embody and draw upon."[23] By returning to Mohican ancestral homelands and encouraging tribal members to reconnect with and claim space within these places, the Historical Committee provided opportunities for tribal members to gather information and shape a felt knowledge about their tribal history. Moreover, by recovering stories that remain embedded in Mohican ancestral homelands, teaching them to other tribal members, and learning them as a community, the committee worked against assimilation policies that discouraged gener-ations of Mohican children from learning or taking pride in their heritage.

The process of recovering these stories and regrounding themselves with these places is one that many tribal members have written or spoken about,

Figure 17. Tribal members who traveled east on the 1989 bus tour pose for a group photograph. Courtesy of the Stockbridge-Munsee Community, Cultural Affairs Department, Arvid E. Miller Library Museum.

Figure 18. (*left to right*) Linda Miller Kroening, Dorothy Davids, and Bernice Miller aboard the group bus on a historical trip in the 1980s. Courtesy of the Stockbridge-Munsee Community, Cultural Affairs Department, Arvid E. Miller Library Museum.

describing a distinct "feeling" they have upon arriving in their ancestral homelands. Leah Miller explained, "The first thing about it is, it's a spiritual thing. When you go out there to the homeland, you can feel your ancestors, and everyone who goes there says that."[24] Jo Ann Schedler made similar comments, emphasizing that

> when you get into the Berkshires [mountains in southwestern Massachusetts], into Stockbridge, Massachusetts, and you walk places that your ancestors were, it's just a deep feeling of knowing that your family was there . . . looking at the ground they walked on . . . on the Hudson River, knowing that they were in canoes, they fished, they lived along the shores, they're buried there. That is just an amazing, amazing feeling . . . this feeling of very deep pride.[25]

For many, the specific sites of former Mohican villages like Peebles Island and Schodack Island especially held this quality. In her reflections on these places, tribal secretary Ruth Gudinas wrote that "folks talked about the spirit of the place, the possibility of walking on the graves of their ancestors, the 'feeling' of the island."[26] Similarly, tribal member Jim Davids wrote, "As soon as we pulled in here I felt the presence of our ancestors."[27] Other Mohicans reflected that it "felt good just being there" and that "the route of the whole trip was easing, to know that our ancestors had touched, walked, learned upon these lands."[28]

Some tribal members connected these feelings directly to pride and belonging. Reflecting on her trip, Arminta Chicks Hebert remarked that "each day brought a feeling of awe and wonder—almost a sacred feeling. There was a special feeling hard to describe as though someone from long ago [was] sharing a feeling of togetherness—as though someone from long ago was sharing a feeling of happiness—as though they were waiting for us. I have never experienced such a feeling of well-being."[29] Ruth Peters wrote that what she and others learned on the trip "made us feel proud to be part of the Stockbridge tribe," while Arlee and Jim Davids remarked that they

> felt humble; [we] felt proud and [we] felt sad at each of these places. It is a feeling that is hard to describe to stand upon the very spot that you[r] ancestors lived and died. You feel you finally found yourself as far as where you are from if that makes any sense to you. [We] have the feeling of being Indian in more than name only. And Proud [sic] of it!![30]

These feelings spanned generations and not only built a sense of Mohican identity and belonging among individuals, but also contributed to shared experiences among tribal members, which supported the production of collective memory among those who made the trip. As Gudinas noted in the closing paragraph of her 1989 journal of the trip, "We have become in a sense, a community through our shared experience."[31] Feelings of ease, familiarity, and belonging are common reactions for Indigenous people returning to their ancestral homelands.[32] In spite of removal and the fact that few tribes control significant land bases in lands they were removed from, returning contradicts erasure narratives by signaling that tribal nations maintain connections to these places, and within communities it builds collective experiences and attachments to places that inform a shared sense of identity—a feeling of kinship and of nationhood.

The Historical Committee reinforced these natural connections by using the trips as an opportunity to teach tribal history, educating tribal members

Figure 19. Tribal members look out from the top of Monument Mountain, a common stop on the historical trips that is located just outside Stockbridge. Courtesy of the Stockbridge-Munsee Community, Cultural Affairs Department, Arvid E. Miller Library Museum.

about each area's significance and its place within the Mohican past and present. For example, Gudinas recalled that on Peebles Island, tribal member Steve Davids "told us about the ancient Mohican village in the Albany area—we're right across the H. [Hudson] River from Albany, are north about 10 mi and are on Peebles Is. [Island]. He told us about Mohican history as well as about non-Indian history."[33] Other tribal members described this trip as "very educational," "very informing and educational," and "a good historical lesson."[34]

Teaching youth and young people about tribal history is of particular importance to the tribe. As Gudinas noted, the younger tribal members on the 1989 trip were "interested in where we are and where we are going. We show the map now and then and give them lessons in geography [and] in history."[35] The success of these teaching practices is clear in the reflections younger tribal members wrote. For example, Denall Gardner noted that "although I was going to be a junior in college, I have not absorbed so much history and information about my people before in my life."[36] Similarly, Gudinas wrote that she heard a young Stockbridge college student say that "she had learned more about her Indian heritage on this one trip than she had learned in all her classes combined."[37] In this way, learning history outside of the classroom in specific, significant Mohican places is key for these younger tribal members as they work to reverse the effects of U.S. assimilation policy and recover their tribal histories. As tribal member Steve Comer noted, providing them with these educational experiences in these important places at a young age will "give them a taste of our past and perhaps the motivation to learn more about it."[38]

Returning to Stockbridge-Munsee homelands allows tribal members to claim space for themselves within these places.[39] To do so, Mohicans leave tobacco, leave and take items like stones and soil from places they visit, and conduct tribal ceremonies as a way to reinscribe meaning and value for themselves in these landscapes. Enacting these types of changes creates what Christine DeLucia calls "memoryscapes," or "constellations of spots on the land that have accrued stories over time, transforming them from blank or neutral spaces into emotionally infused, politically potent places."[40] Grounding themselves within this network of places works directly against settler-colonial attempts to remove them from and sever their ties with these places. One of the more public ceremonies occurred in 1989 on Schodack Island, where tribal member Bruce Miller and non-tribal member Oscar Pigeon honored Mohican ancestors by laying tobacco in a public ceremony that later appeared on the nightly news in New York.[41] Some tribal members even camped on the island overnight, and emphasized that "to be back where our ancestors held their last Council Fire before being moved[,] we were perhaps the first Mohicans to camp there again after two or three hundred years had passed. To camp beside the Hudson River and know that they had lived there was quite an experience."[42]

More privately, Mohicans have also engaged in the practice of laying and taking stones from specific places, which tribal members say is something they have been doing for years, and something that was passed down from their ancestors. According to Bernice Miller, "Whenever we visit an ancestral place, we take a stone back with us to remember our ancestors. I don't know how it started, just that my father did it, his father did it, and his father and so on."[43] Indeed, the custom of laying stones is well documented among other Algonquin tribes within the Mahicannituck Valley.[44] Multiple sources confirm the existence of a significant rock cairn, or pile, "some six or eight feet in diameter" near Stockbridge at Monument Mountain, one of the locations tribal members still consider sacred and climb on each trip.[45] To the Mohicans, Monument Mountain is Maaswuseexay, or "fisher's nest/standing up nest," and the cairn is Maaswuseexay Wuwaana'kwthik, or "place of arranged stones at the fisher's nest/standing up nest."[46] Though the cairn was destroyed at some point in history, the Mohicans have worked to rebuild it on their trips to Stockbridge. Tribal members have also brought stones from their home in Wisconsin to add to the pile and have taken a few stones back to Wisconsin with them, drawing important physical connections between the two locations. As one tribal member wrote, "We try to keep up this unknown tradition.... To us now it means we've returned to the land of the ancestors."[47]

Today the cairn resides in its original location, which is, fortunately, well into the woods off one of the popular trails that hikers use to climb Monument Mountain. I would not have found it had I not been hiking with Rick Wilcox, who, in addition to his research with and advocacy for the tribe, helps maintain the pile and keep it free of debris. While the cairn is not off

Figure 20. The stone cairn rebuilt by Mohicans on the historical trips. Photograph by author, August 24, 2021. Reprinted with permission from the Stockbridge-Munsee Community Historic Preservation Office.

limits to nontribal members, Wilcox explained that he always checks with the tribal historic preservation manager, Bonney Hartley, before leading non-tribal members to it and allowing them to take photos. Hartley manages these requests on a case-by-case basis. She and other tribal members welcome those who want to admire the cairn, but they also want to ensure it is not vandalized.[48] In their own moments of laying tobacco and piling rocks, tribal members on the trips not only stop to reflect and think about the history of their ancestors in these places but also create a space that is distinctly Mohican, placing stones from the reservation and places the tribe visited and lived in a single location, and honoring that space with tobacco. Bringing tribal members to these places, teaching history there, and enacting these practices of reclaiming space together, across generations, are all particular types of "place-making" that help tribal members construct or reconstruct the importance of these places in relation to their tribal history and tribal identity.[49] Place-making helps forge collective community identity and connection to land, opposing settler-colonial efforts to separate Mohicans from these places and serving as critical elements of Indigenous nation-building.

Encountering the Painful Legacies of Settler-Colonial Violence

Returning to ancestral homelands has the potential to induce significant pride and a shared sense of belonging among Stockbridge-Munsee tribal members—feelings that are critical to Indigenous nation-building. However, returning to these lands and learning the histories of forced removal and assimilation can also be incredibly painful. Though the returning Mohicans did not experience removal from their homelands themselves, as Dorothy Davids noted in one of her reflections of the trips, "We personally carry some of the genetic materials of our ancestors. So even if I am talking about the present, the past isn't very far behind. In fact, it is embedded in our present."[50] In fact, the phenomenon Davids describes is backed by science. Historical or transgenerational trauma is the cumulative impact of past traumatic experiences that are passed through multiple generations and visible in epigenetics.[51] On the trips, tribal members encounter places that hold significant meaning for their people, as well as those that are embedded with trauma. Sometimes those locations are the same place, like the town of Stockbridge. Before it was Stockbridge, it was Wnahktukuk, an important Mohican village site that fostered peace and diplomacy in Mohican homelands. And yet, it is also the place that is most aligned with attempted assimilation through the mission that was founded there and the eventual removal of the Mohicans that occurred when they were forced to leave this place. While contemporary Mohicans acknowledge that their ancestors made the best decisions they could with the information available, to many this place still signifies the first concession that Mohicans made to colonialism. For example, Steven James Davids wrote that upon arriving in Stockbridge, "my chest filled with both pride and sorrow. Pride because my ancestors chose a most beautiful place to call home and sorrow because they weren't able to keep it and we weren't able to keep all of the rich culture that was ours."[52] Though these feelings may seem at odds with the joyful and happy emotions described previously, they too serve an important (if unintentional) role in shaping a common Stockbridge-Munsee identity that is grounded in an understanding of and experience with historical trauma. As difficult as reflecting on these histories is, it can also be used to process historical loss and think of it as a shared experience, so that as tribal members are reflecting on what removal may have been like for their ancestors, they are also forming collective memories that lead to a shared sense of history and identity.[53]

In memoirs from the trips, it is clear that many of the retraumatizing experiences occurred in the context of public history spaces, particularly museums that held Stockbridge-Munsee ancestors or sacred items. In one such instance in 1975, thirteen-year-old Carmen Cornelius encountered "a trunk with the skeleton of an Indian child who died without burial" in a small museum in Ohio near the site of the Gnadenhutten Massacre, an event that left nearly one hundred Munsee people who were living at a Moravian mission dead.[54] Journalist Eileen Mooney noted that upon seeing the remains, Cornelius was especially upset. "Her eyes filling with tears," she remarked, "I want to start a petition to have her buried."[55] Though we do not know what kind of effect this had on museum curators, Dorothy Davids indicated that the trunk had been removed the next time the Mohicans visited the site.[56]

The Mission House Museum, which held the Bible and Communion set that were stolen from the Mohican reservation in the 1930s, was also a painful place for many tribal members to visit before the items were returned in 1990 and 2006, respectively. Yet because the items are sacred, visiting them was a regular part of each journey before then. In these encounters, the Mohicans were forced to travel hundreds of miles to see the items, many for the first time, and then endure the pain and frustration that inevitably accompanies reckoning with the fact that these items were stolen and are being held by nontribal members. On a couple of the trips, this pain was deepened by encountering *John Sergeant and Chief Konkapot,* a Norman Rockwell painting that depicts John Sergeant meeting with Mohican chief John Konkapot. Rockwell spent the last quarter of his life in Stockbridge, and what is perhaps one of his most recognizable paintings, *Stockbridge Main Street at Christmas,* depicts the quintessential town. The Mohicans were able to meet him and see *John Sergeant and Chief Konkapot* in progress. Rockwell spent time with the tribal members and pointed to some of the smaller details of the work, such as John Sergeant's wife, Abigail Williams, who is shown peeking around the corner of the room, apparently angered by the presence of a Mohican in her living room.[57] The message that they were not welcome in the Sergeant home was a painful reminder for tribal members, one that stuck with them across multiple trips and as they toured the Mission House itself, where the painting is set.

The Mohicans encountered the painting again on their 1989 trip after Rockwell had passed away, this time visiting the museum in Stockbridge that

Figure 21. Norman Rockwell's *John Sergeant and Chief Konkapot,* which Ruth Gudinas refers to in her account of the 1989 trip. As Gudinas mentions in her account, Abigail Williams, John Sergeant's wife, can be seen angrily peeking around the corner, signaling that Konkapot and the other Mohicans were not welcome in her home. Printed by permission of the Norman Rockwell Family Agency. Copyright 1976 the Norman Rockwell Family Entities.

was established in his honor. Immediately after the Rockwell Museum, they visited the Mission House. With this painting and the (at the time) unreturned Bible and Communion set in mind, Gudinas wrote that the tour of the Mission House in 1989

> was hard; the first thing we saw as we entered were the Bibles. We weren't allowed to take flash pictures but I wanted to record the faces of the Stockbridgers as they looked at their Bibles, wanting to come home. The tour is always interesting and I had Norman Rockwell's painting in mind as we went through the "Indian part" of the house. Mim [their tour guide] is funny; she says "They thought the Indians would like a special room of their own." We all know that the Sergeants, or at least Abigail Williams Sergeant, didn't want the Indians in their house. They could go no further than that room.[58]

Traveling through a space their ancestors were not allowed to enter and reckoning with the fact that *their items* remained in the house was frustrating and sad for Mohicans on the trip. Yet simultaneously, these trips marked the first time that some tribal members were able to see the Bible and Communion set. Many were excited and joyful at seeing the items, and in the various accounts of this particular trip, seeing the Bible set is perhaps the single event almost every tribal member mentioned. Aminta Chicks Hebert wrote, "When we saw our Bibles again there was a happy feeling. It seems that in the not too far future we may again have them in our possession."[59] Likewise, Kelly Davids noted that "the best part of the trip was when we went to the Mission House to see our Bibles."[60] Engagement with public history sites like the Mission House are often exciting opportunities for tribal members to gain greater access to materials related to their history and relatives, but they can also be deeply frustrating.

Though these emotions are seemingly in tension, they also activated a resolve for action.[61] Tribal members have used the trips to create meaning in and gain understanding from these sites of violence and embed them within larger Stockbridge-Munsee Mohican geographies, where they find a sense of belonging and shared identity. Though collective reliving of trauma is not an intended aspect of the trips, experiencing the return to this land and the often-problematic representations of Mohican history in these colonized spaces cultivates Mohican identity formation and stimulates the types of activist efforts I discuss in the final section of this chapter. In a speech given at a conference in Mohican homelands, Dorothy Davids wrote, "I remember that each time we crossed the Mahicannituck we viewed the water and the hills with a sad longing, as though forgotten memories became restless and urged us to remember."[62] In returning, the Mohicans are urged to remember, and these restless memories drive the larger efforts to recover and reclaim Mohican national history; they drive Mohican archival activism.

Testimonies as a Part of Archival Activism

While stirring and at times traumatic, these emotions were not an intentional outcome of the trips. Yet, the Historical Committee understood that these reactions were valid and that they shed light on the intergenerational impacts of removal that were still felt in their community today. So as they processed these feelings, they were intentional about documenting their own experiences, actions, and emotions and providing other tribal members with journals to do the same. These accounts were never meant to be private. Rather, they were produced specifically for the purpose of being archived in the Arvid E. Miller Library-Museum. Much like earlier efforts to record personal narratives in writing and oral history, this initiative to create new sources of knowledge is an important part of archival activism and a crucial aspect of reshaping Mohican narratives about Mohican history. However, the journals produced as a part of the historical trips are unique in that they specifically aim to record Indigenous feelings and memories of violence and trauma being formed in the context of returning to ancestral homelands.

On each trip, the Mohican Historical Committee either assigned individuals with the responsibility of documenting tribal members' thoughts and reactions or asked each traveler to keep a journal of his or her own. Historical Committee secretary Ruth Gudinas and tribal members like Bernice Miller and Kristy Miller were entrusted with documenting the group's travels on a number of occasions. As Dorothy Davids notes in her own account of a trip, "We had supplied everyone with a notebook and pens and asked them to keep a journal for historical purposes."[63] Without specific prompts, tribal members of all ages were asked to simply reflect on their experiences on the trips. These testimonies include descriptive accounts of landscapes and experiences, but they also include tribal members' reactions, emotions, and *feelings.*

These feelings often include reflections of trauma and loss, emotions that are seldom easily defined or recorded in historical documents, in part because those who experience trauma often purposely try to forget or disassociate from these emotions.[64] This response to trauma is understandable but means that historians must find new ways to record and recognize trauma to ensure that it *is* present in the historical record and thus remembered. As Ann Cvetkovich argues, the absence of trauma from official sources means that historians must focus on "new genres of expression, such as testimony," prioritizing personal memories and bearing witness to undocumented events and feelings.[65] In their journals, Mohicans create testimonies of their own feelings, emotions, and imaginaries upon returning to land from which their ancestors were forcibly removed. Doing so brings light to trauma that has so seldom been acknowledged and recorded and provides additional context for future narratives that discuss Mohican removal.

These testimonies document feelings, which scholar Dian Million reminds us are a distinct type of Indigenous knowledge because they communicate experiences that only Native people separated from their ancestral homelands can experience.[66] They are cataloged in the Mohican tribal archive on the reservation, where they are new primary sources that have become an important mode for recognizing the impacts of historical and intergenerational trauma.[67] Following Cvetkovich's assertion that trauma "demands an unusual archive" that incorporates personal memory in all forms, the Mohican tribal archive cultivates the collection of these important felt histories. In doing so, it articulates the importance of these personal narratives and ensures that those accessing the archive will be able to see, read, and perhaps even feel the ongoing connection Stockbridge-Munsee people have to their homelands. The creation of the journals and their preservation is a powerful reminder of ongoing Mohican connections to history and place, and an important piece of the Historical Committee's efforts to shift the sources from which Mohican historical narratives are constructed.

We Are Still Here: Direct Action among the Returning Mohicans

Mohican efforts to collect and produce documents for the archive, reaffirm ties to ancestral homelands, and teach tribal history through place constitute a distinct type of activism that works to undo the ramifications of settler colonialism and cultivates a shared sense of place-based Mohican national identity. These efforts also facilitate direct action that disrupts erasure narratives and reclaims Indigenous geographies in the Northeast. Chapter 5 focuses on interventions within public history, while here I focus particularly on broader critiques of colonialism Mohicans have made during the historical trips and land-based historic preservation projects that the returns have helped facilitate. These interventions are, at first glance, less directly connected to the archive. Much like the legal battles discussed in chapter 3, they often use the archive as an arsenal for evidence, but many rely less on archival documentation. Instead, their chief connection to the archive lies in the fact that the interventions have emerged out of the historical trips, which have long been a key component of the Historical Committee's larger efforts to shift the way Mohican history is collected, accessed, and represented. The archive serves as the hub from which all of these projects have grown, and it continues to serve as a resource for many of them.

Contesting Erasure Narratives

While erasure narratives are prevalent throughout the United States, they are particularly salient in the Northeast. The vast majority of tribes in this area were forcibly removed, and early settlers crafted definitively false narratives about being the "first" to arrive in a new land while the "last" of Native people were disappearing.[68] James Fenimore Cooper's *The Last of the Mohicans* is a classic example of the latter type of narrative and is of course particularly relevant here. The towns the Mohicans visit on their trips often romanticize Native history, and many white settlers are even shocked when they meet living Native people.[69] The Mohicans refute these common attitudes by making themselves as visible as possible on the trips. On at least one journey they traveled with a "Returning Mohicans" sign at the front of their bus, which was the name of a tribal youth group in the 1980s and also quite literally represented all those returning on the trip. Additionally, several of the trip records indicate purposeful interactions and conversations with settlers to make non-Native residents aware of their ongoing connection to their ancestral homelands.[70]

One of the ways the Mohicans have made themselves most visible is by issuing press releases about their returns to local newspapers and accepting interview requests where they often explicitly dispute erasure narratives. In

Figure 22. The "Returning Mohicans" sign that was placed in the front windshield of the Mohican bus on the 1989 historical trip. Stockbridge-Munsee Community, Cultural Affairs Department, Arvid E. Miller Library Museum.

many cases, they also use this platform to launch various critiques against settler-colonial policies and practices. For example, when asked what the motivation behind the trips was in 1975, Bernice Miller frankly explained that "We've been discouraged from remembering anything but what missionaries wanted us to remember."[71] Likewise, when asked about whether or not this trip to the Northeast was also in honor of the United States' bicentennial celebration, she scoffed, "We don't have any feeling for the 200th anniversary of this land."[72] Dorothy Davids made similar comments in a 1991 interview, explaining, "When I drive through the Berkshires and see what a beautiful place it is, I just have this deep sadness for the injustice of it all. People there tell me I shouldn't be sad. 'After all,' they say, 'we're preserving it.' Well, they're not preserving it for us. They're not going to give that land back."[73] While these statements would have undoubtedly been uncomfortable for the majority-white readers who live around Stockbridge, where these articles were published, Miller and Davids used the media platforms to educate this population on settler-colonial assimilation policies and remind them that Native people are continuing to oppose settler colonialism.

Similarly, Mohican tribal members have been clear with their discomfort and at times their anger at the failures to acknowledge the importance of Indigenous pasts and presents in public spaces. For example, regarding discussions of human remains being unearthed during land development projects, James Davids, the chief conservation officer for the tribe in 1996, told a newspaper, "I don't feel comfortable with people coming across our ancestors. . . . I don't want [the remains] to go to museums."[74] Similarly, in 1975, tribal members told the *Berkshire Eagle* newspaper that if an organization in the Northeast wanted to work with the tribe, they ought to start by "returning the Bibles from the Mission House" (or convincing the Mission House Museum to do so).[75] The article goes even further to suggest that the Mohicans "would appreciate a scholarship for historic [*sic*] research, perhaps at a college in this area."[76] Like Bernice Miller's previous statements, these assertions remind white settlers that their homes were built at the expense of Mohican people who were dispossessed of their land, and that they continue to live in a settler-colonial nation.

Still, while the Mohicans have used the media as a tool, it is certainly a double-edged sword. As Bernice Miller notes in her account of the 1968 trip, reporters did not always base their stories entirely on Mohican press releases and interviews, writing that one reporter in Stockbridge "wrote what he thought he heard."[77] Likewise, tribal member Kristy Miller seemed disgusted with the way reporters treated her and others on the 1972 trip, writing that "getting your picture taken right and left gets really sickening."[78] On that particular trip, the *Berkshire Courier* published a photograph of tribal members posing with one volume of the Stockbridge Bible (Figure 23). Examining the facial expressions of the women in the photo, we might conclude that they were less than enthusiastic about being asked to pose next to this sacred, stolen item, which was at the time held by the Mission House Museum. In her account of another trip, Gudinas goes as far as calling interactions with the press a "spectacle," noting, "the press was all over the place."[79] Many reporters also exploited the "Last of the Mohicans" trope, with titles like "'Last' of the Mohicans Looking for the 'First'" or "The Latest of the Mahicans."[80] Unfortunately, some of the trips even became a sort of tourist experience for white settlers who now live in these towns. White residents of Stockbridge published several reports of tribal visits, and their commentary, such as a photograph labeled "The Indian War Canoe" (Figure 24), exemplifies the extent to which some white settlers exoticized the returning Mohicans and continued to classify them within existing racist stereotypes and tropes. Many of the newspaper articles covering trips in the 1970s and 1980s focused more on the experience of the Stockbridge residents than on the returning Mohicans, such as one article that noted: "The host families were just overwhelmed with how much they got out of the experience."[81]

At times, the articles also reinforced narratives that glossed over settler-colonial violence, using terms like "retreated," "moved," or "left" when describing how the Stockbridge-Munsee Mohicans ended up in Wisconsin, but never saying that they were *forced to leave*.[82] In other words, these newspapers capitalized on the spectacle of the returning Mohicans while obstructing the violent history that led to a reality in which the Mohicans return to, rather than live in, their ancestral homelands. As with any aspect of the media, it would be impossible for the Mohicans to control every part of these articles. For them, the chance to use the media to intervene in existing erasure narratives seems to outweigh the negative effects the media might have.

Figure 23. (*left to right*) Blanche Jacobs, Bernice Miller, Dorothy Davids, Kristy Miller Malone, Tina Gardner Williams, Lonnie Kroening, and Karolyn Raasch pose with a volume of the Stockbridge Bible for a newspaper article published by the *Berkshire Courier* in 1972. Stockbridge Indian Collection, Stockbridge Library.

Figure 24. Tribal members John Miller (*far left*) and Pewehsen Dodge (*second from right*) take part in a canoe trip on one of the Mohican historical trips. This photograph and its caption, "The Indian War Canoe," appear in a report published by Stockbridge residents. Photograph by Clemens Kalischer.

Claiming Space and Emphasizing Ongoing Connections

The ongoing connections Mohicans maintain to their homelands are also clear in the continued fights they have waged against land development or construction projects and in the way they have exercised their right to be involved as a sovereign nation when human remains or cultural items are unearthed from the ground.[83] While federal laws such as the Native American Graves Protection and Repatriation Act (NAGPRA) and Section 106 of the National Historic Preservation Act (NHPA) now mandate certain types of consultation, Mohican commitment to these issues began before either of these laws was passed and extends beyond the legal obligations. Their activism around these issues has significantly evolved since the coordinated trips started in 1968, and at times the tribe has even used the trips to transport delegations of tribal members east to meet with state and local officials. In

2015 they founded a satellite Historic Preservation Office to have a permanent presence in their homelands, and placed their Tribal Historic Preservation Officer (THPO) in this office so that they can readily consult on historical preservation and repatriation projects. By returning, remaining, and asserting their right to be involved in these projects, the Mohicans have reinforced the continued ties to these lands that are foundational for direct interventions. Moreover, these efforts tie directly to the Historical Committee's broader efforts to shift the way their histories, or in this case historical items and ancestors, are collected, accessed in public spaces, and used to craft narratives about Stockbridge-Munsee history.

In Stockbridge the Mohicans have directly involved themselves in the historic preservation of sites, including the Indian Burial Ground, a plot of land on the edge of town that was historically used by the Mohicans to inter their dead. Though the Mohicans were forced to leave Stockbridge in the late eighteenth century, they continued to return to Stockbridge and care for the burial ground throughout the early nineteenth century. Minister Timothy Woodbridge, who was born in Stockbridge in 1784, noted that the Mohicans continued to winter in Stockbridge and "loved to rekindle the fire upon the old hearthstones, and linger about the ancient cemetery."[84] In 1808 they also submitted a successful petition to prevent the town from building a road that would have cut through the burial ground.[85] However, likely fearing that they would eventually be forced to leave New York and have a more difficult time returning to Stockbridge in the future, the tribe deeded the burial ground to Dr. Oliver Partridge, a local physician, in 1809 and asked him to take care of it and ensure their ancestors were not disturbed. Still, three tribal members also returned again in 1869, well after the tribe had been forced to leave the Northeast and been relocated to Wisconsin, and erected living structures on the burial ground in an attempt to claim it, before they were ultimately evicted.[86] In other words, tribal members always returned to care for this space. Today the burial ground includes a monument dedicated to the Mohicans, and more than two hundred years after the land was deeded to Partridge, one of his descendants has partnered with the Mohicans to restore and continue to help preserve the area today.[87]

That descendant is Rick Wilcox—the same town resident who has worked with the tribe to locate and transcribe key archival materials and to preserve the stone cairn at Monument Mountain. Wilcox is the retired police chief of Stockbridge and has dedicated much of his life to researching local history.

Since 2010 he has worked on several other projects with THPO Office staff in Stockbridge. He and former THPO Sherry White began their collaboration by writing a grant to restore the burial ground, asking for funds to do standard maintenance like removing brush, leveling sinkholes, and attending to trees. During the project, White traveled to Stockbridge and "provided advice on how to 'clean up' the site without violating the burying grounds," and ensured the Tribal Council approved the specific aspects of the restoration.[88] White and Wilcox also worked together on another project in 2012, when they convinced the town of Stockbridge to designate another plot of land with known human remains as a protected burial ground.[89]

More recently, beginning in 2019, Wilcox has worked with the Stockbridge-Munsee Historic Preservation Office on two other archaeological projects in Stockbridge. The first involves searching for the 1739 meeting house, a building that is well documented in archival records but unrecognized on the land itself. The second is a search for the site of a ceremonial ox roast hosted by then general but later president George Washington on the homesite of Mohican "King" Solomon Uhhaunaunauwaunmut to thank Mohican warriors after the Revolutionary War.[90] The THPO Office charged Wilcox with searching through archival records to determine where to start digging, and while the meeting house is clearly marked on a survey, the location of the ox roast has been more difficult to pinpoint.[91] In our 2021 conversation he described this as "putting together pieces of a jigsaw or a crossword puzzle." Every piece of evidence helped to narrow the search. From there, he and tribal historic preservation manager Bonney Hartley worked together to write several grants to fund both archaeological projects and applied for the appropriate state permits to begin digging.[92] The permit process in particular was arduous, and as Hartley noted, it was frustrating that "we have to ask for permission to dig for our own materials."[93]

Still, the Stockbridge-Munsee Department of Cultural Affairs, the archaeological team they hired, and affiliated volunteers broke ground on both projects in July 2021. At the site of the meeting house they located "soil discolorations that suggest a building's foundation from the right time period and several wrought-iron nails," as well as a building trench near where the meeting house stood. They also uncovered some unexpected things: a thinning flake from a resharpening tool and two original floors from Mohican homes that date much further back than the eighteenth century. These discoveries provide important evidence that the tribe had been in Wnahktukuk long before Stockbridge was a colonial town. At the site of the ox roast they also found what is likely the original floor and firepit of a Mohican long-house near where the ox roast is believed to have taken place. As of this writing, carbon dating is being completed on "burned material" found in the firepit area to determine if this could indeed be the site of the ox roast.[94] Through these projects, the Mohicans have continued to demonstrate a vested interest not only in the preservation of their homelands but also in how the materials that represent their history—whether in archives, museums, or uncovered from the ground—are used to inform tribal understandings of heritage and historical narratives for the broader public. As Hartley explained in the context of the meeting house, "So many petitions, really eloquent letters and things . . . that we know and love from our sachems were composed here," so discovering evidence of the meeting house "just brings that to life. . . . Of any physical structure that there could be, this is the one that encapsulates all of that history."[95]

This continued interest is also evident beyond Stockbridge in other parts of Mohican ancestral homelands. Both the Historical Committee and the THPO Office have used the trips to research important sites that hold historical importance, to collect information on possible land development or construction projects in these places that the tribe might oppose, and to meet with officials for these projects when possible.[96] For example, in 1987, nine tribal members traveled east to represent the tribe and present archival evidence concerning the importance of Schodack Island, a historical Mohican meeting place in present-day New York. In her account, Dorothy Davids noted that "the tribe was asked if we had an interest in this and of course we do. . . . It is our wish that our history will somehow be commemorated with a museum or visitors' center and that the natural wildlife of the islands will not be destroyed."[97] Historical Committee members also insisted that tribal members be involved in any archaeological digs, and used their trip to emphasize that the island is "sacred ground."[98] Though there was no museum when I visited the island in 2012, the area is a public, undeveloped park and includes interpretive signs that attest to Mohican ties to this area—representations that are likely a result of Mohican activism.[99]

In a similar instance in 1996, the tribe also fought plans to build a Wal-Mart in Leeds Flat, an area in the Catskill Mountains where human remains were unearthed the previous year.[100] Dorothy Davids noted, "We were never consulted. Only told how our dead would be buried."[101] In the same article, she emphasized "This land is sacred to the tribe," underscoring that the Mohicans have an ongoing connection to these spaces in spite of removal. In a letter to Wal-Mart President and CEO David Glass, Tribal President Virgil Murphy underscored the historical importance this site could hold for the Mohicans, writing that "because of assimilation efforts our people have lost much of the knowledge of our history and culture and have lived for all these years with an emptiness and yearning to regain what was lost. . . . Can you imagine our excitement when we learned of the find at your development site, and upon hearing that it could be one of the most important archaeological finds in the northeast?" He continued, emphasizing, "This letter is to urge you to consider our position and try to understand the immense value the site holds for our people."[102] Again, the Mohicans were successful. They forced Wal-Mart to forgo their plans to build a store on the site and successfully petitioned to have the area designated as a Historic Place on the National Register of Historic Places in 1998.[103]

Since this and other incidents, the tribe has also worked hard to ensure they have a voice when human remains or cultural items are unearthed within the bounds of their ancestral homelands or when land development projects have the potential to unearth such remains or items.[104] When remains are unearthed, tribal members commonly return east to reinter them within Mohican original homelands, using these events as a way to educate attendees about the Mohican Nation. In some instances they have even participated as volunteers in archaeological digs at larger village sites.[105] In the case of the Wal-Mart Leeds Flat site, since both the Mohicans and the Haudenosaunee Confederacy believed the remains could be their ancestors, both groups led a collaborative reburial ceremony.[106] The Mohicans have participated in many reburials since then, and they have worked with institutions in their ancestral homelands to ensure they are consulted when remains or cultural items are unearthed.

In another successful example, the tribe, led by the Historic Preservation Office, established a working collaboration with the West Point Military Academy in New York. In a ceremony on October 28, 2005, representatives from the Stockbridge-Munsee Band of Mohicans signed a Memorandum of Understanding with the U.S. Army Garrison at West Point, recognizing that the Army Garrison resides on Stockbridge-Munsee ancestral homelands and "that the Stockbridge-Munsee Tribe of Wisconsin possesses a unique experience in both written and oral history to identify and evaluate historic properties of religious and cultural significance." The agreement also created a protocol for the tribe and the Army Garrison to work together on repatriation matters should they arise and notes that West Point will "maintain the confidentiality of all information pertaining to cultural properties where possible" and contact the Stockbridge-Munsee tribe for approval and consultation before "any proposed undertaking that will involve any new excavation of previously undisturbed soils."[107]

Commenting on the ceremony and the agreement, Tribal President Robert Chicks noted, "We look forward to working with West Point in this new capacity so that we may all enjoy a greater understanding and respect for Stockbridge-Munsee history in New York, our ancestral homeland."[108] The ceremony also included an exchange of gifts, during which President Chicks presented a wampum belt made by tribal member Lynn Welch to the Colonel and Garrison Commander Brian Crawford. Likewise, after the ceremony,

Figure 25. Historical Committee member Leah Miller gives a speech at a reburial in New York State in 1996. Miller appeared at the reburial as a representative of the Tribal Council. Courtesy of the Stockbridge-Munsee Community, Cultural Affairs Department, Arvid E. Miller Library Museum.

Figure 26. (*left to right*) Tribal members Steve Comer, an unnamed individual, Susan Davids, Dorothy Davids, and Kim Pecore participate in an archaeological dig in New York State. The individual standing behind the group was also not identified by name. Courtesy of the Stockbridge-Munsee Community, Cultural Affairs Department, Arvid E. Miller Library Museum.

tribal members and a group of officials from West Point traveled to Van Cortlandt Park in the Bronx, where a monument to the Continental Army Company of Stockbridge Mohicans was erected in 1906. Together, the West Point officials and tribal members participated in a wreath-laying ceremony to honor the Mohican veterans who fought in the American Revolution with the colonists.[109] In these and other collaborations, the Stockbridge-Munsee people not only maintain an active connection with these places their ancestors lived but also continue to assert that they have interest, and should have a voice in decisions made about these sacred places.

This agreement was no doubt facilitated by both Section 106 of the NHPA and NAGPRA, both of which require consultation with Indigenous nations in relation to historical items and human remains that are unearthed from the ground. Passed in 1990, NAGPRA requires that all institutions that receive federal funding consult with Indian tribes and Native Hawaiian organizations *if* human remains or certain cultural items (i.e., funerary objects or items of cultural patrimony) are unearthed on federal or tribal land or have been acquired by an institution that receives federal funding.[110] On the other hand, Section 106 of the NHPA requires federal agencies or those receiving federal funding to consider whether an "undertaking" (or project) will affect historic properties *before* they break ground on federal, state, or private land, and requires that they consult the appropriate THPO throughout the process. If the federal agency and THPO identify "adverse effects" that the project might have, the law dictates that the agency and tribe work together to "avoid, minimize, or mitigate the adverse effects."[111]

Neither of these laws is without its flaws. Among other issues, NAGPRA has little power to enforce timely communication between institutions and tribes, so a direct agreement between the Mohican Nation and an institution like West Point ensures the Mohicans will be involved in each step of the process. Likewise, Section 106 can be difficult to enforce. Indeed, it is the federal law that should have required extensive consultation between tribal representatives from the Standing Rock Sioux and Cheyenne River Sioux Nations before the Dakota Access Pipeline was streamlined. Instead, failure to initiate timely consultation with tribal representatives led to what sources called an extreme "lack of transparency" around the site evaluation process, which should have involved tribal representatives throughout.[112] While the law requires that federal agencies notify THPOs of potential historic sites within development projects, the onus of demonstrating how sacred or important a site is and advocating for its protection falls on tribes, and they often have to conduct significant archival research to do so.[113] As former THPO Sherry White noted:

> if you're working with a federal agency on a federal project and you know an area is sacred to the tribe, you have to prove that it's sacred, when everyone else on that project is doing everything in their power to get that project completed. As the tribal representative for these federal projects, you're sitting in meetings with a wide range of people, from city planners and lawyers to politicians and architects, and you're there by yourself. So, you really had to do the research to ensure these areas were sacred and you could prove that.[114]

Moreover, while consultation is required, reaching an agreement that no historic properties will be affected is not (except when the project is on tribal land).[115] Federal agencies can request additional investigations be completed to substantiate tribal information about sites, and can even streamline projects based on the supposed greater "public benefits."[116] This means that for tribes like the Mohicans who consult on projects in their ancestral homelands rather than current reservation lands, federal agencies ultimately have the power to determine if historic properties or adverse effects merit the movement of a land development project.[117] Even when consultation processes are collaborative and successful, they often involve a lot of time and require tribal consultants to physically travel to sites, making the process even more difficult for tribes like the Mohicans, who are hundreds of miles away from where these land development projects are taking place.[118]

When the Tribal Historic Preservation Office was opened, White was flying back and forth between the Northeast and the reservation in Wisconsin. She noted that many repatriations during this time "took years. Not just because I was the only one doing it and going back and forth. It takes time to conduct research on each item and at the same time, the museum you're trying to reclaim the item from is often fighting you, so you are answering their questions. Plus, you are working on Section 106 projects on top of that."[119] To combat these issues, the Stockbridge-Munsee Mohican Nation opened a satellite Historic Preservation Office in 2015, ensuring that the Mohicans have a permanent presence in their homelands and are readily available to support repatriation cases and consult on development projects.[120] The office was originally located in Troy, New York, but is now based at Williams College in Williamstown, Massachusetts. When Bonney Hartley moved to New York in 2015, she was serving as the THPO for the Mohican Nation, and her main role became working on projects that fall within the regulations of Section 106.[121] Having a THPO readily available to consult on projects on the East Coast increases the chance that the Mohicans will be consulted throughout the process of new development projects and that they will be able to identify any adverse effects of development early on. The thirty-day comment period can slip by quickly for a single THPO who has multiple things on his or her plate, and again, for tribes who do not live in their ancestral homelands, identifying and explaining the historic importance of a site in enough detail may take significant time and research. Hartley now serves as manager of the Tribal Historic Preservation Office and is focusing more on repatriation. Jeff Bendremer, the current THPO, focuses on reviewing land development projects that fall under the Section 106 guidelines for federal land or state preservation laws and then meeting with project representatives to assist in the evaluation process. Bendremer contracts directly with an archaeologist on projects where there is a high potential for discovering human remains or other cultural items, and then makes recommendations about the site on behalf of the tribe. At its best, collaboration allows tribes and federal agencies to work together to come up with solutions to any "adverse effects" projects might have. For example, when Hartley served in the role, in some cases she was able to negotiate that upon completion, land development projects include educational signage or historical interpretations of Mohican history as a part of the Section 106 consultation process, but she emphasized that these interpretations "have to say that the tribe still exists."[122]

These efforts and the continual Mohican presence in their homelands has already started to pay off. In addition to the numerous consultation and collaboration efforts discussed, the Mohicans have started to reclaim ownership over land, starting with the return of Papscanee Island in the spring of 2021. Donated by the Open Space Institute, the 156-acre land preserve, named for Mohican sachem Papsickene, is an important cultural and historical site for the Stockbridge-Munsee Nation. It is a place the Mohicans have long returned to, and their presence on the land is well documented in both archival and archaeological sources as well as tribal oral histories. The Stockbridge-Munsee Department of Cultural Affairs has installed new signage on the site and is in the process of further protecting it by applying to have the land listed on the National Register of Historic Places as a Traditional Cultural Property.[123] They also worked with the Open Space Institute to create a Story Map website explaining the history of the island, the removal of the Stockbridge-Munsee people, the tribe's survival and resilience today, and the importance of returning land to Indigenous people.[124]

The fights the Mohicans and other tribal nations wage to be consulted on land development projects exemplify bigger shifts in how Native nations, historic and cultural preservation personnel, and land developers are approaching questions of cultural heritage. Though these projects often represent major clashes between Native interests and those of academic or state institutions, the processes of collaboration are improving as Indigenous people insist on their right to historical materials and remains in their homelands.[125] The Mohican case makes this clear. While the tribe initially faced significant resistance to requests to be more involved in the preservation of their cultural heritage, the creation of the satellite Historic Preservation Office has made a significant impact in ensuring they are viewed as the main authority and resource on their own history. Rick Wilcox emphasized this in our 2021 conversation. Reflecting on the progress the tribe has made in the last five years, he said, "It's because of Bonney [Hartley]. Her patience and advocacy on behalf of the tribe has made the biggest difference."[126] In these direct endeavors, the Mohicans build on their efforts to improve access to and reclaim authority over the management of their historical and cultural materials, shifting the way these materials are accessed and used to create public historical narratives in and out of archives.

Though the Mohicans have not been further removed since the 1930s and their children have not been placed in boarding schools since the early twentieth century, the legacies of removal and assimilation policies have not disappeared. Moreover, these policies have contributed to the scattering of Stockbridge-Munsee archival materials and the common erasure myths that suggest Native people like the Mohicans left the Northeast and have not maintained connections to these places. Addressing these outcomes of colonialism must, then, be an ongoing, multipronged initiative, and the historical trips to Mohican homelands are a key element of this process. The journeys to Mohican homelands span the last fifty years of Mohican archival activism and are intertwined with the other activities led by the Historical Committee. By continually returning to their homelands and reclaiming places as their own in both private and public ways, the Mohicans work to restring the ties with the Northeast that settler colonialism sought to sever. By collecting documents and teaching tribal history through place, they work to undo the legacies of assimilation and instill a shared sense of pride and Stockbridge-Munsee heritage in future generations. By establishing a foundation for further direct action, the tribe disrupts erasure narratives and demands consultation and collaboration in future projects concerning their histories. Together, these efforts shift how both tribal and nontribal members learn Stockbridge-Munsee history: building a shared sense of identity and nationhood among tribal citizens, and articulating Mohican sovereignty and survival to external audiences.

The tribal archive is foundational for planning these returns, and the trips themselves are an essential part of Mohican archival activism. Knowledge in the archive that the Historical Committee spent years collecting and making accessible to tribal members is foundational for teaching tribal history in Mohican homelands and cultivating a collective sense of Mohican national identity. The tribe's demands for collaboration and consultation allow the Mohicans to exercise sovereignty over how their historical materials are collected. Through their returns, tribal members shift how Mohican history and historical materials are made accessible, who controls their use, and how they are used to create public narratives. As we will see in the following chapter, these trips are only the beginning of the significant interventions the Mohicans have made in the representations of their history in Wisconsin and beyond.

5

New Narratives for Public Audiences

We wanted, you know, for people to become aware that we weren't the Last of the Mohicans. They act like we're dead people. You know, oh here's an Indian mummy over here, or here's a weapon that they used to use. It's like we're dead and this is just our history, and we don't need to worry about them anymore. They're gone now. And we just wanted to make sure that the information that they were letting people know wasn't just historical and that we're still here, we're a living people, and we have our own culture, we have our own ways. And again, it's a way of making sure that those misrepresentations don't continue.

—Leah Miller, Historical Committee member, interview with author, 2016

As the Mohicans traveled through their homelands on dozens of historical trips, they frequently encountered misrepresentation of their histories in public spaces. Exhibits or signage that mentioned the tribe typically placed them and their presence on the land in the past, and few if any interpretations laid bare the harms of settler-colonial policies like removal and forced assimilation through missions. These representations are detrimental to the tribe for several reasons. First, the assertion that Stockbridge-Munsee people disappeared and no longer exist makes many skeptical that those returning to and advocating for their right to represent their own histories are "real Indians." Compounding the *Last of the Mohicans* myth, the more the public is presented with the notion that Native people have disappeared from the Northeast, the harder it is for them to believe that living Mohicans care about or have a claim to sacred sites or have a right to be consulted when significant cultural items and human remains are unearthed. Second, the failure to reckon with colonial harm absolves white settlers in the Northeast of the responsibilities they have to recognize how they have benefited from settler colonialism and support Native efforts to reclaim land. This lack of recognition for settler-colonial history creates significant barriers to collaboration and consultation. Finally, these misrepresentations are harmful to returning tribal members who encounter these narratives, are presented with false notions of their own disappearance, and are made to feel like they do not belong. Together, these public erasure myths challenge Mohican sovereignty and nationhood: they make it difficult for the tribe to exercise their sovereignty when working with non-Native land developers and institutions, and they threaten the tribe's efforts to cultivate a shared sense of pride and identity within their community.

The Historical Committee quickly realized this as they led groups of people back to Stockbridge-Munsee ancestral homelands. Their efforts to be recognized as the best representatives of their history and to cultivate a shared sense of heritage among their own citizens would always be more difficult if the general public did not recognize Mohican survival and nationhood. And so, they turned to public history and public education—mediums beyond academia that include K-12 schools, educational programming presented in documentaries and books, museum exhibits, and other types of place-based public heritage representations such as signage and monuments. In their interventions within these spaces, the pillars of archival activism are evident. The Historical Committee, and later the Department of Cultural Affairs, have used their newly assembled archival resources to change the way both Native and non-Native audiences access tribal history, assert the tribe's sovereignty and right to represent their own stories, and intervene in existing and craft new narratives of Mohican history.

This chapter highlights several of these public history and education efforts to show how the tribal archive serves as an essential resource for contesting existing erasure narratives and producing new histories that emphasize Mohican survival and nationhood for primarily external audiences. Beginning with public education, I discuss several curriculum efforts in Wisconsin and in the Northeast that have sought to target one of the largest sources of Native misrepresentations: K-12 education. In developing their own and contesting existing curriculum, Mohican tribal members use evidence within the archive to point out inaccuracies in existing representations, conduct research as part of their production of counternarratives, and present alternative sources that off-reservation schools can use to teach Mohican history in collaboration with the tribe. I then move to public history spaces, especially focusing on a series of new projects produced in Stockbridge, Massachusetts.

In new exhibits, a walking trail, and public signage, the Mohican Department of Cultural Affairs relied on extensive archival research to shift representations of their history in several formats. The projects show how the creation of an archival collection that collects previously scattered sources and establishes the Mohicans as the leading experts on their own history is as an essential piece of contesting dominant narratives and constructing new histories that emphasize Mohican survival and nationhood. Contesting and writing new narratives of Mohican history in public education and public history spaces are important types of Native political action that exemplify the types of historical interventions tribal archives can facilitate.

Mohican History in Public Education

From the moment the Historical Committee was formed in 1968, members prioritized changing false narratives of Mohican history. They immediately connected their efforts in gathering archival materials to their ability to contest these narratives, and eventually they worked across Wisconsin and the Northeast to change how Mohican history was taught in schools, even creating their own curricula in 1979, 1995, and 2008. But these efforts started locally—focusing on the content that their own children and those who lived near the borders of the reservation were taught in school.

In spring 1972, the U.S. Congress passed the Emergency School Aid Act (ESAA), a program designed to make financial aid available for schools with high populations of "minority group students" to eliminate and prevent minority group segregation, discrimination, and isolation.[1] Though it was not specifically designated to schools with high populations of Native students, the ESAA was passed at a time when the federal government was newly recognizing the historical marginalization of Indigenous students, and therefore it was one of a few resources that schools with high Native populations could draw on to improve Indigenous education.[2] The ESAA designated resources for different kinds of grant funding and programming in schools that had significant populations of so-called minority students. Schools, or local education agencies (LEAs), as they were termed in the act, could request funds with the intent of developing new education standards by working directly with members of the communities that made their school populations more diverse.[3] In 1974, Bowler Public Schools created such a proposal. Bowler is a small town about five miles southwest of the Stockbridge-Munsee

Mohican reservation (Map 3). Though its small population is predominantly white, children from the neighboring Mohican reservation were integrated into Bowler Schools in 1947, following the closure of the Stockbridge Day School on the reservation. The high population of Mohican students (the "minority group") in Bowler Schools made it a good candidate for ESAA funds.[4] In theory, these funds were designated to support Stockbridge-Munsee students. The only problem was that the Bowler School District did not bother to include Stockbridge-Munsee community leaders in the development of their proposal.

The Mohican Nation had worked directly with Bowler Schools previously, such as in 1972, when the Historical Committee led a "Teach-In" after Mohican

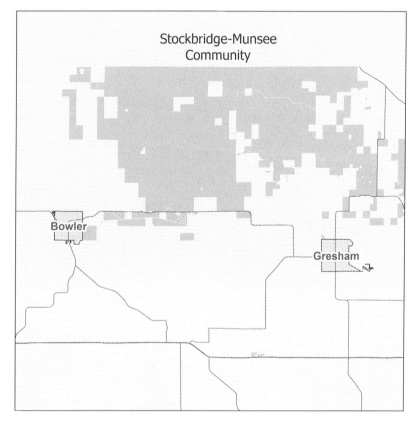

Map 3. This map shows the proximity of Bowler and Gresham, towns bordering the Stockbridge-Munsee reservation, where many tribal members attend school.

community members expressed concern that they were not involved in the planning or implementation of American Indian Week at Bowler Schools.[5] Therefore, the school district was by no means ignorant of the Historical Committee's existence or their commitment to educating others about the Mohican Nation. Yet Bowler's ESAA proposal listed four non-Native faculty members from the University of Wisconsin–Stevens Point as the paid consultants who would educate Bowler teachers about Stockbridge-Munsee students, and neither the Historical Committee nor the tribe was ever contacted to help shape or implement these trainings. In fact, the committee only found out about the project when the Bowler home school coordinator (who was also a tribal member) brought the proposal to a Historical Committee meeting, after it had already been partially funded.[6] Outraged, members of the Historical Committee demanded a meeting with the superintendent and members of the Bowler School Education Committee and prepared feedback on the funded proposal that outlined "apparent violations of federal regulations," "the over-balance of budgetary allocations to non-Stockbridge persons," and "various statements of questionable truth."[7] As Dorothy Davids recalled, "We told [them] that if anyone was going to teach our culture, it would be done in our community, our buildings, and our people would be involved." According to Davids, the superintendent replied, "Over my dead body."[8]

In response, members of the Historical Committee meticulously combed through the *Comprehensive Manual for Local Education Agencies* administered by the U.S. Department of Health, Education, and Welfare's Office of Education to highlight where the Bowler School District had violated federal regulations, especially those that were meant to ensure the involvement of the "minority group" that made them eligible for ESAA funding, members of the Stockbridge-Munsee Nation. The committee noted that while the act required the formation of an advisory committee with at least five civic or community organization leaders who "are broadly representative of the minority and nonminority communities to be served by the project," no members of the Mohican Tribal Council or Historical Committee were asked to be involved, and no Stockbridge-Munsee people were at the advisory committee meetings that developed the proposal.[9] The few Mohican people who were placed on the committee (mostly teaching aides already working in Bowler Schools) never received copies of the act's regulations as Bowler School District was developing the proposal, another requirement of the

ESAA that the district had avoided. These teachers' names were placed on the grant proposal, yet they were never invited to meetings or directly consulted about the curriculum content. These actions were especially frustrating given that, as Dorothy Davids emphasized, "This act was established for the very purpose of preventing the isolation of groups from one another."[10]

After combing through the federal requirements, the Mohicans, along with their lawyer, notified the superintendent that they had gathered enough evidence in Bowler's proposal alone to initiate a civil rights case.[11] To avoid this, the district conceded to create a district advisory committee chaired by Historical Committee member Sheila (Miller) Moede and change how the funds the ESAA granted to Bowler would be distributed.[12] The Historical Committee recommended that the training outlined in the original proposal take place on the Mohican reservation and use the awarded ESAA funding to pay members of Mohican Historical Committee (instead of non-Native professors) to lead the program. Again, the district agreed, and the training became a two-week teaching seminar on the reservation that was attended by thirty-five school staff members and sixty-five Mohican community members.[13] Like the originally proposed trainings, the workshop was meant to combat the root causes of segregation at Bowler Schools. But to do so, the Mohicans had to critique Bowler's assumptions about what the root causes of segregation were.

In their original proposal, the Bowler School District highlighted what they identified as the causes of Native students feeling isolated by noting that "most of these students live on the reservation so their lifestyles and close friends are Indian. We constantly urge them to 'reach out' but many do operate in small Indian cliques. Their cultural background is different from the rest of our student body."[14] In the revised workshop, Mohican tribal members challenged these assumptions specifically, noting that "all of these are positive factors for the tribe. All are results of the collective effort of the tribe to preserve its identity as 'a people.'"[15] Moreover, they criticized the one-sided nature of Bowler's assessment, noting that "nowhere in the proposal are school personnel or the Bowler community perceived as isolated" from the Mohicans, and that "nowhere are the behaviors of school personnel viewed as possible causes of the low self-image" of Native students.[16] The workshop also aimed to "build a greater sense of understanding of the relationships between Native Americans and later Americans," "build a comfortable trust level between the school and community," create "a strong inter-community relationship through which conflicts can be examined and resolved," and "gain insight into stereotypes that exist, how they become norms in society, and how they are perpetuated."[17]

When I asked Historical Committee member Leah Miller about these efforts, she also emphasized that the main goal was simply to foster harmony between the Mohicans and their non-Native neighbors. She explained:

> It helps them to understand us, and it helps us to understand them.... It's good for them to learn about us and to learn that we're, maybe we're different, but we're not any better or any worse than anybody else. We just want people to understand that and to help them get rid of these stereotypical ideas that some people have.[18]

Indeed, the white children in these reservation border towns and their parents were the neighbors that the tribe would eventually contest reservation boundaries with in the 1990s. While we do not know if those contesting Mohican land claims were ever exposed to the Historical Committee's interventions in local schools, it is clear that the committee recognized the value in educating their neighbors about tribal history.

In addition to these goals, the workshop also emphasized that the newly established tribal archive was an important local resource that Bowler teachers, administrators, and students could and should be using as a part of their educational curriculum, especially in connection to any lesson about the Mohican Nation. To do so, the Mohican workshop leaders made spending time in the Mohican tribal archive and library a central part of the two-week seminar, establishing teams that conducted research on topics such as the formation of the Stockbridge-Munsee reservation, their removal from their ancestral homelands, and the incorporation of the town of Bowler. Other topics included the history of education among Mohican tribal members (including colonial missionization, boarding schools, and mission schools), Stockbridge-Munsee treaty rights, and other subjects meant to increase Bowler staff's understanding of the history of the Stockbridge-Munsee Mohican Nation and decrease segregation and discrimination in Bowler Schools.

This two-week teaching seminar was a significant step forward and laid the foundations for future educational interventions. However, the fact that consulting Mohican historians before creating a curriculum about Mohican history was not an obvious step for Bowler School District administrators called attention to a larger problem. Much of what was taught (or not taught)

in local and national schools was out of Mohican control, and even in situations like this, in which the Mohicans did eventually provide direct training
to teachers, changing the curriculum itself was another matter entirely. This
was made clear just two years later when Historical Committee Member
Leah (Miller) Heath wrote a letter to the Bowler School District to challenge
its use of the book *Caddie Woodlawn* in their curriculum. The book tells the
story of a young white girl from Wisconsin who lives in a village where
Native people "scare most of the neighbors."[19] (Miller) Heath called attention
to the way that Native people were situated in the book as violent savages and
suggested that these types of stereotypes were dangerous and could encourage prejudice among young children. She suggested that a diverse evaluation
committee be established to review educational materials within the district.
Unfortunately, instead of using the communication channels that the Mohicans had sought to establish in the recent 1974 training on the reservation,
Bowler Schools simply forwarded (Miller) Heath's letter to the publishing
company, which responded that a committee such as the one she suggested
"could hobble efforts for innovative education and only succeed in exchang-
ing the hypothetical prejudice you complain of for a very real kind of prejudice called censorship."[20] Much like the comments made in 1974 about tribal
members being the source of their own discrimination, Bowler administrators continued to claim that any efforts to give Mohican tribal members
more power within educational materials and decisions was in itself a form
of prejudice. In other words, in spite of the small steps forward that had
been facilitated by the on-reservation workshops, many perceptions about
the Mohicans and their right to shape the curriculum and educational materials that their children learned with remained. There was still much work to
do to educate Bowler teachers and administrators.

The Mohican Historical Committee's next step in this ongoing effort was
to establish an educational resource office at the Arvid E. Miller Library-
Museum and begin making plans to create an "educational and dissemination arm" of the Historical Committee, which would later be known as
Muh-he-con-neew Inc.[21] In 1978, committee members Dorothy Davids and
Ruth Gudinas made this dream a reality by establishing Muh-he-con-neew
as a nonprofit organization through which they would ultimately publish new
Mohican curricula in collaboration with the Historical Committee. The first
opportunity to write a curriculum came just a year later, when the Wisconsin Department of Public Instruction helped pass the Title IV-C Elementary

and Secondary Education Act, which provided grant funding for various educational institutions. Instead of responding to an existing problematic proposal like Bowler's 1972 plan, this time the Mohican Historical Committee secured their own funding in conjunction with the Great Lakes Intertribal Council, the School District of Rhinelander, and other Wisconsin tribes to develop a distinct curriculum for elementary and middle school students. Davids served on the statewide Native American Curriculum Development Committee that created this material, designed to "develop an awareness of and sensitivity to American Indian history, culture, and lifestyles, with an emphasis on Wisconsin Indian tribes."[22] The Mohican Historical Committee designed the Stockbridge-Munsee portion of the curriculum and used the space to develop new educational materials that relied on Mohican historical documents in the Mohican tribal archive and sought to radically shift how Mohican histories were regularly taught in Wisconsin schools.

We can see this curriculum unit as a clear attempt to generate new narratives that emphasize Mohican nationhood and survival by attending to its clearly outlined goals and objectives, which emphasized changing existing misrepresentations and stereotypes and assisting students to better understand Native histories and cultures. In teaching students "how a specific group of people can be changed both culturally and geographically because of historical events," the curriculum highlighted Indigenous survival and the dynamic nature of Indigenous cultures. By encouraging them to "appreciate the differences between cultural groups without applying their own value system," the committee sought to dismantle stereotypes and misrepresentations. By "help[ing] students understand the meaning of reservation land and see[ing] how it affected and still affects Indian people," the tribe stressed the significance of settler-colonial policies while emphasizing Native sovereignty. Finally, by emphasizing "how important the preservation of cultural heritage can be for any group of people," the Mohicans made a strong case for the future of their nation.[23] These objectives outline the crux of Mohican goals to change the way their history is presented, objectives that were realized in this education curriculum that they would eventually help implement in schools around Wisconsin.

In the body of the Mohican section of the curriculum, the Historical Committee constructed educational materials and activities that emphasized Mohican ancestral homelands and culture but also named the devastating effects of settler colonialism. An entire section of the curriculum that focuses on the "Coming of the Europeans" includes subsections on the fur trade, diseases, missions, and violence in Mohican homelands. Subsequent sections include the history of removal, activities that challenge students to define treaties, and explanations of significant policies like the General Allotment Act and the Indian Reorganization Act. The curriculum ends with a focus on the present-day Mohicans, highlighting the sovereignty of the Mohican Nation as well as the tribal offices and organizations that make up the vibrant Mohican community. The curriculum even includes a small section on the Munsee language, which was the primary focus of language revitalization at this time.[24] This section of the larger Title IV curriculum was created by a team of Historical Committee members who conducted significant research in the tribal archive—a feat that would have been significantly more difficult if committee members had been forced to travel to archives across the United States to collect this information. Moreover, the statewide curriculum committee used the tribal archive as an important resource throughout the curriculum development process, and local Title IV programs continued to use the tribal archive as an important resource for their students through the 1980s.[25] The Mohican unit within the larger curriculum was reframed into its own curriculum in 1993, which the Mohican Nation distributed to interested parties until they created a new curriculum specifically for fourth and fifth graders in 2008. In each of these curriculum projects, the archive made the materials needed for research more accessible and helped locate expertise on the reservation and with tribal members, instead of in university and school officials who are non-Native, encouraging others to see tribal members as the best resources on their own history.

The earlier interventions in Bowler Schools as well as the initial development of the Mohican curriculum in 1979 were further supported in 1990, when the Wisconsin Legislature passed Act 31, requiring Wisconsin schools to teach tribal history, culture, and sovereignty/treaty rights in grades four, eight, and twelve. The act was passed after the statewide American Indian Language and Culture Board issued a statement recognizing connections between racism and lack of education around American Indian treaty rights, specifically after clashes between Ojibwe spear fishermen exercising their treaty rights and non-Native Wisconsin residents became increasingly hostile. After the U.S. State District Court for the Western District of Wisconsin upheld Ojibwe treaty rights, the Language and Culture Board called on the Wisconsin Department of Public Instruction to work with tribes to develop and implement a curriculum that would be instituted statewide in schools.[26] While this legislation sets Wisconsin ahead of numerous other states in terms of requiring the teaching of Native history, scholars have argued that its implementation is still problematic in the sense that it gives little detail on what should specifically be taught within the scope of the tribal history, culture, and sovereignty of Wisconsin tribes and provides little training in Native studies for teachers who receive education degrees in Wisconsin.[27]

Likewise, though the Wisconsin Department of Public Instruction did work directly with Wisconsin tribes, including the Mohicans, to create a curriculum that addressed Wisconsin Native history and treaty obligations, it did not always incorporate feedback from tribes. For example, in 1995, Dorothy Davids and Ruth Gudinas wrote to the department on behalf of the Mohican Historical Committee to restate recommendations they had made *three years prior* that had yet to be implemented in the draft of the Mohican section of the department's publication, "Classroom Activities on Wisconsin Indian Treaties and Tribal Sovereignty." Davids and Gudinas critiqued the curriculum's grouping of the Stockbridge-Munsee, Oneida, and Brothertown Nations as "New York Indians" as well as the fact that the curriculum sometimes referred to the Mohicans as the "Mohegans," an entirely different tribal nation. They carefully cited their critiques and corrections with research materials and included a note emphasizing that these sources could all be found in the Arvid E. Miller Library-Museum and that "the Stockbridge-Munsee Historical Committee, which has been researching Mohican/Stockbridge-Munsee history for many years can offer workshops in that history to teachers in . . . any district in the state."[28]

Though most of Davids's and Gudinas's corrections were made after they notified the Department of Public Instruction of these issues a second time, in 1996, Tribal Chairman Virgil Murphy had to write the department again to notify them of another "critical error" that had not been changed. In the published version of the new curriculum, the Stockbridge-Munsee Mohicans were said to have moved from western Massachusetts to New York's Hudson River Valley. As Murphy explained in his letter, the Hudson River Valley *is* the ancestral homeland of the Mohican peoples. They in fact moved south to western Massachusetts only after European settlers encroached on their homelands. Murphy noted that "we are deeply concerned that those who use this curriculum will never realize that members of the great Mohican confederacy, the Peoples of the Waters That Are Never Still, met Henry

Hudson on the banks of the Muh-he-con-ne-tuk and were the Native force to be reckoned with along that great river."[29] In this instance the ultimate outcome was positive, in that the Mohicans received a sincere apology from the director of the curriculum project along with a promise that this error would be updated in the next version of the publication.[30] Davids and Gudinas also worked within the Act 31–funded American Indian Program at the Department of Public Instruction over the next thirteen years. Starting in 1989, the program put on a Summer Institute at which Davids and Gudinas presented their workshop "Bias Is a Four-Letter Word," a program they created as a part of the consulting firm Full Circle: Education for a Diverse Society, which they formed in their "retirement."[31]

After the passage of Act 31, Davids and Gudinas continued working on educational efforts for the Historical Committee. In particular, they devoted a significant amount of their time to completely redesigning the 1993 Mohican curriculum, developing a new model, titled *The Mohican People: Their Lives and Their Lands,* that would fulfill the fourth grade requirements of this new legislation. The curriculum was published in 2008.[32] Davids and Gudinas spent fifteen years redesigning the new curriculum, which was nearly triple the size of the 1979/1993 models and is divided into seven parts, each of which includes multiple activities and lesson plans. Like the older models, this new curriculum includes sections on Mohican ancestral homelands, settler colonialism, removal, the formation of the Mohican reservation, and tribal sovereignty today. It also includes two more specific sections on Mohican participation in the American Revolution and incorporates short vignettes and photos of "present-day Mohicans," perhaps to emphasize that, in addition to the importance of history, the Mohicans are still here.[33]

The curriculum grounds several specific themes in the introduction and encourages teachers to emphasize them throughout their implementation of the lessons in their classes:

> One is ADAPTATION, most obvious after the arrival of the Europeans and the changes in living styles that were forced on the Mohicans by these invading strangers in their midst. The second is SURVIVAL, which follows from the first. It drove the necessities of adaptation and change as a result of the COLONIZATION of the Mohican people—a process that is meant to result in such control over the lives of the colonized, their decisions and choices, that

almost total dependence on the powerful is created. Evidences of RESISTANCE are to be found in the Mohican story also.[34] (emphases in source)

This curriculum was redesigned in direct response to new Act 31 standards and, in that sense, was meant to be applicable for implementation around the state. Still, the Mohican Historical Committee sought to make additional inroads with Bowler Schools, especially given continued issues with how Mohican history was represented.[35] Therefore, shortly after the curriculum was redesigned and ready to be implemented, the Historical Committee worked closely with University of Wisconsin–Eau Claire professor James Oberly to apply for a substantial grant from the Wisconsin Improving Teacher Quality Program.[36] In their successful proposal, Oberly and the Mohican Historical Committee outlined the staggering achievement gap between white and Stockbridge-Munsee students in the border schools near the reservation, as well as their concern that both Native and non-Native students were being taught inaccurate Mohican history. Upon receiving the grant, the committee then worked in conjunction with the University of Wisconsin–Eau Claire to design a year-long program that sought to comprehensively change how Mohican history was taught in Bowler Public Schools as well as Gresham Public Schools, another local school district on the southeast border of the reservation (Map 3). The program funded twelve education specialists from the University of Wisconsin–Eau Claire and seven members of the Stockbridge-Munsee Historical Committee, who put on a five-day retreat on the Stockbridge-Munsee reservation to allocate teaching responsibilities within the newly designed Mohican curriculum. The grant also provided funding for a series of other meetings over the next year, including a weeklong intensive curriculum training session for twenty-four teachers and support staff from Bowler and Gresham Schools, a two-day seminar to evaluate the implementation of the new curriculum, and a final two-day gathering to discuss the results and next steps following the first year of teaching the curriculum in local schools.[37] In this way, the Mohican Historical Committee sought not only to design the materials that would be used to teach their history but also to educate teachers about their history, present, and the importance of understanding their Stockbridge-Munsee students.[38]

Since the implementation of this curriculum, students from Bowler and Gresham Schools have visited the tribal archive to conduct research, view historical manuscripts, and explore the tribe's historical collections.[39] Many classes even require students to conduct oral history interviews with Mohican elders.[40] These engagements have been led by Historical Committee members who are also staff at the Library-Museum and illustrate how beneficial having the Mohican archive on the reservation can be for engaging local students and potentially changing their perspectives about the Mohican Nation. Much like the connections between representations and repatriation in the Northeast, the Historical Committee understood that their ability to enact their sovereignty locally was dependent on their white neighbors understanding their history and their status as a sovereign tribal nation. Therefore, their increased collaboration with schools on the borders of the reservation is an investment in everything from their ability to enact sovereignty in land battles to ensuring their children feel pride in their heritage and a sense of belonging in the community. In each of these interventions, the Mohicans advocated to have their histories reflected accurately and comprehensively and connected these efforts directly to how their students belonged (and thus performed academically) in these predominantly white communities. While this work is never finished, in advocating for their place in these schools, the Mohicans advocated for their place in the community and more comprehensively, created new counternarratives that sought to emphasize their distinct culture and legal status as a sovereign nation to the surrounding white communities. These types of activist efforts are based on years of archival research and a reliance on historical documents and materials that are made accessible in the tribal archive. In other words, these significant changes in local education policies and curriculum exemplify the kinds of positive change that can grow out of tribal archives and demonstrate the broader shifts in how Mohican history is taught and represented as a result of Mohican archival activism.

Beyond Wisconsin: Reforming Public Education in Mohican Ancestral Homelands

As the Mohicans developed their education curriculum, their ultimate goal was not only to change the way their histories were taught to their own children on the borders of the reservation and other students throughout Wisconsin, but also to change the way their history was taught across the United States, particularly within their ancestral homelands throughout the Northeast. As outlined in chapter 4, the erasure narratives articulated throughout the Northeast are particularly damaging because of the tribe's removal from that area. The Mohicans defy these representations by continually returning to and making claims to their ancestral homelands and engaging in numerous efforts to change the way their history is taught in Northeast K-12 and higher education institutions. For example, in 2002, Tribal President Robert Chicks made a presentation to Bronx elementary school children. It was arranged by a public relations firm in New York that the tribe hired to more comprehensively communicate the message that the Mohican Nation had not disappeared and still held strong connections to their ancestral homelands, including New York City.[41] Members of the media were also invited to the presentation, "to emphasize the presence of the Mohicans, past and present, in that area."[42] Moreover, since the completion of their 2008 curriculum, the Historical Committee has marketed these materials to schools not only in Wisconsin but also in New York and Massachusetts.[43]

While in situations like these the Mohicans have been able to produce new educational narratives of their own and maintain control over their content and distribution, other collaborations have brought significant challenges. For example, in 1996, Mohican tribal members worked directly with Columbia-Greene Community College in Hudson, New York, to create the Institute for the Study of Native Americans of the Northeast. Though it is no longer in existence (and it is unclear why this is the case), the institute sought to "initiate studies in the social history, geographic boundaries, laws, and cultures of various original inhabitants of Northeastern America, with special emphasis on the Mohican Nation . . . since the site of the college exists on the very land where the Mohicans resided prior to European encroachment."[44]

The institute formed a steering committee that was meant to be composed of two-thirds Native peoples (half of whom had to be from the Mohican Nation) and one-third Columbia-Greene faculty. It was intended to serve as a vehicle through which the college could support existing Mohican research efforts and through which the Mohicans could reclaim space and assert their ongoing presence in their homelands. The institute also proposed to put on a conference in September 1997 that was meant to recognize Native nations of the Northeast; review the history of these nations, particularly the Mohicans; and develop guidelines and plans to build a living village on Mawanagwassik (Rogers Island).[45]

However, as the institute developed, it appears that only two Mohican tribal members were actually placed on the steering committee. Perhaps lured by the

prospect of funding, the institute decided to partner with the New Netherland Museum, an organization that manages the *Half Moon,* a replica of the
ship explorer Henry Hudson (the first representative of European colonization that the Mohicans came into contact with in their ancestral homelands) sailed on.[46] While members of the institute first proposed that the ship
would sail down the Hudson River to be closer to the college and become
the "centerpiece" of the event in a "recreation of first contact," they soon can-
celed their original conference in favor of participating in an event the New
Netherland Museum had already created, which was meant to be a commemoration of Henry Hudson's landing.[47]

Dorothy Davids had originally agreed to speak at the event when it was
still meant to be a conference about Mohican and Native history, but she was
hesitant after the event became a commemoration for Hudson. In a letter to
institute coordinator Richard Powell, Davids explained that the tribe would
only be willing to participate if the event was to be educational. She wrote
that the tribe "does not wish to celebrate the arrival of Henry Hudson to our
homeland," "does not want to be token Indians on exhibition," "DO want
as much of the truth about Dutch trade and subsequent land fraudulent
acquisition by the Renssaellers, Livingstons, and other Dutch settlers," and
do want truthful education about "the use of rum as an exploitive item of
trade in spite of supposed law prohibiting it" (emphasis in original).[48] Davids
emphasized that while she would be willing to address these points in her
speech, it was important to her that the organizers also include it in their
materials. While it is unclear to what extent Davids's suggestions were implemented, her niece Molly Miller did present her speech after she was unable
to attend, and the institute did publish her text in the April 1998 edition of its
journal.[49]

The Mohican tribal archive includes minutes of institute meetings through
May 1998, but it is unclear if they stopped meeting at this time or if the single
Mohican tribal member remaining on the steering committee simply stopped
participating and therefore stopped sending copies of the minutes to the
tribal archive. After the 1997 Henry Hudson Commemoration event, the institute went on to produce a speaker series in 1998 without a single Mohican
speaker, offer a Native American–themed summer camp led by non-Native
instructors, and propose a Native American Society that would "provide
more hands-on experience of culture and lifestyle" to learn about "Native
American habitat and way of life."[50] Like many collaborative efforts, this one

was certainly imperfect, and as the non-Native faculty members took control of the institute it clearly moved away from what the Mohicans had initially envisioned. Still, we should read Davids's critique of the event and the speech she wrote for it as key interventions in common narratives that celebrate white settlement. Even within a problematic event, Davids was able to represent Mohican history and, perhaps, disrupt the viewpoints of white listeners who came to celebrate Henry Hudson and subsequent Euro-American settler colonialism. This was certainly not the last event that the Mohicans would have the chance to speak at within their homelands, and indeed tribal members participated in a subsequent "Mohican Seminar" in April 2000, where Dorothy Davids was able to give another speech on Mohican survival and perseverance as the keynote speaker.[51]

A recent collaboration with Williams College has had much better results. Williams was named for and founded with the bequest of Ephraim Williams Jr., an early settler who directly benefited from Stockbridge-Munsee dispossession. Williams's father, Ephraim Williams Sr., illegally claimed Mohican land as his own in the mid-eighteenth century, and Elijah Williams, the brother of Ephraim Williams Jr., seized political control in Stockbridge without significant tribal input. Moreover, the college sits on Stockbridge-Munsee Mohican ancestral homelands. As a part of reckoning with this history, Williams College began providing office space for the tribe's satellite Historic Preservation Office (previously located in Troy, New York) in February 2021. The college is also funding student interns to support research projects with the Stockbridge-Munsee Community Department of Cultural Affairs. Williams students have already assisted with "research to protect cultural sites and repatriate historical items" as well as the two archaeological digs in Stockbridge discussed in chapter 4.[52] Though this office and its staff are not positioned in close proximity to the tribal archive, they work closely with staff in the Arvid E. Miller Library-Museum, who are also part of the Department of Cultural Affairs, to exchange archival documents, co-conduct research, and expand the tribe's ability to serve as experts on their own history.

Though these collaborations with colleges have had mixed results, they demonstrate that as tribal members continue to return to their ancestral homelands and as the Historical Committee and Department of Cultural Affairs continue to make these ongoing connections clear, non-Native people and institutions have noticed and contacted the tribe directly to consult with them on their interpretations of Mohican history. While some of these efforts were no doubt sincere, others seemed to hope the Historical Committee would simply affirm, rather than challenge, the narratives produced by non-Native museums and other public history institutions. Many of these institutions sought to include Mohican historical narratives within a larger story about white settlement but were unwilling to listen or respond when the Mohicans responded critically. Still, the Mohicans maintained their educational goals, pushing for historical truth-telling about violence and illegality and advocating for a centering of Mohican history and Mohican voices.[53]

Like their efforts in Wisconsin, the Historical Committee also worked with K-12 institutions in the Northeast to correct misrepresentations of Mohican history. In one particularly frustrating case from 2009, the Mohicans received a proposal for an elementary school curriculum designed for fourth and fifth graders in schools and library programs across New York State. The curriculum, titled "Voyage of Discovery, Indians of the Hudson Valley," was designed by the New Netherland Museum of Albany, New York (the same institution from the Henry Hudson commemoration). It narrates the "discovery" of the Hudson River as well as the interactions that followed between Euro-American settlers and Native nations in the region.[54] Contrary to the hopes of those at the New Netherland Museum, the Mohican Historical Committee refused to support the curriculum, calling its perspective biased, and questioning the "authenticity" of its content in a letter dated May 15, 2009. The committee wrote, "Although it has some good activities on the history of trade between the Northeastern Native peoples and the Europeans, it appears to be biased in its perspective and falls short of living up to its intent to be the story of the Northeastern people in the valley of the Mahicannituck, in particular the Mohicans."[55]

More specifically, the committee wrote that the entire curriculum appeared to be a "discourse on the takeover of Native people and their lands" and included "a subtle bias favoring the Europeans."[56] They wrote that the curriculum seemed to assume "that Native people were pagan, primitive, savage, and in many ways eager to please their white colonizers."[57] In response to these issues, the Mohicans emphasized the importance of Native self-representation, writing, "Histories are rooted in the stories of the people themselves. . . . We have no recollection of anyone from your group contacting the historians of this community."[58]

The committee concluded the letter with the following statement:

In conclusion, we wish to say that we are delighted that scholars in the East are at least recognizing the presence of the Mohicans in the valley of Mahicannituck. Thanks to James Fenimore Cooper, the Mohican people usually get comments such as "I thought you folks were long gone!" when they say who they are. This is why we wish that your curriculum would reflect the feelings, thoughts and motivations of the Mohican people, rather than so much about non-Mohican assumptions about their way of life before and just after the invasion of the non-Native colonizers. As we said at the beginning, the stereotypes about Native people are embedded deep in children's consciousness, and they need to be displaced by strong and true images of the people who were here for so many centuries before the Europeans came. We are sorry to say that we believe your curriculum does not do much to replace stereotypes with accurate and authentic images of the peoples of the valley of the mighty Mahicannituck.[59]

In their response, the Mohicans suggested that the museum rely on the 2008 curriculum created *by* the Mohicans, since this was also designed for fourth and fifth grade students, but more importantly educated students about Mohican history from a Mohican perspective and emphasized Mohican survival and sovereignty.

In spite of this clear disapproval of the curriculum and the Mohicans' urging that the material needed significant revision, the curriculum was indeed released and is still promoted and used throughout schools in New York as of 2021. Though the content of the series of textbooks is unavailable online, we can still gather the following. The series is still problematically named "Voyage of Discovery," and centers the original journey of Henry Hudson, and the replica ship, the *Half Moon,* which retraces Hudson's journey every year, conducting programs as a traveling museum.[60] In a series of three, the final textbook, *Indians of the Hudson Valley: An Exploration of Indian Life: Before, during and after European Contact, 1550–1750,* is distinct from the other two "Voyage of Discovery" texts. This separation of content suggests that Native people are somehow a side story rather than an integral component of the colonial history of the Northeast. Both the title and separate textbook in the series exemplify the New Netherland Museum's view that Native people are not central to both the history and present of the Northeast. The image on the cover of the textbook makes this all the clearer, with Native people represented as ancient objects unearthed.

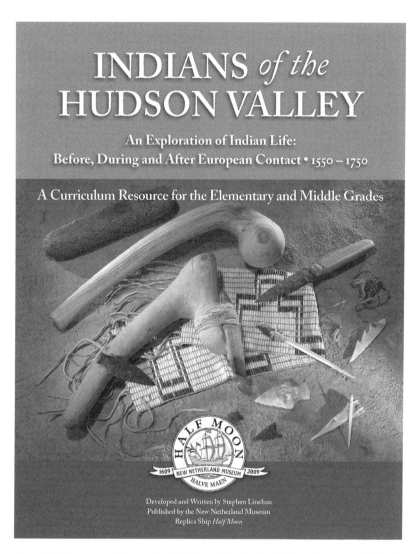

Figure 27. The cover of the textbook *Indians of the Hudson Valley*, which was published in spite of failing to receive approval from the Mohican Nation.

Instead of being represented as people who are very much still alive, the cover of the textbook represents Native people in the same way most museums do, through objects.[61] Despite Mohican interventions, the New Netherland curriculum seems to be portraying the exact message the Mohican Historical Committee feared: that Native people, and in particular the Mohicans, are part of an ancient past. Still, in spite of the perpetuation of these negative stereotypes, what matters is that because they have established themselves as the best resource on their history, the Mohicans have resisted and begun the work of disrupting dominant narratives of disappearance, creating the possibility that someday, even if not today, these narratives will change. Though the New Netherland curriculum is still rife with problems, the response the Mohicans wrote made a difference. Though the cover image, the separate text, and the problematic title of the series remain in use, a chapter titled "Mohican and Lenape Tribes Today" was added to the book following the response from the Mohican Historical Committee in 2009.[62] There is still work to do, but these small victories along the way matter and exemplify how the Mohicans and other tribal nations continue to challenge dominant narratives, educate others, and assert the importance of centering their own histories and voices. Moreover, as the Mohicans have continued to be vocal about these and other representations, more and more non-Native organizations throughout the Northeast have contacted them, and the Mohicans have seized many of these opportunities as a way to continue educating a broader public. Indeed, by 2009 the Mohicans started receiving so many requests for speakers that they developed a directory of speakers to fulfill as many of these requests as possible.[63]

When I interviewed Historical Committee member Jo Ann Schedler in 2017, she emphasized how important these efforts are, while noting that the tribal archive is crucial for these types of presentations. As one of the speakers the tribe often relies on, Schedler had recently been asked to give a presentation to the Daughters of the American Revolution on the East Coast. While she has some knowledge of the colonial era, she explained how helpful it was for her to be able to conduct research on the reservation in preparation for the event. Moreover, she credits these types of presentations with making a huge difference in how the people who live in Mohican ancestral homelands understand Mohican history. Referencing presentations the tribe has made in New York City as well as Stockbridge, Schedler noted that following Mohican engagement in these places, local residents applied for and received historic preservation grants to preserve Mohican sacred sites and monuments to Mohican history.[64] In other words, these educational engagements and acts of self-representation matter. While the Mohicans maintain more control over some representations than others, in each of these instances, they have made the best of options that are not always ideal. They have challenged dominant narratives of peaceful white settlement and Mohican disappearance, and instead they have not only asserted new narratives of Mohican survival and nationhood but stressed their right to do so.

Mohican Public History Representations

Beyond educating the public about Mohican history and culture in schools and other public educational programming, the Mohicans have also intervened in and developed their own educational narratives in public history, such as those in museum exhibits and other public heritage sites. The Historical Committee's use of public history started early in 1975, when they built a fourteen-panel exhibit that traveled throughout Wisconsin as a part of the state's bicentennial celebration.[65] Since then, they, and more recently the Stockbridge-Munsee Department of Cultural Affairs, have created their own on-reservation museum and been involved in several exhibits in the Northeast, each of which they have used to contest representations that erase ongoing Mohican presence and instead present narratives of Mohican nationhood and survival.[66] As a 2021 article covering some of these initiatives put it, "the Stockbridge-Munsee Band of Mohicans wants you to know their story. And they want to be the ones telling it to you."[67]

These initiatives are particularly important because they change how the public accesses Mohican history—intervening in the frequent practice of non-Native people representing Native people without consent and collaboration. In public history settings, which are still often conceptualized as very Western, white spaces—places for "ancient Indian artifacts," not living Native curators—Mohican self-representation has an even greater impact. By contesting existing public history narratives and asserting their right to represent their histories in these spaces, the Mohicans defy the notion that they are either unable or unwilling to represent themselves and instead assert that they are the best experts on their own histories. Like earlier efforts, they have grown out of years of Mohican archival activism, which has laid the foundation for the Historical Committee to be able to provide key input, expertise, and educational materials on their tribal history. Since the tribe created the Department of Cultural Affairs in 2018 to unite staff in the Library-Museum, the Tribal Historic Preservation Office, and the Language and Culture program, they have taken up much of the work that the Historical Committee set out to do. Three recent projects in Stockbridge, Massachusetts, provide a glimpse into the way the Mohicans are using these public history and heritage spaces to create new public narratives that emphasize Mohican survival and sovereignty.

As we know from chapters 3 and 4, Wnahktukuk, or Stockbridge, has been a significant place in Stockbridge-Munsee Mohican history for thousands of years. As a village site, the location of the two-volume Bible set and a four-piece pewter Communion set before they were repatriated, and the place of several other sacred and historical sites, it is important for its historical connection to the tribe and its contemporary representations of Mohican history. However, prior to 2020, accurate representations of Mohican history in Stockbridge were still minimal. The Mission House Museum, where the Bible and Communion set were previously kept, was largely devoid of representations of the Mohicans, instead focusing on the missionary John Sergeant. The smaller "Indian Museum," which sat a short distance behind the Mission House, focused primarily on other objects collected by museum founder Mabel Choate in the 1930s. There was no other recognition of the tribe or its ongoing connection to Stockbridge in town beyond the Indian Burial Ground and other markers in the Stockbridge cemetery. As of 2021, this has changed significantly. The Mission House Museum now includes historical interpretation about both Sergeant and the Mohicans in Stockbridge, and the Trustees of Reservations, the preservation agency that manages the museum, handed complete interpretive control over the "Indian Museum" to the Mohican Nation. In town, the Department of Cultural Affairs has created a walking tour of the village that includes individual tribal members talking about their ancestors' homesites and their ongoing connections to Stockbridge. And at Monument Mountain the tribe successfully renamed the mountain peak, whose name previously included a racial slur, and installed new signage to educate the public about the importance of the mountain to Mohican people. While these projects are only a few of several initiatives that members of the Historical Committee and Department of Cultural Affairs have been involved in over the past fifty years, they highlight ways that Indigenous archival activism can begin in archives and extend to significant shifts in the representation of Native history.

The Mohican Miles *Exhibit: Reclaiming the "Indian Museum"*

Prior to 2021, the Stockbridge Mission House Museum focused almost exclusively on the missionary John Sergeant Sr. The carriage house, a smaller building that sits a short distance behind the Mission House, was named the "Indian Museum" and was dedicated to the history of the Mohicans in Stockbridge. Both buildings have been run by the Trustees of Reservations since the museum's founding by Mabel Choate in 1929. Choate is the collector who bought the stolen Bible and Communion set from Reverend Westfall shortly after founding the museum, and prior to 1991 these items were on display in the Mission House Museum in the context of Sergeant and the mission he founded. The carriage house underwent renovations in 1987, and the Historical Committee created some materials for the museum in the early 2000s, but the most significant changes happened in 2021, when the Trustees of Reservations handed complete control of the carriage house over to the Stockbridge-Munsee Community. In its form as of this writing, the new carriage house exhibit, titled *Mohican Miles,* and new signage in the Mission

Figure 28. The Mission House Museum in Stockbridge, Massachusetts. Photograph by author, August 5, 2012.

House itself strongly articulate ongoing Mohican presence in and connections to Stockbridge, directly critique previous misrepresentations of Stockbridge-Munsee history, and outline Mohican survival and nationhood.

Understanding the significance of these changes requires a sense of the carriage house museum's past. While there are no museum exhibit records prior to 1987, the renovation plan from that year tells us a great deal about how the Stockbridge-Munsee people have been represented in this space over the last thirty years. Renovated exhibits included an "Assimilated Indian" section with a map showing the forced removal of the Mohicans, an "artifact wall" where the proposed takeaway was that "The Stockbridge Indian was a viable culture," and another space to recognize John Sergeant (beyond his central treatment in the Mission House itself). The renovation plan also included a "Kids Corner" where children were invited to try on headdresses, apply makeup "to duplicate war paint symbols," and "view themselves as the Stockbridge Indians did in an adjacent puddle/basin of water-mirror." Not shown on the blueprint but detailed in the complete renovation plan was a small section titled "Modern Indian," which featured three photographs of present-day Stockbridge-Munsee Mohicans.[68] Astoundingly, this was twelve years after the Historical Committee initiated efforts to retrieve the Bible and Communion set, and they had coordinated at least five returns to Stockbridge by this point.

When I visited the carriage house museum in 2012, then called the "Indian Museum," some of this had changed, and some of it had not. While there were (thankfully) no opportunities for children to don redface and nothing in the museum focused explicitly on assimilation, the wall of artifacts remained, and the posters about removal were still displayed. Notably, the museum did include two posters contributed by the tribe to educate museumgoers about historic preservation work in Mohican homelands. While one poster explained NAGPRA, showcasing the rights that sovereign Native nations have over human remains, funerary items, and objects of cultural patrimony, the other poster discussed archaeological historic preservation efforts both on and off the reservation. The poster clearly illustrated Mohican ancestral homelands to emphasize their continual connection to these places and listed areas of historical, cultural, and archaeological importance the tribe has throughout New York, Connecticut, Vermont, Pennsylvania, and parts of Wisconsin. Likewise, the tribe created a seven-minute video for the museum that included interviews with tribal members who discussed Mohican history and the ongoing connections they maintain with Stockbridge and their home-lands in the Mahicannituck (Hudson) River Valley. The video told a story of Mohican survival and perseverance in spite of removal, assimilation, and subsequent policies that attempted to break up Mohican land in Wisconsin. The speakers emphasized that they are not the last of the Mohicans.

As of 2012, the Mission House itself included no content about the Stockbridge-Munsee Mohicans. Visitors walked through the two-story build-ing to learn about the clothing its white inhabitants wore, their religious rituals, and cultural practices. The absence of Native people and stories dis-tinctly asserted that this was not a Native place but rather one for Euro-Americans. In fact, the one mention of the tribe within the museum was an open, empty ledge with a sign indicating that it was the previous location of the two-volume Bible set and Communion set. Since Christianity was a main theme within the Mission House's exhibits, these items were significant pieces in the narrative they presented about missionizing and Stockbridge as a significant site of conversion. Leaving an empty shelf not only communi-cated how symbolic these items were in the presented missionizing narrative but also conveyed that a significant part of the museum was "taken," that the museum was even perhaps grieving a loss and memorializing these items with a notable absence.

Figure 29. A view inside the "Indian Museum." Photograph by author, August 5, 2012.

When I visited the museum in 2012, our tour guide addressed the vacant space by explaining, "This is where we used to keep two Bibles and a Communion set that were given to the Indians as a gift. But a few years ago, the Stockbridge Indians asked for them back. We just couldn't say no to such a sweet request. So now, the Bibles are in Wisconsin on the reservation." As is evident from the thirty-one-year fight that the Mohicans engaged in to retrieve their Bible and Communion set, recovering these items was by no means a situation in which the trustees simply "couldn't say no to such a sweet request." Describing it as such and emphasizing the loss and absence of these items by continuing to display an empty ledge was yet another instance in which white settlers were deemed generous and Native people are relegated to "sweet" recipients. In the initial story of the Mohicans receiving the Bible as a gift, the non-Native museum displays of Native objects across the country, and the previous display of absence at the Mission House, the narrative is the same: white collectors are generous gift givers or saviors of objects, and Native people are the recipients of these gifts. These narratives continue to paint white collectors and museums as benevolent and obscure their (at best) complacency with housing Native objects and (at worst) their role in actively taking these objects from Indigenous communities. Moreover, they dismiss the activism, labor, and struggles for these sacred objects that Native nations have led. These are the narratives the Mohicans have resisted by fighting to represent their own histories.

And yet, much changed in the nine years since my 2012 visit, likely, as Stockbridge resident and tribal collaborator Rick Wilcox surmised in our conversation about other initiatives in Stockbridge, because of the creation of the satellite Historic Preservation Office in 2015 and the Department of Cultural Affairs' ongoing presence in Mohican ancestral homelands—a presence that stems directly from years of Mohican archival activism by the Mohican Historical Committee. When I visited the Mission House Museum again in 2021, you could no longer walk through the two-story Mission House. The front rooms were visible through a wall of glass, and the only portion of the house that one could enter was a small hallway that runs along the back of the house. It is unclear if this was due to precautions around Covid-19 or historic preservation concerns. In either case, I could not help but feel like there was still a divide between the Sergeants' history and that of the Mohicans, especially since the section of the house you can enter is the "Indian part" of the house, the only portion of the structure that Mohicans were allowed to enter in the eighteenth century. While this back section of the house now features a prominent sign which explains that "the Stockbridge Indians ARE a primarily Mohican people who existed in the region since time immemorial" (emphasis in original), tribally produced posters about important tribal leader John Quinney and the tribe's many removals, and a few remaining Mohican-made objects (some collected by Choate and others gifted by the tribe), the walled-off portion of the house features antique furniture and colonial objects.[69]

The most significant changes are visible in the previously named "Indian Museum," which has been completely renovated by the Mohican Department of Cultural Affairs. The first visible poster, titled "The ~~Indian Museum~~ Carriage House," addresses this change directly, calling attention to the problematic segregation of the Mohican story from that of the Sergeants, and calling out some of the previous exhibits from the 1987 renovation. The poster goes on to explain that "the tribe has influenced many changes and additions to the Carriage House" since 1987 and that it has now been turned over to the Department of Cultural Affairs to curate their own exhibits as they see fit. Other panels in the redesigned space highlight local cultural heritage projects and repatriation, feature contemporary photos of tribal members in Stockbridge, and provide information about the Stockbridge-Munsee Community today.

Another panel within the exhibit does not mince words when explaining that "the relationship between The Trustees and the Stockbridge-Munsee Community has not always been a positive one." This panel outlines the theft of the Bible and Communion set and speaks plainly about the trustees being "unwilling to meet with the Stockbridge-Munsee Community" until NAGPRA was being debated in Congress. It ends by emphasizing that the successful return of these items demonstrated the tribe's "agency as a nation and resistance to narratives of their disappearance" and that the "self-representation of our stories in this space and throughout our homelands has been made all the more imperative due to the painful removal and erasure from our original homelands by European colonial settlers and their descendants." The artifact wall has been replaced by photos of elders and quotes from tribal members that were taken from archival records, tribal members' narratives, and present-day leaders. A perpendicular wall features a massive timeline outlining Stockbridge-Munsee Mohican presence in their ancestral homelands for at least the last 12,500 years, along with significant events in Stockbridge and eventually the forced removal of the tribe.

Figure 30. The new panel in the Carriage House Museum outlining the theft and return of the Stockbridge Bible and Communion set. Photograph by author, August 23, 2021.

Figure 31. In the new Carriage House Museum, photos of elders and quotes from historic and contemporary tribal members have replaced the "artifact wall." Photograph by author, August 23, 2021.

The complete renovation of the carriage house is significant. First, and perhaps most important, it is yet another example of the Mohican Nation's resolve to change the way their histories are collected and represented in public spaces. At face value, the new exhibit directly challenges erasure narratives, critiques and educates viewers about common misrepresentations in museums, and clearly articulates Mohican nationhood and resilience. However, the tribe's intervention in this space has also changed, and aims to change the broader problems around how Native histories are collected and put on display. The new exhibit represents the Mohican Nation through stories and photographs rather than objects. Content within the exhibit educates visitors about the importance of Mohican involvement in cultural heritage projects. It also notes that the tribe is in the process of retrieving all of the items that were previously displayed in the carriage house through repatriation. These decisions push back against the history of non-Native institutions misrepresenting Native people and seek to change the way people understand and interact with Native history in museums.

The exhibit's incorporation of archival materials is also noteworthy. Several panels mention that items used in the exhibit were "curated from the archives of the Arvid E. Miller Memorial Library-Museum," and some even feature images of archival documents. The panel section on repatriation outlines the importance of retrieving original copies of archival documents as part of the tribe's larger repatriation efforts.[70] Though this exhibit is based in Stockbridge, its connection to the Mohican tribal archive and the decades of work put in by the Historical Committee and the Department of Cultural Affairs to reunite Mohican tribal members with their homelands is clear. The fact that the Mission House, which at one point questioned whether the tribe was capable of caring for the Bible and Communion set, has now turned a portion of their museum over to the tribe shows just how much the Stockbridge-Munsee Community has accomplished in terms of positioning themselves as the experts on their own history. While these types of collaborations can certainly have their fair share of challenges, as the history of communications with the trustees can attest to, these new representations are an example of what can happen when tribes are able to represent their own histories and non-Native institutions begin to listen.

The Stockbridge Walking Tour, "Footprints of Our Ancestors"

The significantly improved relationship between the tribe and the Trustees of Reservations has extended to the town of Stockbridge itself and prompted several other local projects, including a new walking tour that articulates ongoing connections and claims to space and invites residents and visitors alike to rethink the land they stand upon. Exiting the *Mohican Miles* exhibit, visitors are encouraged to explore tribal history further by taking part in the "Footprints of Our Ancestors Walking Tour," a guided walking tour of the town that takes participants from one end of Stockbridge's Main Street to the other, exploring Mohican homesites, significant places, and representations along the way. Brochures for the tour are available in the *Mohican Miles* exhibit and at the Stockbridge Library down the street. By scanning the QR code on the signage or the brochures, participants can read about and hear living Mohican tribal members discuss the significance of returning to the lands of their ancestors. Visitors to the Stockbridge Library can also watch these videos on-site if they are not interested in completing the walking tour. For those outside of Stockbridge, the tour is also available online.

Like many of the efforts the Historical Committee and Department of Cultural Affairs has taken up in the last fifty years, the walking trail began as in intervention in a project that failed to consult Mohican people. In this case, the Upper Housatonic Valley National Heritage Area sought to develop a Native American Trail Project. The Upper Housatonic Valley National Heritage Area is an organization that seeks to "assist communities, organizations,

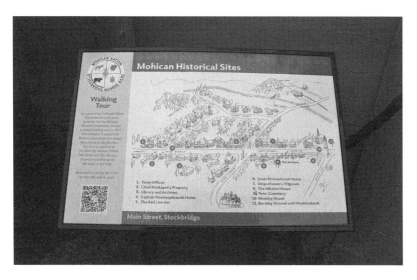

Figure 32. Signage directing museum visitors to the "Footprints of Our Ancestors Walking Tour." Photograph by author, August 23, 2021.

and citizens in the State of Connecticut and the Commonwealth of Massachusetts in identifying, preserving, interpreting, and developing the historical, cultural, scenic, and natural resources of the region for the educational and inspirational benefit of current and future generations." The Heritage Area includes 964 square miles and contains nine towns in Connecticut and twenty in Massachusetts. As part of its mission, the group's website provides suggested itineraries for travelers in the region, bike tours, and various hiking and walking tours for visitors who want to explore the history of the Upper Housatonic River Valley.[71]

Though the Housatonic River Valley is a key portion of Mohican ancestral homelands (it is the area in which Stockbridge is situated), Housatonic Heritage did not initially consult the Mohicans in planning the tour. In fact, it was not until the current librarian at the Stockbridge Library in Stockbridge, Massachusetts, Barbara Allen, mentioned the project to tribal historic preservation manager Bonney Hartley that the tribe became aware of the project at all. Hartley was stationed in New York at the time, and though her job responsibilities do not always permit time to work on projects such as these, she believed it was important for the project to have Mohican representation. As she put it, "HRV [the Housatonic River Valley] is our original homeland and if the Housatonic Heritage is proposing a NA [Native American] Heritage Trail, they should have, as a first priority, reached out to the tribe whose history they are seeking to represent."[72] After Hartley made the Upper Housatonic Valley National Heritage Area aware of the importance of consultation at one of their meetings, they followed up with the Mohican Nation and formally requested the tribe's involvement and support for the project. Since then, Hartley has attended as many of their meetings as possible to ensure the representations of history on the trail align with how the tribe wants their history represented, emphasizing that "We don't want a trail with misinformation . . . the tribe also benefits from local residents and tourists knowing about our history and having it be accurately presented." She also emphasized that it is important that projects like these are not just designed with a white audience in mind but should also be tailored to the Native peoples on whose lands they sit. Elaborating, Hartley explained that if those creating the trail did the legwork of finding and designating important sites, the tribe can truly benefit from being able to easily access and visit those sites: "It needs to be something that if our people come out to this area, we are also learning more about our history here."[73]

The larger Native American Heritage Trail Project is still in progress and could include representations throughout Massachusetts and Connecticut, but Hartley has especially focused on the portion of the trail that goes through Stockbridge, Massachusetts, what has now become the "Footprints of Our Ancestors Walking Tour." Again, Hartley worked closely with Stockbridge resident Rick Wilcox to develop the tour, and after significant archival research to identify each of the sites, the Department of Cultural Affairs debuted the self-guided brochure and map in 2018, before developing web and video components of the tour in 2019. That July, seven tribal members traveled to Stockbridge to narrate the specific histories of their ancestors that aligned with each stop on the tour.[74] In their videos, tribal members primarily focused on articulating the history of their ancestors and their homes in Stockbridge and what returning to those places meant to them. For example, standing on the homesite of his ancestor "King" Solomon Uhhaunaunauwaunmut, tribal member Jeff Vele articulated the same "feeling" that so many other tribal members have recounted on their trips home:

Upon crossing the bridge, I saw that this was the place that I had come in 2006. There on the water is a rather large, flat rock. And when I was there in that 2006 trip, I looked off of that bridge at that rock and I could feel my ancestors there fishing from that rock. It was later, while we were on this same [2019] trip to see the artifact that was recovered that I learned the location was the site of the homesite of King Solomon, who is a direct ancestor of mine. And that just really brought to heart the feeling that I had had thirteen years ago when I had looked down at that rock and felt my ancestors there fishing.[75]

Similarly, Bonney Hartley comments on the significance of knowing that the eastern half of what is now the town cemetery belonged to her ancestor David Naunauneecannuck:

To know that this was the land of my direct ancestor, to think about him, to feel his presence, to think about our other relatives, his family here, his children, to know about the other relatives across Main Street, and to think about the kind of lives that they had that led to us still being here today and all the sacrifices that they've made along the way. . . . It's a very direct connection, and I still feel their presence and personally, you know feel that their spirits are still here and that they are still looking out for my family and our tribe today.[76]

In the video about the Indian Burial Ground, Odessa Arce further emphasized the importance of these continued returns to Stockbridge:

> It's crucial to come back and set foot on these land that my ancestors set foot
> on because it gives you a sense of where you came from and what your people
> have been through, and it helps you grow into the person that you are, knowing
> your history. Also, from being separated, it's really meaningful to come back
> and see exactly where we were, because it helps keep everyone together.[77]

In that sense, the videos articulate to both Mohican and non-Mohican audiences that connections to land and a shared sense of heritage are crucial
elements of individual identity formation and ultimately Mohican nation-
building, or as Arce puts it, "keeping everyone together." The last video in the
series ends with a powerful reminder: "The Stockbridge-Munsee Community continues to place great significance in visiting, teaching, and preserving the tribe's heritage in Stockbridge."[78]

In addition to narrating their ongoing connections to the lands in Stockbridge, tribal members also use the tour to educate listeners about the
settler-colonial policies that forced the tribe to leave their ancestral lands
and had a negative impact on their ways of life. Standing on the homesite
of his ancestor Captain Jacob Naunauphtaunk, Robert Little explains that
Naunauphtaunk was a celebrated veteran of the French and Indian War
(1754–63) who helped prevent the invasion of English settlements. He notes,
however, that "rather than receiving gratitude, our ancestors found themselves increasingly unwelcome in New England."[79] A video focusing on Jonas
Etowaukaum's homesite explains that in spite of Etowaukaum's notable role
as a veteran of the French and Indian War, he, like many other Mohicans,
was sued for debt and forced to give up his land. Tribal member Terrie K.
Terrio explains that this was used as a tool to obtain Mohican land long after
Stockbridge, detailing how her grandmother lost her forty-acre lot in Red
Springs, Wisconsin, because she could not afford her grocery bill and was
forced to sell her land.[80] Another video features several tribal members sitting on the site of the Stockbridge Meeting House, one of the archaeological
sites that the tribe is working to uncover. As they sit together, Jeff Vele reads
aloud from a 1763 document that explains how settler Elijah Brown called
a town meeting with no official authority, notifying Mohican officials less
than twenty-four hours in advance, while most of them were working in their

maple sugar houses several miles away. At the meeting, Elijah Williams Sr., whose descendants would go on to found Williams College, was elected, while none of the Mohican candidates who were able to make it back in time were allowed to be heard. Tribal members challenged the decision, but it was dismissed in Boston courts. Tribal members in the video respond to this story in different ways. While Jo Ann Schedler notes that in spite of this history "We are still together . . . and I'm proud of that, I'm proud of our ancestors," Jeff Vele reminds listeners that "It is ironic though, that the same methods that were used in the 1700s to dispossess our people of land were used in the 1800s to dispossess our people of lands in the Red Springs area in Wisconsin."[81]

Several other videos also feature archival documents. Through images, videos, and even filmed interactions with archival records, they emphasize the importance of these sources in uncovering the Indigenous history of this place. In discussing the Town Offices, which sit on the land of tribal member Aaron Sausockhock, Robert Little explained that "to see the manuscripts and the names of our ancestors, it's very, it touches my heart." These documents highlight tribal members' roles in local government before they were forcibly removed, and speak to the important history of diplomacy in Stockbridge.[82] Bonney Hartley makes similar remarks when viewing the original plat plan of the town, which outlines each of the homesites assigned to Mohican tribal members, as well as a 1750 proprietorship document, which she explains "tells the story, the most, of the dispossession here."[83] Hartley explains that the original documents are particularly important to tribal members who return to Stockbridge because the reservation is so far away. The materials bear a unique relationship to this land and tribal history here, and as Hartley put it, that "connects all of us."[84]

By placing these contemporary Mohican tribal members back into the historical representations of Stockbridge, the Mohican Nation emphasizes their ongoing connections to this place as well as the violent ways they were forced to leave. The videos reveal both the joyful and the traumatic experiences of returning that were so clearly articulated in previous historical trips. They also disrupt ongoing myths of disappearance in Stockbridge and beyond. Before the tour and the new *Mohican Miles* exhibit, the only acknowledgment of ongoing Native presence in the town was the Indian Burial Ground, which arguably attests to a Mohican past, not present. As Hartley noted, it suggests that "We're all dead and gone. . . . It doesn't say something about

Figure 33. A still frame of Stop 3 on the "Footprints of Our Ancestors Walking Tour," showing Bonney Hartley, who as of this writing is the tribal historic preservation manager, and Stockbridge Library curator Barbara Allen viewing a 1739 plat of Stockbridge that identifies Mohican land ownership. The plat was a key source in Wilcox and Hartley's research to construct the walking tour. Stockbridge-Munsee Community, Cultural Affairs Department, Arvid E. Miller Library Museum.

what happened, why we were forced from here, where we are today."[85] By bringing living tribal members back to Stockbridge and asking them to narrate the importance of this place to them, the tour contests those myths quite directly. In Hartley's words, "You can say a hundred times that the tribe still exists, but it doesn't have the same impact as looking at a living tribal member talking about their history."[86]

Renaming Peeskawso Peak

Reclamations and recognition of Mohican space in various forms have long been a part of Mohican archival activism. But beyond more private practices like rebuilding the stone cairn, these projects have also included public signage at diverse locations, from mission school sites to trail markers and highway signage.[87] In Stockbridge, a 2021 project to rename two trails at the Mohican sacred site Monument Mountain aimed to correct an offensive misrepresentation and educate hikers about the cultural significance of the mountain.

As outlined in chapter 4, Monument Mountain has long been a sacred place for Mohican people. Though it is known as Maaswuseexay, or "fisher's nest," in the Mohican language, it is believed to have been named Monument

Mountain for the significant rock pile, or "monument," created and maintained by the Mohican people prior to their removal from the Northeast.[88] The mountain has two main trails, which were previously named "Monument Trail," and "Squ*w Peak," and is managed by the Trustees of Reservations, the same preservation agency that manages the Mission House Museum. Though the relationship between the trustees and the tribe has not always been a positive one, this has changed significantly since the establishment of the tribe's satellite Historic Preservation Office in 2015. In 2021, Brian Cruey, who is the director of the trustees' Southern Berkshire properties, admitted that the changes were "long overdue" and that the tribe has "felt that we need to do a better job telling that story, and we are really open to that."[89] The trustees agreed to rename both trails in April 2021, which are now called "Mohican Monument Trail," and "Peeskawso Peak Trail," respectively. The latter change replaces the racial slur "squ*w" with the Mohican word that means "virtuous woman."[90]

In addition to the name changes, the mountain base also includes new signage that identifies it as a sacred site and educates hikers about its history,

Figure 34. New signage at Monument Mountain that includes the two renamed trails. Photograph by author, August 24, 2021.

asking them to be respectful as they hike. Previously, historical representation of the mountain focused entirely on an 1850 picnic between Nathaniel Hawthorne, Herman Melville, and several other writers, a charming story that nonetheless erased a much longer Indigenous history. While signs about the famous picnic remain, they are complemented by additional signage that emphasizes ongoing Mohican connections to the mountain. To tell the story of the stone cairn, Maaswuseexay Wuwaana'kwthik, or "place of arranged stones at the fisher's nest/standing up nest," the sign includes images of archival records, including a diagram of the stone cairn drawn by Ezra Stiles in his 1762 journal and a petition to the Massachusetts General Court signed by tribal leaders John Konkapot, "King" Solomon Uhhaunnauwaunmut, Johannis Mthoksin, "King" Ben David Naunauneekannuck, and Jacob Cheeksonkun that requests permission to remain in their homelands. The sign uses both documents to emphasize the long-held Mohican cultural practices that are still tied to this place and to demonstrate how important this mountain and the surrounding land has always been to Mohican people. The final portion of the new signage speaks specifically to ongoing Mohican returns to this place, noting that in spite of removal, the Mohican Nation has survived and the Mohicans "often return to their eastern homelands for historical trips and remain actively involved in the protection of cultural sites and the return of cultural heritage items." It also emphasizes that the Mohicans never relinquished their connections to this land, stating that "records consistently show tribal members returning to the site of the offering place [the stone cairn] throughout the 1800s to offer stone prayers, and tribal members continue to carry on the tradition to this day."

The new signage at Monument Mountain works to further preserve this site, contests narratives that claim the tribe has disappeared, and reclaims space so that when tribal members return, they know that they belong here, and that they are home. Like the *Mohican Miles* exhibit, and the "Footprints of Our Ancestors Walking Tour," the signage is yet another example of new narratives that have grown out of Mohican archival activism: tribal members' efforts to reclaim their histories and change how they are represented in public spaces. Through each of these projects, the Department of Cultural Affairs has made historical preservation a key theme not only to emphasize their ongoing connections to this place but also to enlist those visiting these spaces to respect them and aid in their protection. Their reminders throughout each of the projects that the Mohicans have always and continue to return to these lands support these efforts by positioning the tribe as the best cultural stewards of their own lands and histories, and continually work to undo the pervasive myths of Mohican disappearance. Finally, for Mohicans who return to Stockbridge, the projects cultivate a sense of ownership and belonging among tribal members—supporting ongoing efforts to create a shared sense of heritage and belonging that is rooted in land and bolsters Mohican nation-building. Like other projects within Mohican archival activism, these public history representations change the way both Native and non-Native audiences access Mohican history, exemplify the way the tribe is enacting their sovereignty in various contexts, and craft new narratives of Stockbridge-Munsee history that change public understandings of the past.

When I interviewed Historical Committee member Leah Miller in 2016, she emphasized how important it is to educate non-Indigenous people about Native histories:

> Apparently, there are a lot of ignorant people in our country who aren't aware of the fact that this land was originally Native land, or they just don't want to believe it because they just, I don't know, I hate to use the word hateful, but that's what comes to my mind when I think about how some non-Native people treat Native people.[91]

When I interviewed Miller, we were in the midst of the NO DAPL protests in North Dakota. Within the last month, members of the National Guard had sprayed freezing water on protestors in icy November conditions, fired rubber bullets at peaceful protestors, and attempted to forcibly remove people who were simply trying to keep their water source clean. These actions stemmed from a refusal to understand and respect Native sovereignty and a failure to see Indigenous people as real, modern human beings. In other words, they stemmed from a likely constant exposure to misrepresentations of Native people and history.

Though the contestations over Mohican representations have never become violent, the range of public history projects the Mohicans have contested have certainly been both hurtful and harmful. In Bowler Schools' assessment of Mohican children as isolating themselves *because* of tribal culture, in the representation in the "Indian Museum" of the Mohicans as a "once viable culture," and in the Upper Housatonic Valley National Heritage

Area's failure to initially consult the Mohicans in their representation of the region, these educational institutions produced damaging representations that influence understandings of Native people throughout society. And yet, in each of these situations, the Mohicans asserted their right to represent their own histories and sought to generate new educational narratives of survival and nationhood anyway. The Historical Committee implemented their Act 31 curriculum in Bowler and Gresham Schools in 2008, redesigned the "Indian Museum" as *Mohican Miles,* and designed the walking tour: a powerful digital public history project that corrects colonial erasures of Native land ownership and presence and emphasizes Mohican survival.

Still, it is important to recognize how inequitable these partnerships can truly be and attest to the work the Mohican Historical Committee put in to initiate these new narratives and educate others. For every new Mohican-led representation, there is certainly a Henry Hudson commemorative event or an *Indians of the Hudson River Valley* textbook covered in artifacts. Building equitable relationships between Native and non-Native organizations and institutions is not something that happens overnight, and it is impossible without non-Native institutions' willingness to listen, learn, and change in dialogue with Indigenous nations. In the instances I have presented here, the Mohicans have done the bulk of the work to educate others about their existence when it is not their responsibility to do so. They have gone above and beyond to protest, challenge, and replace damaging stereotypes when these representations should not exist in the first place. In other words, it is time that non-Native institutions begin responding more regularly to this activism and recognize the damaging power dominant narratives of Native history can have on the way we interact in society today.

In the final section of the book, I return to the importance of archival collections and emphasize the importance of non-Native institutions in the larger scope of Native nations reclaiming and representing their own histories. While Native people can make, and have been making, these interventions without the support of settler-colonial archives, as this book has shown, their work becomes significantly easier when they have access to and control over their own archival records. Those of us who work in settler-colonial archives can and must enable this access and create equitable partnerships with Native nations that ultimately lead to more accurate and more responsible narratives of Native history.

Conclusion

Indigenous Archival Activism beyond Tribal Archives

Meaningful consultation and concurrence are essential to establishing mutually beneficial practices and trust. Through dialogue and cooperation, institutions and communities can identify mutually beneficial solutions to common problems and develop new models for shared stewardship and reciprocity or for the appropriate transfer of responsibility and ownership for some materials.

—First Archivist Circle, "Protocols for Native American Archival Materials," 2007

Tracing Mohican archival activism shows us how one tribal nation has approached the question of who has the right to represent Native history for decades, but that work is far from complete. After centuries of preserving Mohican history for future generations and more than fifty years of recovering additional knowledge and materials from archival institutions, the Mohican historical project continues. Members of the Historical Committee who have been at this work for decades continue their efforts, while working with and passing the torch to younger staff members of the Department of Cultural Affairs. Together, they continue to identify and recover archival collections, produce new primary and secondary narratives from the perspectives of tribal members, and revise the way Stockbridge-Munsee history is represented in public spaces. Their work to strengthen a shared sense of Stockbridge-Munsee Mohican identity and belonging and enact data sovereignty over their historical materials is an important element of Indigenous nation-building. Still, the nature of settler-colonial collections and representations can make this feel like a never-ending process: the tribe continues to search for relevant collections of materials that remain elusive after being bought and sold several times, and many harmful and inaccurate representations of Mohican history remain present in public institutions and spaces.

In many ways, the tribe is more equipped than ever to continue taking on these challenges. In addition to the Historical Committee, which still meets to discuss and advise tribal leaders on matters of historical importance, the Department of Cultural Affairs includes several paid positions that are continuing the work started by Bernice Miller, Dorothy Davids, and others on a full-time basis. The Tribal Historic Preservation Office at Williams College in Massachusetts has two staff members working to represent Mohican interests in the Northeast, the Mohican and Munsee languages are being taught to Mohican children for the first time in several generations, and the Department of Cultural Affairs is continuing to find new ways to reach tribal and nontribal audiences through social media, public advocacy, and expanded collaborations with non-Native public humanities institutions.

Yet, as much as the Mohican Historical Committee and Department of Cultural Affairs have accomplished and continue to pursue, much of the incomplete work depends on the cooperation of non-Native institutions and organizations. Tribal archives and museums are the result of Native nations taking matters into their own hands in spite of settler-colonial collecting policies. But these institutions can only go so far if non-Native museums and archives refuse to repatriate Native knowledge and materials and continue to enact barriers that make it difficult for Native people to access these spaces. While chapter 5 highlighted how the Mohicans initiated and continue to build collaborations with several public humanities and educational institutions, this Conclusion looks forward by assessing some of the broader collaborative work that has begun between tribal nations and non-Native institutions. In particular, I consider how the tenets of Indigenous archival activism—access, sovereignty, and new narratives—might guide settler-colonial institutions, as they undertake this work in collaboration with tribal nations.

Most collaborations between tribes and settler-colonial archives began after the publication of the "Protocols for Native American Archival Materials" in 2007, and the movement around "Indigenous data sovereignty" was formally launched by the U.S. Data Sovereignty Network in 2016. The protocols were published by the group First Archivist Circle, an organization formed to promote collaboration among tribal and nontribal archivists, and have since been endorsed by the Society of American Archivists (SAA) and the Association for College and Research Libraries (ACRL). Still, SAA only endorsed the protocols in 2018 after much debate, followed by the ACRL in 2019, and as of this writing, most archives are still determining how and to what extent they will implement the practices.[1] In part, the slow implementation is due to a significant disinvestment in libraries and archives over the past several decades and the resulting precarity of library and archival workers.[2] These institutions are understaffed, and their employees are over capacity. Still, many have started to address these issues as they are able and are continuing to learn through organizations like the Association for Tribal Archives, Libraries, and Museums, which was founded in 2010. These efforts were certainly bolstered by earlier conversations about who has the right to collect and represent Native history—conversations spurred by the Red Power movement, the debate over and eventual passage of the Native American Graves Protection and Repatriation Act (NAGPRA), and of course grassroots activism like that of the Stockbridge-Munsee Mohican Nation. While the work that many settler-colonial archives are now undertaking does not amount to Indigenous nation-building (as I argue Indigenous archival activism stemming from tribal archives does) settler-colonial archives do have a significant role to play in shifting the collection, production, and representation of Indigenous histories. Until research at tribal archives in collaboration with Native communities becomes a standard best practice, the majority of historical scholarship is still being produced in the context of settler-colonial archives. Those of us working in these institutions are therefore on the front lines of the production of Native history, and we have both the ability and responsibility to make Indigenous histories more accessible to Native people, set higher and new standards that respect Indigenous data sovereignty, and promote tribal collaboration to aid in the production of new narratives that center Indigenous voices and knowledge.

I approach this call to action as a historian working in one such settler-colonial collecting institution, the Newberry Library in Chicago, which houses a world-renowned collection of rare book and manuscript materials related to Indigenous people across the globe. As the director of the D'Arcy McNickle Center for American Indian and Indigenous Studies at the library, I and my colleagues regularly collaborate with tribal nations and help them access archival and rare book materials that record or represent their histories. This work has expanded further since 2020, when the library received a grant from the Mellon Foundation to pilot expanded collaborations with several communities and make internal changes to the library's cataloging and archiving protocols that would improve access to Indigenous collections and better represent Indigenous protocols. As such, I rely on my own experiences to highlight some of the challenges this work presents, as well as its potential outcomes. I also weave in the work being completed at other settler-colonial institutions, but the examples discussed here are by no means exhaustive. The efficacy of the many initiatives settler-colonial archives have established in the twenty-first century merits significant future study. Instead of providing a set of best practices, which are bound to shift in the coming years, I aim to pose larger questions about the role of settler-colonial collections. I invite librarians, archivists, and others who work in collecting institutions to consider how they might approach their work through the tenets of Indigenous archival activism, that is, how they can increase access for Indigenous communities and prioritize tribal sovereignty to support the creation of new narratives that respect and prioritize Indigenous knowledge. Overall, this is not meant to be a definitive survey of settler-colonial archives but to gesture to what is possible and to further understand what is at stake in these battles for control and fights to reclaim Native history.

Access

When Arvid and Bernice Miller began the work of collecting their historical materials in the 1930s, the most significant problem they faced was geographic distance. For most tribes, especially those without substantial tribal archives, this is still a persistent issue. However, digitization technology has enabled increased sharing of materials between settler-colonial archives and tribal nations, and for many archives this has been the easiest and most common way to increase access to materials.

Large-scale digitization is by no means cheap or easy, but access to high-quality cameras and scanning software on most smartphones means that I and others who work in settler-colonial archives are frequently requesting items from Special Collections, snapping a few photos, and emailing them to tribal archivists, historians, and historic preservation officers in a matter of minutes. Many institutions have also taken up larger-scale digitization and sharing projects as they are able to receive funding for such work. For example, beginning in 2011, the American Philosophical Society (APS) received a grant from the Mellon Foundation to create close partnerships with four tribal communities. They have since expanded this work into an approach they call "Digital Knowledge Sharing," which they define as "an approach of equitable knowledge exchange and relationship building." Since then, the APS has founded a Center for Native American Research, worked with dozens of tribal nations to help identify relevant materials in the collection, and committed to providing free digital copies of materials to tribal communities.[3] Northern Arizona University's Cline Library has completed similar work, comprehensively combing through its collection to create a LibGuide to "Indigenous Peoples in Special Collections and Archives" and deaccessioning materials and returning them to tribal communities when possible.[4] Other projects take this work even further by using digital tools to recontextualize historical materials. For example, on the Plateau Peoples' Web Portal, a collaboration between eight tribal nations and Washington State University, at least eight non-Native institutions have digitized material culture, photographs, and archival documents not only to make them more accessible but also to give tribal nations the ability to provide further, or corrective, information about the materials. The portal uses the Mukurtu content management system, which allows tribes to determine access protocols and restrictions for their items online and add additional traditional knowledge or information that may have been left out of the original data accompanying the items.

Some of this work to increase access goes back even further but has been reinvigorated by the ongoing conversations about these issues in the field. For instance, the D'Arcy McNickle Center for American Indian and Indigenous Studies was founded in 1972 at the Newberry Library, around the same time the Mohican tribal archive was founded. One of the McNickle Center's original goals was to support the work of tribal historians using the vast Indigenous collections at the Newberry. The collection has also always had a designated librarian for the Edward E. Ayer Indigenous Studies Collection since it was donated in 1911; this staff member is on hand to assist tribal communities with locating relevant materials. As of 2023, this work continues under another Mellon Foundation grant which provides funding for the Newberry to cultivate relationships with three tribal communities so that we can learn how we might make the collections more accessible to communities in support of tribally led initiatives and investigate what internal changes are needed to make the library a more welcoming space for Indigenous researchers.

While digital sharing seems to be the major focal point of most collaborations between tribal nations and settler-colonial archives, institutions have
been much more reticent to actually repatriate items to tribes. While the
Newberry did repatriate a Kwakwaka'wakw house plank in 1997, which was
one of very few traditional objects in our collection, the Cline Library, the
Peabody Museum of Archaeology and Ethnology, Dartmouth College, and
Cornell University are the only institutions I am aware of that have actually
deaccessioned archival records and returned them to tribal nations.[5] All of
these returns were quite recent, with the Cline Library beginning a deaccessioning project in 2016 and the remainder of the institutions completing
repatriations in 2021 and 2022. This is primarily the case because NAGPRA
does not explicitly refer to documents in its list of items that institutions
that receive federal funding must inventory. Therefore, most settler-colonial
archives and libraries have never completed NAGPRA inventories; they do
not believe, nor have they been told, that the law applies to them. This does
not mean that a NAGPRA request could not be made. Many documents held
in settler-colonial archives were created by Indigenous people and contain
information about sacred sites and funerary ceremonies, and they could be
interpreted as cultural patrimony. It is unclear whether or not such a case
would be successful, and it would likely vary from institution to institution.

Repatriation from libraries and archives is also complicated for other reasons. Even if settler-colonial archives began creating NAGPRA-style inventories or even evaluating their collections for items that should be repatriated
outside the law, they would face the same, if not greater, issues of capacity
and time that museums have been struggling with since the 1990s. The collections amassed by settler-colonial collectors are simply enormous. They are
far greater in magnitude than the number of items in museums, and evaluating each book or archival record, consulting with tribal nations, and making
determinations takes significant staff time. Ironically, the fact that NAGPRA
has not been interpreted as applying to settler-colonial archives makes allot-
ting time to this type of inventory and evaluation even more difficult. While
museums are under a clear federal mandate to create collection inventories
and consult with tribes, archives are not required to take up this work, and
they have thus been much slower to hire the staff that would be needed to
complete these kinds of evaluations. Moreover, while ancestors and museum
objects are more commonly associated with a single tribal nation (or deemed
culturally unidentifiable), many materials in archives are more complicated.

While some items are clearly associated with a single group, others, such as the journals of settlers that contain observations of Indigenous people, often contain knowledge extracted from several communities. Whom should the item be returned to if the information contained within it originated from several different tribal nations? Issues of provenance and the reluctance to split up archival collections make repatriation even more challenging. Archival principles of *respect des fonds* and original order dictate that archival collections are maintained in the organizational format in which they were donated and are grouped by donor to preserve the context in which they were collected. Since many collectors assembled materials from multiple Indigenous nations, repatriating archival materials can require breaking up an archival collection, which would defy archival standards and, in some cases, go against the wishes of donors. How should a collecting institution weigh its responsibilities to tribal nations against standard archival principles and best practices? Could we recognize that splitting a collection could cause the loss of important context but also remember that we are talking about traditional knowledge that was already extracted from the context in which it was created? How might we reckon with the context of creation and community origin in addition to the context of collection when making these decisions?

In spite of these challenges, repatriation of archival materials is a worthy action that every settler-colonial archive should take seriously. We have seen throughout this book the enormous value that access to copies of archival materials can have, and those impacts are even more significant when tribal members have access to the original items. As several Mohican tribal members articulated in the "Footprints of Our Ancestors Walking Tour," there are few parallel experiences to seeing the signature or writings of one's ancestor with your own eyes. These documents connect Indigenous people to significant moments and people in their histories and inform their sense of self-identification and belonging within an Indigenous nation. While the information contained within archival documents can certainly be useful in public history and other legal advocacy projects, the return of physical materials that one's ancestors created can have even greater impacts that support Indigenous identity formation and nation-building. Because NAGPRA is so unclear when it comes to archival records, I urge settler-colonial institutions to think beyond the law when they receive repatriation requests from tribal nations, and simply ask themselves and the tribe(s) they are working with what their responsibilities are given the history and impact of an item. Was the document taken from a tribal nation, or sold under duress as a part of the settler-colonial collecting project? Does it contain the original words or traditional knowledge of tribal members that were removed from important community contexts? And can it positively affect the lives of Indigenous people by returning a critical piece of their history and ensuring they have control over how that item is accessed and used to produce historical narratives in the future? Like everything discussed in this conclusion, these conversations take reciprocal relationship building and significant self-reflection.

For items that remain in settler-colonial archives for one reason or another, additional issues with searchability and access continue to make locating materials related to one's own tribal history difficult. The first is in how items are cataloged and described. The vast majority of libraries and archives use Library of Congress Subject Headings (LCSH), the most widely used subject thesaurus in the world. Subject headings are assigned to library materials to facilitate searching for items on similar topics, and because most settler-colonial libraries and archives use LCSH in their catalogs and databases, it is easier to locate materials on similar subjects across geographically dispersed institutions. Unfortunately, these subject headings were often created based on the names tribal nations were given in settler-colonial documents, and therefore are not always consistent with the names tribal nations use for themselves. They can also lead to confusion if several different names have been used for a single group of people. Each subject heading does have an authority record kept by the Library of Congress, which includes the preferred subject term and variant search terms associated with a particular subject heading, but the authority records are not always comprehensive or up to date. For example, several LCSH will yield materials related to the Stockbridge-Munsee Mohican Nation, including "Stockbridge Indians," "Munsee Indians," "Mahican Indians," "Stockbridge Munsee Community," and "Stockbridge and Munsee Tribe of Indians." However, searching for materials under these subject headings does not yield the same results. To some extent, this is understandable—there are times throughout history when these groups are not the same. However, it *is* surprising that the search results do not have more overlap, given that these communities became one nation in the nineteenth century and have always been related. While a search for "Stockbridge Indians" in the Newberry's catalog currently results in several treaties, petitions, and other legal documents and historical books related to the Stockbridge-Munsee Mohican Nation, searches for "Mahican Indians" and "Munsee Indians" produce significantly fewer results. The authority record for "Stockbridge Indians" does not include Munsee as variant or related search term, and the authority record for "Mahican Indians" does not include Stockbridge.[6] In cases like these, tribal members are forced to search under several names to locate their materials and use settler-colonial language like "Stockbridge Indians" to search for the materials related to their histories.

Solutions to this problem are limited without the Library of Congress changing LCSH terms for Indigenous peoples. While individual libraries can and have created their own local subject authorities, the ubiquity of LCSH and the significant investment in time and expertise to maintain a local vocabulary makes this option prohibitive for many libraries. In some library catalogs and databases it is also possible to change the public display of a term without changing the underlying data, but this approach has the potential to affect searchability. For example, at the Newberry we have considered replacing a subject heading like "Stockbridge Indians" with something like "Stockbridge-Munsee Mohican People" so that the latter is visible to the public but the former is still being used as the subject heading used to generate search results. This would mean that users would see "Stockbridge-Munsee Mohican People" on items that have been cataloged with the subject heading "Stockbridge Indians," but unfortunately, a search for "Stockbridge-Munsee Mohican People" as a keyword would still not present these items. This approach is an improvement in appropriate terms but not in searchability. This option also raises the concern of confusing users, who may think that a search under the phrase "Stockbridge-Munsee Mohican People" would yield all relevant results, when in reality, users would still need to search "Stockbridge Indians" to locate the same materials. Researchers' abilities to effectively search for these items would depend on a librarian explaining how our use of subject headings differs from other, similar institutions'. Other imperfect solutions include adding a "Stockbridge-Munsee Mohican People" local index term or subject heading in addition to the LCSH "Stockbridge Indians" or adding the words "Munsee" and "Mohican" to a free-text note (language that is often not taken directly from the source and can be edited) within the public-facing catalog record. A keyword search for "Munsee" or "Mohican" would then yield these materials in the results. Again, the time and expertise needed to add these index terms, local subject headings, or free-text notes is often prohibitive for libraries, and these options raise questions about whether searchability should be sacrificed for respectful names, or whether this simply creates another barrier for tribal nations to access their historical records. Either way, it points to the ways in which settler-colonial knowledge and sense of belonging are entwined within these institutions and shows why it can be so difficult to disentangle these threads. Solving one problem often leads to another.

The presence of racial slurs within catalog entries is a similar problem. While these words were used by settlers who interacted with Native people and should not be erased from the records themselves, they can be hurtful for Indigenous people to encounter as they are searching for materials. Even if they do not affect searchability, they do have an impact on how Indigenous people feel and to what extent they perceive themselves to be welcome in archival spaces. Again, solutions for this problem are imperfect. Many racial slurs appear in the published titles of works, where changing the word in the title itself would make it unsearchable across library catalogs. In these cases, libraries can add a context note to the catalog record explaining that the title of this material contains a racial slur and that the library does not endorse this language but has preserved it as a historical record, but it does not remove the word itself. In other cases, racial slurs appear in free-text notes, where catalogers copied the language used in the source into the item description (a common practice used throughout the history of library cataloging). In these cases, libraries and archives can and should eliminate racial slurs from free-text notes entirely and replace them with appropriate words.

Another common issue with LCSH is that for items that include information about multiple tribal nations, catalogers historically used general subject headings like "Indians of North America—Great Lakes Region" rather than listing out the subject headings for each tribal nation. This practice originated during the era of the card catalog, in which the limited space on a card influenced the number and granularity of subject headings applied to an item. The application of broad subject headings to Indigenous materials also persists today because many catalogers feel they lack the expertise to appropriately identify specific tribal nations and communities. This issue is a simpler fix, one that the Newberry has taken on for several collection items. For example, prior to 2020, the catalog entry for an eighteenth-century French manuscript that contains descriptions of the traditional lifeways of several tribal nations at Fort Michilimackinac only included broad subject headings like the one above, even though the description listed the "Outaouas, Hurons, Pouteouatamis, Noquets, Sakis, Puans, Outagamis, Miamis of Chicagou, and Sioux" as being described in the item itself. Because the catalog record lacked subject headings pertaining to each of these tribal nations and the description only included this direct transcription of tribal names, a search for "Potawatomi," for example, did not yield this item within search results. To increase searchability, we added eight subject headings (Ottawa Indians, Wyandot Indians, Potawatomi Indians, Sauk Indians, Ho Chunk Indians, Menominee Indians, Miami Indians, and Santee Indians) to the catalog entry.

In each of these cases there is no perfect solution, but improvements can be made to make it easier for tribal representatives to locate the materials that are relevant to their nations. Considering these challenges should be an important part of the work all settler-colonial archives are undertaking today, and it is my sincere hope that more coordination of these efforts can happen on a national level in the future. While at least one repository, the X̱wi7x̱wa Library at the University of British Columbia, has already started to use its own subject headings, and the Brian Deer Classification System has been used by several other repositories within Canada, most libraries in the United States feel unable to make major changes to their subject headings without direction from the Library of Congress, for fear of affecting searchability.[7] Major changes to subject headings such as replacing the headings themselves with the names tribal nations use for themselves should be directed by tribal nations, and to avoid every library in the country flooding Tribal Historic Preservation Offices with requests for guidance on what name they would prefer, a national effort to create a crosswalk from outdated language to names chosen by tribal nations would be significantly more effective.

Beyond Library of Congress Subject Headings, another common issue with searchability in tribal archives is the ways in which individual Native authors and historical actors have been left out of item descriptions. We saw this clearly in chapter 1 when Mohican leader Hendrick Aupaumut was left out of several collection descriptions, even those that include his writing. The Mohican tribal archive's reorganization of Aupaumut's papers into his own collection is the ideal solution to issues like these, but settler-colonial archives can also assist with making these items more discoverable and properly attributing items to Native authors and contributors and listing their names in finding aids so that when tribal members use the names of their relatives and ancestors as search terms, items to which they contributed appear.

Adding the names of Native contributors is one of the initiatives the APS has taken up as part of its work to make materials more accessible to Indigenous communities. The APS holds many manuscripts and writings by anthropologists who worked closely with Indigenous people to record the languages, knowledge, and traditions of hundreds of different tribal nations. Yet in spite of the significant contributions made by Indigenous peoples to these materials, they are most frequently cataloged by the names of the anthropologists, not the Native contributors. As a result, Indigenous knowledge is credited to those who recorded the information, rather than those who "knew it, communicated it, and looked after it," even in cases when information about the Indigenous contributors is available within the item itself. Such was the case with a document called "Clallam Notes, 1917," which was until recently attributed to well-known anthropologist Franz Boas. In reviewing this item, APS curator Brian Carpenter realized the recording could not have been made by Boas and noticed a name, "Mrs. Mahone," scrawled at the top of one of the pages. Using census data, Carpenter was able to determine that Mrs. Mahone was Rose Mahone, a Klallam woman who clearly assisted the linguist who recorded the information in this document and was "the ultimate basis of the information in the document." Rose Mahone's name is now included in the full catalog entry for the item in APS's collection, making it easier for Klallam tribal members who are familiar with Mahone's work to find this item that she helped create.[8]

One additional aspect of accessibility I want to discuss here is the physical spaces of settler-colonial archives, which are frequently sterile, guarded by security, and in some cases accessible only to those with academic credentials. The simplest way for settler-colonial archives to address this issue is to make their collections accessible to everyone—regardless of whether or not they hold advanced degrees. Most repositories have done this. But the questions of sterility and security pose more challenges. Archives in part feel sterile because they are temperature controlled and free of debris that could harm the materials contained therein. They are typically guarded by security measures to prevent the theft of items. While I do not have ready solutions to these issues, I do want to give one example of an archive that has taken up some of these barriers in an effort to make their collections more accessible to Indigenous people. Though located within a settler-colonial institution, the Indian Residential School History and Dialogue Centre (IRSHDC) at the University of British Columbia describes its purpose as honoring and privileging "the experiences of Survivors, to create a Survivor-centered, trauma-informed space for dialogue ... [and] to amplify conversations around the legacies of the Indian Residential School System and the on-going impacts of colonialism in Canada." The building that houses the IRSHDC includes architectural elements that feature Indigenous culture. Within the space, the archive offers comfortable spaces where families can sit together to review materials. It also includes a separate room for reflection that those experiencing the secondary trauma of reading residential school materials can use to take a break, an Elder's room, and a space for children with toys, books, and activities.[9] While not all archives can create identical spaces, it is worth considering what changes can be made to ensure that Indigenous people have space to process any trauma that may come up as they are conducting research, how archival spaces might feature the work of Indigenous artists and architects, and what spaces could be cultivated so that groups and families could more readily visit archival spaces. For many Indigenous communities, intergenerational learning is a key element of passing on knowledge, yet few archives allow for the presence of children in certain spaces without advanced planning.

In each of the access barriers presented here, tribal archives have already made significant progress. It is time now for settler-colonial archives to begin making, or in some cases continue to make, significant changes to how their collections are accessed so that materials are more readily available to and easy to locate for Native people and communities who are working to recover and reclaim their histories. As each of the presented examples has shown, this work is neither easy nor perfect. What matters is that those of us who work in settler-colonial archives continue to make progress on these efforts, are open to solutions that disrupt our understandings of best practices, and, most important, listen to Indigenous peoples and regard them as the experts on their own histories that they are.

Sovereignty

In terms of tribal sovereignty, tribal archives are similarly the repositories where Indigenous people have the most control over the organization of, access to, and use of historical records that include tribal knowledge.

However, they typically cannot control tribal information that is still available in settler-colonial archives, which, as exemplified in the Mohican case, is most original archival materials. The most straightforward way to support tribal data sovereignty over how their knowledge contained in archival records is accessed is to return the original materials to tribes. However, for the many reasons explained here, the repatriation of archival documents is not always straightforward; for the foreseeable future, many of these items will likely remain in settler-colonial repositories. In these contexts, settler-colonial archives can prioritize tribal sovereignty and protocols in their decision making about how Indigenous materials are accessed, and thus affect (even if it is impossible to control) how they are used to create historical narratives. Some of this builds on concerns outlined in the previous section that are still works in progress for most settler-colonial archives: tribal nations should be able to determine what vocabulary is used to identify their knowledge and histories in archival collections and provide feedback on how the materials that contain their knowledge or were written by their citizens are described. Other issues lie more in how materials that contain information about or images of sacred ceremonies, funerary customs and human remains, and other knowledge that was never meant to be removed from tribal contexts is accessed by researchers.

In response, many settler-colonial archives have developed culturally sensitive materials policies that detail how items will be identified as culturally sensitive and who can access these materials. The policies of two such institutions provide insight into how settler-colonial archives might think about these questions. In its "Protocols for the Treatment of Indigenous Materials," the APS outlines how items will be classified as culturally sensitive and the effect this will have on how these materials are accessed. For items that have been classified as culturally sensitive in coordination with or at the request of a tribal nation, the APS may place restrictions on the item, such as not allowing photographs or requiring that a staff member is present if a researcher wants to view an item. The APS will also not reproduce items that are culturally sensitive or give permission for the item to be published in print or digital form without the explicit consent of tribal representatives. As of this writing, however, they do not restrict access to any of the items in their collections as long as a researcher has a "legitimate need" to view the item. They also explain that they will continue to identify items as culturally sensitive or potentially culturally sensitive in coordination with tribal nations.[10]

The Newberry Library's policy on culturally sensitive materials is similar, and indeed the original version created in 2016 was based on APS's protocols. However, the policy was revised in 2021 with support from the previously mentioned grant from the Mellon Foundation, and thus it contains some significant departures. Like the APS protocols, the Newberry's policy emphasizes its commitment to open access. However, we are clear that this commitment must be balanced with "respect for rights of tribal nations and Indigenous communities to protect materials created by them, materials created by others that depict their cultures, and traditional knowledge preserved in these materials." Accordingly, items that have been identified as culturally sensitive may be restricted from public access at the request of a tribal historic preservation officer or similar tribal official, and other materials without this request can be flagged as culturally sensitive in several different ways. First, any material identified as culturally sensitive by Newberry staff or tribal partners will be flagged, notifying researchers of the sensitive nature of the materials and requesting that they do not photograph or reproduce the item in any way. Like the APS, the Newberry also commits to not digitizing these items or presenting them to the public without consent from affiliated tribal nations. Second, a traditional knowledge (TK) label that further clarifies the nature of the sensitivity and specific protocols for the items may be added to the catalog record in consultation with tribal officials.[11]

While the Newberry's application of TK labels is still in process as of this writing, other repositories like the Library of Congress (LOC) have begun to do so. For a collection of Passamaquoddy wax cylinder records recorded by anthropologist Jesse Walter Fewkes in March 1890 and donated by Harvard's Peabody Museum, the LOC worked with tribal representatives to assign three labels—"Attribution," "Outreach," and "Non-Commercial"—to the collection of recordings. The recordings taken by Fewkes include "songs, legends, creation stories, and linguistic terms provided by Passamaquoddy community members, principally Peter Selmore and Newell Josephs."[12] Though the recordings were not inappropriate for nontribal members to listen to, Passamaquoddy tribal members still wanted to ensure that those who listened to the recordings understood that the materials should only be shared for educational purposes and should never be used for profit. TK labels allow for the communication of such guidelines. Tribal nations choose from a selection of labels that can provide information about the provenance of an item, protocols that are associated with it, and permissions that should be considered. However, the texts of the labels are customizable by tribe and are meant to be flexible to fit the differing needs of tribal nations. For example, the "Attribution" label attached to the Passamaquoddy sound recordings is given a second name, "Elihtasik (How it is done)," and a description below requests that those who use anything within the collection correctly attribute it, which "may include individual Passamaquoddy names, it may include Passamaquoddy as the correct cultural affiliation, or it may include Passamaquoddy Tribe as the tribal designation." Likewise, the "Non-Commercial" label's second name, "Ma yut monuwasiw" (This is not sold), instructs researchers that the material may not be used for any purposes that "derive profit from sale or production for non-Passamaquoddy people."[13] TK labels can also be used to identify seasonal protocols, whether an item should only be viewed by men or women, or whether an item is reserved for community use only.[14] TK labels are available to and used by some tribal archives to help both Native and non-Native researchers understand how to use a collection, but in the context of settler-colonial archives they are a valuable tool for tribal nations who want to exercise data sovereignty over how materials that represent their histories are accessed and used to created narratives.

While few settler-colonial archives have gone beyond this, some have created unique ownership agreements with tribal nations regarding storage, access, and use. For example, Northern Arizona University's Cline Library refers all requests to view culturally sensitive materials related to the Hopi people (the primary representatives in their collection) to the Hopi Tribe of Arizona so that the tribe can consult with researchers directly to determine appropriate use for their materials and build relationships of trust.[15] In another collaborative relationship, the Myaamia Center at Miami University holds the physical materials related to Myaamia culture, but ownership remains with the tribe, and there is a formal process of tribal review that requires approval prior to items being accessioned. The tribe also retains intellectual control over the items.[16]

In conversations about tribal sovereignty, the biggest barrier for most settler-colonial archives to overcome is that of equal, open access—a foundational concept within museums, libraries, and archives alike.[17] Open access is an admirable goal, but it does not account for the fact that many of the items these institutions contain were taken from tribal communities without permission from their owners or extracted from the contexts in which they rightfully belong without consent. In these cases, it is up to libraries and archives to undo the harm that has been done by returning these items to tribal contexts and control. In some cases that means repatriating the item directly to tribal communities, but in cases where that is not possible or is not the preference of the tribal nation, culturally sensitive materials policies, TK labels, and unique ownership agreements can support tribal nations' data sovereignty and create more reciprocal, respectful relationships between tribal nations and settler-colonial archives.

Narratives

In broad strokes, archives aim to share knowledge, cultivate learning, and support the production of historical narratives that help society better understand our pasts. The initiatives discussed throughout this conclusion do not deviate from those goals; they merely emphasize that for those of us who work with collections that hold materials by and about Indigenous peoples, our goals must not just be geared at the broader public but give special attention to Indigenous access and sovereignty. Everything we do to improve access and support Native sovereignty is ultimately about the creation of new narratives that more accurately depict and respectfully represent Native communities. In facilitating better access to historical materials through digital sharing and repatriation, we have the ability to support tribal language and cultural revitalization efforts and enable the production of more historical narratives written by Indigenous people. In working to make the collections we work in more accessible, welcoming, and supportive of Native researchers, we can challenge the settler-colonial histories of our institutions and academia that have long privileged white voices and perspectives and instead, support Native-produced books, exhibits, art, and other types of research. By working toward ensuring that Native nations are represented respectfully and with correct terminology in our institutions, we can be a part of efforts to better educate the public about Native histories, cultures, and lifeways. By developing policies and practices that respect data sovereignty, we endorse and help to educate others about the fact that Native people are the best representatives of their own histories. Each of these efforts is a type of new narrative, and together these actions are an important type of activism. This work will and should continue to be led by Indigenous nations like the Mohicans, but it is our responsibility to determine how we can contribute.

In my work at the Newberry, one of the questions I consistently ask myself is, Am I contributing to colonial harm, or am I working to undo it? This work is not easy or straightforward, and we will all make mistakes. I certainly have. But our responsibility as those who work in these institutions with colonial pasts is to work to undo some of that harm every day. We might not complete this work; in fact, it will probably continue long after most of us cease working and living. What matters is that we make progress every day and that we continue to listen and be led by the priorities of the Indigenous people whose materials are held in these archival collections. For my fellow historians, archivists, librarians, and curators, I hope the ideas here give you a place to start, and that the rest of this book demonstrates how powerful archival materials can be when they are back in the hands of Indigenous nations. For Native nations, I hope this book can serve as an example of what tribal archives can do, and that it makes a strong argument for why support of those institutions by funders, settler-colonial archives, and historians alike is so important. While the colonial roots of settler-colonial archives and the narratives produced in these spaces run deep, I hope this book reminds us all that Native people have been collecting, preserving, and sharing their histories in innumerable ways since time immemorial. It is up to all of us to support the continuing recovery and reclamation of those histories, which have always been and will continue to be a vital part of Indigenous nation-building.

Acknowledgments

I would not have completed this book without the mentorship, support, and help of so many individuals, and I feel grateful to be able to thank them here. I owe significant thanks to the individuals who first sparked and fostered my interest in history and writing: my father, John Miron; my high school teachers, Meaghan (Harvey) Swanson and Dawn Moyer; and my undergraduate mentor, Jason Stahl. The first iteration of this project began in 2010 through the Undergraduate Research Opportunity Program at the University of Minnesota. After cold-emailing a handful of professors and asking them to work with me on a project, I was fortunate enough to receive my first reply from Jean O'Brien, who would become my project adviser and help me structure my first exploration of this topic. Jeani also encouraged me to take one of her graduate seminars, where I met a group of graduate students who would mentor me, help me with my graduate school applications, and ultimately become some of my closest friends. Thank you to Katie Phillips, Kasey Keeler, Akikwe Cornell, and Jimmy Sweet. I feel lucky to have known you all for so long and that you were some of my first role models in academia. The members of my undergraduate thesis committee (Jean O'Brien, David Chang, Brenda Child, and Darlene St. Clair) also provided invaluable advice about the project. Upon entering graduate school at the University of Minnesota, I was grateful to continue working with Jean O'Brien and add a co-adviser, Kevin Murphy. Jeani and Kevin gave me careful feedback on countless drafts, encouraged me with positive guidance, and shaped this project in enormous ways. Their support for my writing, their care for me as an individual, and their advice in my career development over the past eleven years have been invaluable. The other members of my dissertation committee, Katherine Hayes, Brenda Child, and Christine DeLisle, also played a significant role in shaping this project.

At Minnesota, I participated in the American Indian and Indigenous Studies Workshop, where I received instrumental feedback on my own work and had the opportunity to participate in intellectual discussions that shaped my understanding and engagement with the field of Native American and Indigenous studies. Thank you to Amber Annis, Akikwe Cornell, Sasha Suarez, Jimmy Sweet, Sam Majhor, John Little, Jill Fish, Bernadette Perez, Jessica Arnett, Evan Taparata, Marie Balsley Taylor, Mike Dockry, Mattie Harper, Hana Maruyama, and Kai Pyle for your instrumental feedback and friendships. In particular, I cannot thank Katie Phillips, Kasey Keeler, and Joe Whitson enough for their feedback, encouragement, and support within and beyond the workshop. They have each read countless drafts of book chapters and, beyond colleagues, they have become some of my best friends.

After graduate school, I worked for the National Native American Boarding School Healing Coalition and the Newberry Library. I owe enormous thanks to my colleagues at both of these organizations for their support and patience as I took time away from my day job to conduct additional research, visit with community members, and revise my dissertation into this book. I'm especially thankful to my colleagues Will Hansen and Jessica Grzegorski, who were kind enough to help me learn about and provided feedback on sections of the book pertaining to best practices within cataloging, archiving, and library services, and to the Newberry Library for financially supporting the publication of the book.

In Chicago, I have been fortunate to participate in the Native American and Indigenous Studies Working Group, whose members are too numerous to name. Thank you to those of you who read my work on multiple occasions, and in particular to Kelly Wisecup, Matthew Kruer, Hayley Negrin, SJ Zhang, Joe Whitson, and Teresa Montoya, who not only gathered over Zoom to provide feedback on several chapters outside of the workshop but have become dear friends.

Several other colleagues and friends have also been instrumental to the completion of this project. Thank you to Meredith McCoy, who logged onto Zoom daily through much of the pandemic for simultaneous writing as we both pushed our respective book projects forward. Kelly Wisecup, along with my former Newberry colleagues Daniel Greene and Liesl Olson, read a full draft of the book prior to submission and provided incredibly rich and helpful feedback that shaped the project in important ways. Fred Hoxi was also generous enough to read and provide feedback on the full manuscript, and I owe him additional thanks for also being an all-around outstanding mentor. Thank you to my editor, Jason Weidemann, for his guidance and feedback throughout this process, and to the reviewers selected by the University of Minnesota Press, who offered critically important feedback on the manuscript.

Fellowships from the Newberry Library, the American Philosophical Society, and the University of Minnesota provided vital support for this project, and I want to thank the archivists at the Newberry Library, the American Philosophical Society, the Wisconsin Historical Society, the Massachusetts Historical Society, and the Archives and Research Center in Sharon, Massachusetts, for their help as I conducted research for this project. I owe special thanks to the archivist at the Stockbridge Library in Stockbridge, Massachusetts, Barbara Allen, who took time to talk with me about the relationship and history between the Mohican Nation and Stockbridge, and introduced me to Rick Wilcox, a Stockbridge resident who has worked in collaboration with the Mohicans on several local projects. Rick sent me countless materials from his personal records, provided transcriptions and scanned copies of many archival documents related to the history of Stockbridge, and took significant time to answer my many questions about his work with the tribe (over email, but also while hiking Monument Mountain).

Most important, I owe an enormous amount of thanks to the staff who have worked at the Arvid E. Miller Library-Museum on the Mohican reservation over the years. Nathalee Kristiansen, Yvette Malone, Leah Miller, Heather Bruegl, Monique Tyndall, and the late Betty Groh were incredibly helpful and supportive as I conducted research over the past fourteen years. These women not only helped me navigate the collections but also became friends with whom I shared laughs, frustrations, and excitement. As I began to attend more Historical Committee meetings and conduct additional research for the tribe, they were invaluable in giving me direction and always picking up the phone or quickly answering an email when I needed guidance. Likewise, I want to especially thank the individuals I spoke with at length on the phone and formally interviewed for this project. Leah Miller, Heather Bruegl, and Jo Ann Schedler were kind enough to spend more than an hour answering my questions, and their interviews provide a more complete understanding of the labor required to build an archive and the projects that can grow from a collection. The Mohican Nation's historic preservation manager, Bonney Hartley, was also generous enough to talk with me on the phone several times and to provide careful feedback on sections of this book on more than one occasion. Former tribal historic preservation officer Sherry White offered similar guidance via phone and email, in addition to reading and providing feedback on a full draft of the book. The chapters on the Native American Graves Protection and Repatriation Act and the National Historic Preservation Act would have undoubtedly been incomplete and inaccurate without Bonney's and Sherry's input. My phone conversations with former Library-Museum manager Nathalee Kristianson, former director of the Department of Education and Cultural Affairs Jolene Bowman, and former Library-Museum staff members Stephanie Bowman, Jessica Boyd, and Carlton Stevens were also instrumental. I am grateful to these individuals for sharing their experiences with me and helping to enrich this story.

I also owe an incredible debt to the other members of the Mohican Historical Committee, who welcomed me into their meetings and provided crucial guidance and feedback on my work. In particular, I want to thank Molly Miller, Leah Miller, Sheila (Miller) Powless, Jo Anne Schedler, Heather Bruegl, and Monique Tyndall, all of whom read the full manuscript before publication and provided critical feedback. I am incredibly grateful to everyone listed above for taking the time to read and help improve my work. Any remaining errors are entirely my own. I am also indebted to the entire Stockbridge-Munsee Mohican Nation, who welcomed me into their community. In particular, thank you to the Mohican Tribal Council and the Mohican Legal Department, whom I have worked with at various stages of developing this project. Driving the eight-hour round trip between Minneapolis and Bowler, Wisconsin, during graduate school and the eight-hour round trip between Chicago and Bowler thereafter has not been easy, so I am also indebted to the people who made this travel and my time in Bowler easier. Thank you to Pam Laking and Blaine Koch, who allowed me to stay in their home for the majority of my research trips and provided the best company I could ask for with dinners and Wisconsin Old Fashioneds, as well as Cindy Gloudemans, who allowed me to stay at her cabin near the reservation. I also want to thank my friend and environmental consultant Jake Fahrenkrog. His explanations of what happens on the ground in Section 106 consultations provided me with irreplaceable information that ultimately shaped much of my fourth chapter, and he kindly gave me feedback on multiple drafts of that section. Thank you to Andrew Lamers as well, who created the three maps for this book.

Finally, I never would have completed this project without the emotional support and love of my friends and family, who constantly encouraged me to persevere. Thank you to Abby Vanevenhoven, Rhianna Deering, Jillian Kissinger, Kelly Zoran, Jessi Miller, Russell Johnson, Matt Hanson, Katie O'Grady, Sibel Dikmen, Scott Fluhrer, Jenna Anderson, and Elyse Christofanelli for always keeping me in good spirits and reminding me that my best was enough. Thank you especially to Michael Hoffmeister, who not only provided emotional support but also accompanied me on my first cross-country road trip to Stockbridge, Massachusetts, and to Bri Bergstrom, my best friend, who has always been there to ground me when I have lost my way. I also want to thank my godmother, Janet Bell, who has always provided me with humor and good coffee, and my late grandparents, Robert and Charlotte Bell (who taught me the importance of education and strength in the face of challenges) and Jack and Nancy Miron (who instilled the value of hard work and the importance of kindness in me at an early age). I could not have completed this book without my sisters, Gretchen, Alison, and Jaclyn Miron, who have always been my three biggest supporters. They are the women I have talked to every day about the importance of this work, and they have always inspired me to keep fighting to make the world better. I owe everything to my parents, John and Lori Miron, who have not only inspired me to constantly look for ways to learn and grow but have also loved and supported me for my entire life. From childhood basketball games to my dissertation defense, they have been there with me every step of the way. Finally, I never would have made it through any of this without my immediate family: my husband, Andrew (AJ) Souers, our daughter, Neva, and our beloved dog, Sully. AJ has seen me at my lows and my highs with this project and been with me through the daily work that writing a book requires. His ability to ask thought-provoking, intellectual questions has ultimately made this project better, and his love and support has meant more to me than I could ever express in words.

Notes

Introduction

1. Bernice Miller remarried after the death of her first husband, Arvid Miller, and thus throughout some primary sources she is also referred to as Bernice Pigeon; her collection in the Arvid E. Miller Library-Museum is called the Bernice Miller (Pigeon) Collection. Throughout this book, I always include her first married name (Miller) in parentheses if needed to clarify to whom I am referring. Bernice's maiden name is Davids, but I do not refer to her as such, since the timeline of this book begins after her marriage to Miller.

2. Dorothy Davids, "History of the Historical Library Museum," Miscellaneous, Letters, History folder, DDC; Jane McBride, "Stockbridge-Munsee Museum: A Fire Helped Make This Dream," *Shawano (Wisc.) Leader,* 1970s, folder 1, BMPC.

3. Gary Dodge, "Chief's Hopes Coming True," *Milwaukee Journal,* Arvid E. Miller Memorial Library-Museum folder, box 5, DDC II.

4. Dorothy Davids, "Wherever We Were, Here We Are!," box 6, DDC II; Dorothy Davids, "Rambling through History with Dot Davids, History of the Historical Library Museum," 2009, 2009 Historical Committee folder, CHLMC.

5. Davids, "Wherever We Were, Here We Are!"

6. "Public history projects" refer to a number of projects the Historical Committee created that seek to reclaim authority over Mohican history and produce new Mohican historical narratives to two publics: the "inside public" of Mohican peoples and relatives themselves and the "outside public," a non-Mohican audience. Given the broad public audience of these projects and the specific use of methods common within public history, such as museums, archives, and oral history, I group these projects together as "public history projects." For quoted text, see "NEH Application, Mahican History," box 3, DDC II.

7. Andrew Flynn, "Archival Activism: Independent and Community Archives, Radical Public History, and the Heritage Professions," *Interactions: UCLA Journal of Education and Information Studies* 7, no. 2 (2011): 1; Mathias Danbolt also uses the phrase "archival activism" to describe the archiving of activist activities, which departs from how I use it here. See Mathias Danbolt, "We're Here! We're Queer? Activist Archives and Archival Activism," *Lamda Nordica* 15, nos. 3/4 (2010): 90–118.

8. Jennifer R. O'Neal, "'The Right to Know': Decolonizing Native American Archives," *Journal of Western Archives* 6, no. 1 (2015): article 2. Brooke M. Black has also argued that tribal archives allow tribal nations to control their own materials. My definition of Indigenous archival activism includes but extends beyond this. See Brooke M. Black, "Freeing the 'Archival Captive': A Closer Look at [Native American Indian] Tribal Archives" (Master's of Library and Information Science paper, San Jose State University, 2005), http://www.provenance.ca. Other scholars have also made similar arguments about self-representation as a form of activism in the context of tribal museums. See Brenda J. Child, "Creation of a Tribal Museum," in *Contesting Knowledge: Museums and Indigenous Perspectives,* ed. Susan Sleeper-Smith (Lincoln: University of Nebraska Press, 2009), 251–56; Amy Lonetree, *Decolonizing Museums: Representing Native America in National and Tribal Museums* (Chapel

Hill: University of North Carolina Press, 2012); Kristina Ackley, "Tsi?niyukwaliho?ta, the Oneida Nation Museum: Creating a Space for Haudenosaunee Kinship and Identity," in *Contesting Knowledge: Museums and Indigenous Perspectives,* ed. Susan Sleeper Smith (Lincoln: University of Nebraska Press, 2009), 257–82; Gwyneira Isaac, *Mediating Knowledges: Origins of a Zuni Tribal Museum* (Tucson: University of Arizona Press, 2007); Mary Lawlor, *Public Native America: Tribal Self-Representation in Museums, Powwows and Casinos* (New Brunswick, N.J.: Rutgers University Press, 2006).

9. Also see Lara Leigh Kelland, *Clio's Foot Soldiers: Twentieth-Century U.S. Social Movements and Collective Memory* (Amherst: University of Massachusetts Press, 2018). Kelland's concept of "memory practices" as "the enactment of collective memory . . . to rewrite dominant historical narratives" (8) overlaps with my definition of Indigenous archival activism, but again, my definition extends beyond this.

10. In *Spiral to the Stars: Mvskoke Tools of Futurity,* geographer Laura Harjo makes an important distinction between what she categorizes as two schools of thought in relation to sovereignty. The first emphasizes tribes' engagement with the nation-state, while the second, "radical sovereignty" focuses on agency and power within communities to make change without permission from the federal government. Tribal archives support both of these types of sovereignty. They arm tribal nations with the materials they need to make themselves legible in legal cases with the U.S. government and also give them the tools to create a new sense of shared identity and belonging within their own communities. See Laura Harjo, *Spiral to the Stars: Mvkoke Tools of Futurity* (Tucson: University of Arizona Press, 2019).

11. Dorothy Davids, *A Brief History of the Mohican Nation Stockbridge-Munsee Band,* 3rd ed. (Bowler, Wisc.: Stockbridge-Munsee Historical Committee, 2017). Multiple spellings of Mahicannituck occur throughout literature, but I have chosen to rely on the one used by the Mohicans on their tribal website. See Stockbridge-Munsee Community, "Origin and Early History," Stockbridge-Munsee Community, accessed May 14, 2018, http://mohican-nsn.gov.

12. Davids, *A Brief History.* The name *Mohican* (sometimes also spelled Mahican or Mahikan) should not be confused with the name *Mohegan*, which refers to an entirely different tribe whose ancestral homelands are in present-day eastern Connecticut. Although some Mohegans fled west to join the Mohicans at Stockbridge after the Pequot War, the Mohegan and Mohican are still two distinct tribal nations. At times, Muhheconneok is also spelled with spaces as "Muh he con ne ok." See Brad D. E. Jarvis, *The Brothertown Nation of Indians: Land Ownership and Nationalism in Early American 1740–1840* (Lincoln: University of Nebraska Press, 2010); and James Oberly, *A Nation of Statesmen: The Political Culture of the Stockbridge-Munsee Mohicans, 1815–1972* (Norman: University of Oklahoma Press, 2005).

13. Some Munsee people began living with the Mohicans in the early eighteenth century when increasing settler-colonial encroachment on Native lands caused both groups to move farther east into the Housatonic River Valley on the western side of present-day Massachusetts and Connecticut, while others joined the Mohicans in Wisconsin in the 1830s, after both groups had been removed. Some Munsee people

were also removed to Canada. See Munsee-Delaware Nation, accessed May 13, 2020, https://www.munsee.ca/; Delaware Nation, accessed May 13, 2020, https://www.dela warenation-nsn.gov/; and Delaware Tribe of Indians, accessed May 13, 2020, http:// delawaretribe.org/. Both the Mohican and Munsee people were very much situated within a larger network of Algonquian relations. In the eighteenth-century, Mohican leader and historian Hendrick Aupaumut's *Narrative of an Embassy to Western Indians* refers to the Munsee as the Mohicans' brothers, the Delaware as their grandfathers, and the Shawnee as their younger brothers. For more on these relationships, see Lisa Brooks, *The Common Pot: The Recovery of Native Space in the Northeast* (Minneapolis: University of Minnesota Press, 2008), 144. Mohican leader John Quinney's history of the tribe also describes a "great confederacy" on the Atlantic coast composed of the Delawares, Munsees, Mohegans, Narragansetts, Pequots, Penobscots, and Muh-he-con-news; see John W. Quinney, "Celebration of the Fourth of July, 1854, at Reidsville, New York: Interesting Speech of John W. Quinney, Chief of the Stockbridge Tribe of Indians," *Wisconsin Historical Collections* 4 (1859), quoted in J. N. Davidson, *Muh-He-Ka-Ne-Ok* (Milwaukee: Silas Chapman, 1893), viii.

14. Brooks, *The Common Pot;* Linford D. Fisher, *The Indian Great Awakening: Religion and the Shaping of Native Cultures in Early America* (New York: Oxford University Press, 2012); Stockbridge-Munsee Department of Cultural Affairs, "Footprints of Our Ancestors: Mohican History Walking Tour of Main Street Stockbridge," https:// www.nativeamericantrail.org; Rachel Wheeler, *To Live Upon Hope: Mohicans and Missionaries in the Eighteenth Century Northeast* (Ithaca, N.Y.: Cornell University Press, 2013). There are multiple different spellings of Wnahktukuk that occur throughout literature, but I have chosen to rely on the spelling used by the Mohicans on their tribal website, see "Origin and Early History." For more on Wnahktukuk in the scope of Algonquin homelands see Brooks, *The Common Pot.*

15. Davids, *A Brief History.*

16. Prior to this a small group of Mohicans and Munsees feared that they could eventually be removed to Indian Country after the Indian Removal Act was passed in 1830. In 1839 this group made their way to present-day Kansas. Some remain there today, while others returned to Wisconsin. See Davids, *A Brief History.*

17. This final removal in 1936 was from the town of Red Springs to the current location of the reservation in the township of Bartelme (a distance of about ten miles). While parts of the reservation still border the town of Red Springs, the tribe lost the majority of this land and the rest of their reservation land through the Act of 1871 and the subsequent General Allotment Act in 1887. Through the IRA, the Mohican Nation was able to regain 15,000 acres in Bartelme (the western portion of their original reservation designated by the Treaty of 1856) after it had been clear-cut by pine loggers. For the Mohicans this is a seventh removal, because they moved ten miles west from the little remaining land they had in Red Springs to this new land in Bartelme. Moreover, only 2,500 of these 15,000 acres were placed in trust for the tribe at this time, and the remaining acres were not placed in trust until 1972. See Davids, *A Brief History;* Oberly, *A Nation of Statesmen;* and John C. Savagian, "The Tribal

Reorganization of the Stockbridge-Munsee: Essential Conditions in the Re-creation of a Native American Community, 1930–1942," in *American Nations: Encounters in Indian Country, 1850 to the Present,* ed. Frederick E. Hoxie, Peter C. Mancall, and James H. Merrell (New York: Routledge Press, 2001), 289–311.

18. The exact wording on the location of the reservation was provided by the Stockbridge-Munsee Mohican Historical Committee. Yvette Malone, email to author, February 6, 2017.

19. Brooks, *The Common Pot,* 240.

20. Electa F. Jones, *Stockbridge, Past and Present, or Records of an Old Mission Station* (Springfield, Mass.: S. Bowles, 1854), 14, quoted in Brooks, *The Common Pot,* 241.

21. Samuel Hopkins, *Historical Memoirs, Relating to the Housatunnuk Indians* (Boston: S. Kneeland, 1753).

22. For Aupaumut and Konkapot, see Quinney, "Celebration of the Fourth of July." For the adoption of Western literary practices, see Drew Lopenzina, *Red Ink: Native Americans Picking Up the Pen in the Colonial Period* (Albany: SUNY Press, 2012).

23. Brooks, *The Common Pot,* 240.

24. John C. Adams Papers, Wis Mss HP, box 8, Wisconsin Historical Society, Madison, Wisconsin.

25. Brooks, *The Common Pot,* 241.

26. Quinney, "Celebration of the Fourth of July."

27. Quinney.

28. Monique Tyndall, personal communication with author, October 5, 2022.

29. Brooks, *The Common Pot,* 240. For other individuals who served as recorders, see Sheila Miller Powless, "Overview: History of the Mohican People," 2001, History Conference 2001 folder, box 5, DDC II; Bernice Miller, "Her Ideas and Reminder Notes," folder 1, BMPC.

30. For framing of the archive as a colonial tool, see Antoinette Burton, ed., *Archive Stories: Facts, Fictions, and the Writing of History* (Durham, N.C.: Duke University Press, 2005); Ann Laura Stoler, *Along the Archival Grain: Epistemic Anxieties and Colonial Common Sense* (Princeton, N.J.: Princeton University Press, 2009); Michel-Rolph Trouillot, *Silencing the Past: Power and the Production of History,* 2nd ed. (Boston: Beacon Press, 1995).

31. Frederick E. Hoxie, *This Indian Country: American Indian Activists and the Place They Made* (New York: Penguin Press, 2012).

32. Savagian, "The Tribal Reorganization of the Stockbridge-Munsee."

33. Davids, *A Brief History;* "Biography, Bernice Miller," August 10, 2016, 2016 Historical Committee folder, CHLMC.

34. Leon Miller to Whom It May Concern, March 19, 1973, Historical Committee folder, CHLMC; Jim Oberly, "Outline for Nomination of Arvid E. Miller Historical Library and Museum for 2002 Governor's Archives Award," box 5, DDC II.

35. "Stockbridge-Munsee Project Begins; Enthusiasm High as Library-Museum Becomes Reality," February 4, 1974, folder 10, HRC; Oberly, "Outline for Nomination."

36. Oberly, "Outline for Nomination." Miller's travel itineraries include notes about which archives to visit and what kinds of material to locate and copy. For an example, see "Meeting Schedule for Arvid E. Miller," 1961–1964, Notes folder, box 6, AEMC.

37. While the Historical Committee was informally established in 1968 when Miller and her family moved the historical materials from her home to the army tent, it is unclear when they officially began meeting. It was likely sometime in the late 1960s or early 1970s, and the Historical Committee was officially recognized and supported as a committee through a 1972 Tribal Council resolution. See "Stockbridge-Munsee Historical Library Museum Needs," Library-Museum folder, HRC. For funding, see Leah Miller, interview with author, December 15, 2016; Sheila (Miller) Powless interview, *HOS*; Stockbridge-Munsee Historical Committee, "Minutes," October 27, 1988, 1988 Historical Committee folder, CHLMC; Davids, "Rambling through History."

38. L. Miller interview, December 15, 2016. At times throughout this book, Leah Miller is also referred to as Leah Heath, which was her married name. I include her maiden name in parentheses in those cases to make it clear that I am referring to the same person. Likewise, Sheila Powless's maiden name is Miller, and at times throughout this book she is also referred to as Sheila Moede, another married name. I include her maiden name in parentheses throughout to make clear that I am referring to the same person.

39. L. Miller interview, December 15, 2016; Powless, "Overview: History of the Mohican People"; "Untitled" February 4, 1974, Library-Museum folder, HRC; Stockbridge-Munsee Historical Committee, "First Meeting," September 17, 1973, 1973 Historical Committee folder, CHLMC.

40. The subsequent members I have listed here are individuals whom I have either seen regularly at Historical Committee meetings I have attended or seen regularly listed in Historical Committee meeting minutes. There are certainly other tribal members and nontribal members who have also been present at meetings over the past fifty years that I have not listed here. As Leah Miller emphasized in her interview with me, and as has been reiterated in several Historical Committee meetings I have attended, the original committee members dictated that anyone who attended the meetings was a member and could vote. Therefore, this is not an exhaustive list of all Historical Committee members but rather a list of those who most frequently attended meetings and led initiatives over the last fifty years. L. Miller interview, December 15, 2016.

41. Kallie Kosc, "'Caring for Our Affairs Ourselves': Stockbridge Mohican Women and Indian Education in Early America," *American Indian Quarterly* 44, no. 4 (2020): 434–76.

42. Kosc, 461.

43. The library was opened in 1974 with the help of a small grant from the Wisconsin American Revolution Bicentennial Committee. This funding allowed the Historical Committee to repurpose the tribal meeting hall and move documents out of the old craft shop, as well as purchase archival supplies. See Stockbridge-Munsee Historical Committee, "Stockbridge-Munsee Tribal Historical Project," 1973 Historical

Committee folder, CHLMC; "Indians Trying to Save History," May 3, 1974, *Milwaukee Journal*, News Articles folder 4, BMPC; McBride, "Stockbridge-Munsee Museum."

44. Nancy J. Schmechel, "A Labor of Love," *Sweetgrass Review*, September–October 1993, Museums Records folder, box 4, DDC II; Powless interview, *HOS*.

45. Arlee Davids to Theresa Miller Puskarenko, "Memorandum: Five Year Plan for Library Museum Archives," November 1996, Arvid E. Miller Library-Museum folder, DDC II.

46. Sheila (Miller) Moede to Polly Pierce, undated, folder 14, box 4, SIC. Unfortunately, this lack of consistent funding for staff is not uncommon. Not everyone within tribal communities always agrees on the importance of funding historic preservation offices or library-museums, and though many external funding sources, such as the National Endowment for the Humanities, the Institute of Museum and Library Services, the Mellon Foundation, and the Council on Library and Information Resources, are increasingly interested in funding tribally based archive and library projects, their focus is typically on project-based work rather than long-term funding for the expansion of staff. In its 2012 comprehensive study of tribal archives, libraries, and museums (TALMs), the Association of Tribal Archives, Libraries, and Museums found that the majority of TALMs have just one full-time employee. A 2011 study found that just 38 percent of TALMs have on-site paid staff at all, and only 15 percent have established funding bases. See Miriam Jorgenson, "Sustaining Indigenous Culture: The Structure, Activities, and Needs of Tribal Archives, Libraries, and Museums" (Oklahoma City: Association of Tribal Archives, Libraries and Museums, 2012); Bonnie Biggs, "A Place at the Table: California's Tribal Libraries Take Steps toward Inclusion," in *Tribal Libraries, Archives, and Museums: Preserving Our Language, Memory, and Lifeways*, ed. Loriene Roy, Anjali Bhasin, and Sarah K. Arriaga (London: Scarecrow Press, 2011), 8.

47. Jolene Bowman, personal communication with author, November 7, 2022.

48. Sherry White, email to author, October 4, 2022.

49. Monique Tyndall, personal communication with author, January 5, 2023; Heather Bruegl, interview with author, January 21, 2021. Both committees did take a break from their meetings during the Covid-19 pandemic starting in Spring 2020.

50. Robert Sidney Martin, "Introduction: The Role of Libraries in Lifelong Learning," in Roy, Bhasin, and Arriaga, *Tribal Libraries, Archives, and Museums*, xii.

51. Jacques Derrida, *Archive Fever: A Freudian Impression* (Chicago: University of Chicago Press, 1995); Michel Foucault, *The Archaeology of Knowledge & The Discourse on Language* (New York: Vintage, 1982); Trouillot, *Silencing the Past.*

52. David M. Levy, *Scrolling Forward: Making Sense of Documents in the Digital Age* (New York: Arcade, 2001), quoted in Martin, "Introduction."

53. For awikhigans, wampum, oral histories, and land see Brooks, *The Common Pot*, 13, 240–41. For winter counts, see Akta Lakota Museum Cultural Center, "The Lakota Winter Count," Akta Lakota Museum Cultural Center website, accessed September 30, 2021, http://www.aktalakota.stjo.org. For more on other forms of writing and record keeping beyond the United States, see Elizabeth Hill Boone and Walter

Mignolo, *Writing without Words: Alternative Literacies in Mesoamerica and the Andes* (Durham, N.C.: Duke University Press, 1987).

54. Trouillot, *Silencing the Past.*

55. Stuart Hall, "Whose Heritage? Unsettling 'The Heritage,' Re-imagining the Post-nation," *Third Text Reader* 49 (Winter 1999–2000): 13–25. Also see Benedict Anderson, *Imagined Communities: Reflections on the Origins and Spread of Nationalism* (New York: Verso, 1983).

56. This definition is adapted from what Ashley Glassburn Falzetti, Courtney Rivard, and Melissa Adams-Campbell outline as the components of "settler archives" in their special issue of *Settler Colonial Studies.* See Melissa Adams-Campbell, Ashley Glassburn Falzetti, and Courtney Rivard, "Introduction: Indigeneity and the Work of Settler Archives," *Settler Colonial Studies* 5, no. 2 (2014): 109–16.

57. Several other scholars have responded to the characterization of archives as tools of oppression, pointing to the ways communities can create and reclaim their own archival collections as tools of resistance and mechanisms for the production of shared identities. The archives of LGBTQIA community groups are especially well documented. They provide clear examples of activist archives that have saved materials previously deemed unworthy of preservation and created opportunities for new narratives that center the marginalized communities that have consistently been erased in dominant historical narratives. These community archives challenge the legitimacy of a singular national story and demonstrate how archives can be used by marginalized communities to diversify historical sources and narratives. However, they are the archives of communities unified by common identities, not sovereign nations, and thus the argument I make here about nation-building is specific to tribal archives. For more on community archives, see Michelle Caswell, Marika Cifor, and Mario H. Ramirez, "'To Suddenly Discover Yourself Existing': Uncovering the Impact of Community Archives," *American Archivist* 79, no. 1 (Spring/Summer 2016): 56–81; Danbolt, "We're Here! We're Queer?"; Kathy Eales, "Community Archives: Introduction," *South African Archives Journal* 40 (1998): 11–15; Flynn, "Archival Activism"; Daniel Marshall, Kevin P. Murphy, and Zeb Tortorici, eds., *Queer Archives: Intimate Tracings,* special issue of *Radical History Review* 122 (May 2015); Dana A. Williams and Marissa K. López, "More Than a Fever: Toward a Theory of the Ethnic Archive," *PMLA* 127, no. 2 (2012): 358.

58. In the scope of this project, I define tribal archives as those that were created by or serve as the repositories for tribal governments. This is not to say that there are not many other Native archives run by individuals, urban Indigenous communities, Indigenous organizations, etc., that participate in archival activism, but I do not make the same argument about Indigenous nationhood in the scope of those collections.

59. Daniel Heath Justice, *Our Fire Survives the Storm: A Cherokee Literary History* (Minneapolis: University of Minnesota Press, 2006), 8.

60. Justice, 25.

61. Accordingly, the creation of Indigenous national archives and the nation-building projects that emerge from them are not dependent on federal recognition,

and federally recognized, state-recognized, and unrecognized tribal nations can and do participate in Indigenous archival activism as a form of nation-building.

62. Brooks, *The Common Pot,* 67.

63. Library-Museum Staff, "Proposal Submitted to National Committee for the Self-Development of People," February 13, 1978, Library Museum folder, HRC.

64. "Declaration of Indian Purpose: The Voice of the American Indian." Proceedings of American Indian Chicago Conference (University of Chicago, June 13–20, 1961), https://www.files.eric.ed.gov.

65. Molly Miller, personal communication with author, April 20, 2022.

66. Nick Estes, *Our History Is the Future: Standing Rock versus the Dakota Access Pipeline, and the Long Tradition of Indigenous Resistance* (New York: Verso, 2019); Paul Chaat Smith and Robert Allen Warrior, *Like a Hurricane: The Indian Movement from Alcatraz to Wounded Knee* (New York: The New Press, 1996).

67. Julie L. Davis, *Survival Schools: The American Indian Movement and Community Education in the Twin Cities* (Minneapolis: University of Minnesota Press, 2013).

68. Kelland, *Clio's Foot Soldiers,* 151.

69. Kelland, 9.

70. For Deloria's "Right to Know" and the subsequent NEH grant, see O'Neal, "'The Right to Know'"; for the American Indian Libraries Association, see Salvatore De Sando, "Publications: American Indian Libraries Newsletter," American Indian Library Association Archives at the University of Illinois, last modified November 1, 2017, http://www.archives.libary.illinois.edu.

71. Jack F. Trope, "The Case for NAGPRA," in *Accomplishing NAGPRA: Perspectives on the Intent, Impact, and Future of the Native American Graves Protection and Repatriation Act,* ed. Sangita Chari and Jaime M. N. Lavallee (Corvallis: Oregon State University Press, 2013), 19–54.

72. The only institution that receives federal funding that is excluded from NAGPRA is the Smithsonian. This is because the earlier National Museum of the American Indian Act, which was passed in 1989, already included repatriation regulations for the Smithsonian. These regulations were initially focused on human remains and funerary objects but were updated in 1996 to also include sacred objects and items of cultural patrimony. See Trope, "The Case for NAGPRA." As defined by the act itself, cultural affiliation means "a relationship of shared group identity which can be reasonably traced historically or prehistorically between a present-day Indian tribe or Native Hawaiian organization and an identifiable earlier group." See Native American Graves Protection and Repatriation Act, 25 U.S.C. 3001, November 16, 1990, nps.gov. According to the National Park Service NAGPRA website, NAGPRA recognizes "Alaska Native villages that are recognized by the Bureau of Indian Affairs" as falling under the larger category "Indian tribe." For the full definition see National Park Service. "Frequently Asked Questions: Who may claim Native American cultural items under NAGPRA." National NAGPRA, accessed June 7, 2018, nps.gov.

73. Sangita Chari and Jaime M. N. Lavallee, introduction to Chari and Lavalee, *Accomplishing NAGPRA,* 7–18.

74. Jorgenson, "Sustaining Indigenous Culture."

75. For the IRA, see Davids, *A Brief History;* "Biography, Bernice Miller." For the 1968 land claim, see Powless, "Overview: History of the Mohican People."

76. For federal recognition cases, see O'Neal, "'The Right to Know.'"

77. For an account of earlier Indigenous interventions in archival collections, see Kelly Wisecup, *Assembled for Use: Indigenous Compilation and the Archives of Early Native American Literatures* (New Haven: Yale University Press, 2021).

78. Kay Mathiesen, "A Defense of Native Americans' Rights over Their Traditional Cultural Expressions," *American Archivist* 75, no. 2 (Fall/Winter 2012): 456–81.

79. First Archivist Circle, "Protocols for Native American Archival Materials," First Archivist Circle, last modified April 9, 2007, http://www2.nau.edu.

80. Society of American Archivists, "SAA Council Endorsement of Protocols for Native American Archival Materials," Society of American Archivists, last modified August 13, 2018, http://www2.archivists.org; Association of College and Research Libraries, "ACRL Speaks Out," last modified August 2019, http://www.ala.org.

81. The most recent comprehensive list of tribal archives and libraries in the United States is from 2007, but as of 2011 the Association of Tribal Archives, Libraries, and Museums identified at least 412 tribal archives, libraries, and museums as part of a survey they conducted. Of those, 185 ultimately responded to their 2012 survey, and of this number, 10 identified as only archives, 40 identified as only libraries, and 99 identified as either an archive + library, archive + museum, library + museum, or a combination of all three types of institutions. See Elizabeth Peterson, *Tribal Libraries in the United States: A Directory of American Indian and Alaska Native Facilities* (Jefferson, N.C.: McFarland, 2007); Association of Tribal Archives, Libraries, and Museums, "Leadership Directory of Native Cultural Institutions & Programs," Association of Tribal Archives, Libraries, and Museums, https://www.atalm.org; Jorgenson, "Sustaining Indigenous Culture."

82. See Tony Choate, "Chickasaw Documentary Wins Heartland Emmy," *The Ada News,* November 9, 2018, https://www.theadanews.com; Paula Burkes, "Tribal Heritage Center Director Strives to Make Records Globally Accessible," *The Oklahoman,* January 27, 2019, https://www.oklahoman.com; Plateau Peoples' Web Portal, Washington State University, accessed August 20, 2021, https://www.plateauportal.libraries.wsu.edu/; Stephen Warren, ed., *The Eastern Shawnee Tribe of Oklahoma: Resilience through Adversity* (Norman: University of Oklahoma Press, 2017); Elizabeth Joffrion and Natalia Fernández, "Collaborations between Tribal and Nontribal Organizations: Suggested Practices for Sharing Expertise, Cultural Resources, and Knowledge," *American Archivist* 78, no. 1 (Spring/Summer 2015): 192–237; "Catawba Indian Nation," Native American Library Services: Basic Grants, Institute of Museum and Library Services, accessed August 11, 2021, https://www.imls.gov; "Wyandotte Nation," Native American/Native Hawaiian Museum Services, Institute of Museum and Library Services website, accessed August 11, 2021, https://www.imls.gov; Thomas E. Sheridan, Stewart B. Koyiyumptewa, Anton Daughters, Dale S. Brenneman, T. J. Ferguson, Leigh Kuwanwisiwma, and Lee Wayne Lomayestewa, eds., *Moquis and Kastiilam: Hopis,*

Spaniards, and the Trauma of History, Volume II, 1680–1781 (Tucson: University of Arizona Press, 2020).

83. For example, see Linda Tuhiwai Smith, *Decolonizing Methodologies: Research and Indigenous Peoples,* 2nd ed. (London: Zed Books, 2012); Alyssa Mt. Pleasant, Caroline Wigginton, and Kelly Wisecup, "Materials and Methods in Native American and Indigenous Studies: Completing the Turn," *Early American Literature,* 53, no. 2 (2018): 407–44.

84. The decisions I have made in this regard are similar to but distinct from the process of refusal that anthropologist Audra Simpson discusses in her work. Simpson reflects on the decisions she and other Native scholars make to share or not share information about their own communities. See Audra Simpson, *Mohawk Interruptus: Political Life across the Borders of Settler States* (Durham, N.C.: Duke University Press, 2014).

85. In continuing to develop a community-engaged research model, I am indebted to the following publications and especially to Historical Committee members themselves, who were incredibly generous in giving me feedback on not only my manuscript itself but also my research methodologies and positionality as an outside researcher. See Smith, *Decolonizing Methodologies;* National Congress of American Indians Policy Research Center, "Holding Space: A Toolkit for Tribal-Academic Partnerships," accessed August 20, 2021, http://www.ncai.org; National Congress of American Indians Policy Research Center and Montana State University Center for Native Health Partnerships, "'Walk Softly and Listen Carefully': Building Research Relationships with Tribal Communities" (Washington, D.C., 2012).

86. Burton, *Archive Stories,* 6.

1. Indigenizing the Archive

1. "Biography, Bernice Miller," August 10, 2016, 2016 Historical Committee folder, CHLMC.

2. Gary Dodge, "Chief's Hopes Coming True," *Milwaukee Journal,* Arvid E. Miller Memorial Library-Museum folder, box 5, DDC II; Meg Dedolph, "Tribes Reclaim Lost Traditions," *Wausau (Wisc.) Daily Herald,* September 22, 1996, News Articles folder 2, BMPC.

3. Ruth was Dorothy's lifetime partner who lived in the community and served as the Historical Committee secretary for many years even though she was not a tribal member. Sheila Miller Powless, "Overview: History of the Mohican People," 2001, History Conference 2001 folder, box 5, DDC II.

4. Stockbridge-Munsee Mohican Tribal Council, Resolution, February 19, 1980, 1980 Historical Committee folder, CHLMC.

5. Drew Lopenzina, *Red Ink: Native Americans Picking Up the Pen in the Colonial Period* (Albany: SUNY Press, 2012), 10. For a similar discussion of the limits of colonial archival materials, see Marisa J. Fuentes, *Dispossessed Lives: Enslaved Women, Violence, and the Archive* (Philadelphia: University of Pennsylvania Press, 2016).

6. William T. Hagan, "Archival Captive—The American Indian," *American Archivist* 41, no. 2 (April 1978): 135–42. For more on this see Linda Tuhiwai Smith, *Decolonizing Methodologies: Research and Indigenous Peoples,* 2nd ed. (London: Zed Books, 2012), 8.

7. Margaret M. Bruchac, *Savage Kin: Indigenous Informants and American Anthropologists* (Tucson: University of Arizona Press, 2018).

8. Rachel Wheeler, "Hendrick Aupaumut: Christian-Mahican Prophet," *Journal of the Early Republic* 25, no. 2 (Summer 2005): 187–220.

9. Electa Jones, *Stockbridge Past and Present; or Records of an Old Mission Station* (Springfield, Mass.: Samuel Bowles and Co., 1854); Hendrick Aupaumut, "Extract from an Indian History," *Collections of the Massachusetts Historical Society* 1, no. 9 (1804); Hendrick Aupaumut, *A Narrative of an Embassy to the Western Indians* (Philadelphia: Pennsylvania Historical Society, 1827). For an extensive analysis of Aupaumut and his writing, see Lisa Brooks, *The Common Pot: Recovering Native Space in the Northeast* (Minneapolis: University of Minnesota Press, 2008).

10. Mark Rifkin, *When Did Indians Become Straight? Kinship, the History of Sexuality, and Native Sovereignty* (New York: Oxford University Press, 2011), 130.

11. Bernice Miller, "Pages from One of Her Notebooks," Bernice's Notes folder, box 2, BMPC.

12. For an example of this, see Bernice Miller, "Notes in a Small Spiral Notebook" folder 1, BMPC. Several other examples are available throughout her collection.

13. Michel Foucault, *The Archaeology of Knowledge & The Discourse on Language* (New York: Vintage, 1982).

14. Dorothy Davids, "Rambling through History with Dot Davids," folders 1–6, DDC II.

15. Dorothy Davids interview, *HOS.*

16. Huron H. Smith, *Ethnobotany of the Forest Potawatomi Indians,* vol. 7 no. 1 of *Bulletin of the Public Museum of the City of Milwaukee* (Milwaukee: Order of the Board of Trustees, 1933). For the dual names of tag and speckled alder, see U.S. Department of Agriculture National Resources Conservation Service Plan Data Center and Biota of North America Program, "Speckled Alder," Plant Guide, https://plants.usda.gov/.

17. Davids, "Rambling through History."

18. L. T. Smith, *Decolonizing Methodologies,* 146.

19. Jo Ann Schedler, interview with author, January 13, 2017.

20. Jolene Bowman, personal communication with author, November 7, 2022.

21. Kimberly Christen, "Tribal Archives, Traditional Knowledge, and Local Contexts: Why the 's' Matters," *Western Archives* 6, no. 1 (2015): 2.

22. Courtney Rivard, "Archival Recognition: The Pointe-au-Chien's and Isle de Jean Charles Band of the Biloxi-Chitmacha Confederation of Muskogees' Fight for Federal Recognition," *Settler Colonial Studies* 5, no. 2 (2015): 123.

23. Stockbridge-Munsee Historical Committee, "Stockbridge-Munsee Tribal Historical Project," grant application to the Wisconsin American Revolution Bicentennial Committee, 1973, 1973 Historical Committee folder, CHLMC.

24. Elizabeth Joffrion and Natalia Fernández, "Collaborations between Tribal and Nontribal Organizations: Suggested Practices for Sharing Expertise, Cultural Resources, and Knowledge," *American Archivist* 78, no. 1 (Spring/Summer 2015): 192–237.

25. I'm intentionally not using the term *digital/virtual repatriation* here, because this type of digital sharing does not actually return items to or reinstate control over how items are accessed to tribal nations. For more on this see Robin Boast and Jim Enote, "Virtual Repatriation: It Is Neither Virtual nor Repatriation," in *Heritage in the Context of Globalization: Europe and the Americas,* ed. Peter F. Biehl and Christopher Prescott (New York: Springer, 2013), 103–13. For Mukurtu and other types of digital sharing, see *Plateau Peoples' Web Portal:* https://plateauportal.libraries.wsu.edu/; Marisa Elena Duarte, *Network Sovereignty: Building the Internet across Indian Country* (Seattle: University of Washington Press, 2017), 48; Stephen Warren, "Introduction: The Eastern Shawnees and the Repatriation of Their History," in *The Eastern Shawnee Tribe of Oklahoma: Resilience through Adversity,* ed. Stephen Warren (Norman: University of Oklahoma Press, 2017), 9; Kimberly Christen, "Opening Archives: Respectful Repatriation," *American Archivist* 74 (Spring/Summer 2011): 185–210.

26. For example, see the Yakama description added to a photograph identified as showing "Indian weapons." The Yakama description clarifies that "weapons" were also used for hunting and fishing, and some were dual purpose, like a horse quirt. Vivian Adams, "Collection of Indian Weapons," Yakama Records, Plateau Peoples Project, https://plateauportal.libraries.wsu.edu/.

27. Stockbridge-Munsee Community, "S/M Historical Library Special Project," February 24, 1986, folder 10, HRC.

28. Alice Te Punga Somerville, "'I Do Still Have a Letter': Our Sea of Archives," in *Sources and Methods in Indigenous Studies,* ed. Chris Andersen and Jean M. O'Brien (New York: Routledge, 2017), 127.

29. Somerville, 122.

30. Dorothy W. Davids, "Final Performance Report to National Endowment for the Humanities," February 1, 1993, 1993 HC Meeting folder, CHLMC.

31. S. M. Powless, "Overview."

32. S. M. Powless. This policy is no longer in place (likely because most researchers photograph collection materials with their phones or cameras rather than on a copy machine). As of February 2020, the Indiana Historical Society camera policy still requires researchers to obtain permission before taking photographs of any collection materials and record the items that they wish to take photos of during their visit. See Amy C. Vedra (director of Reference Services at the Indiana Historical Society), email to author accompanied by Policy for Use of Cameras, February 4, 2020.

33. Notable examples of this include the Green Bay Indian Agency Collection, which the Historical Committee purchased for an unknown amount in 1970, and information from the Carlisle Indian School about their Mohican students, which the Historical Committee purchased in 1997 for $400. See Stockbridge-Munsee Mohican Historical Committee, "Meeting Minutes," October 9, 1997, 1997 Historical Committee Meetings folder, CHLMC.

34. "Independent Registration," Huntington Library, accessed February 14, 2012, quoted in Rivard, "Archival Recognition," 125. As of February 2020 these restrictions were still in place, but they seem to have been lifted since then. The current policy states that the reading room is open to any individual over eighteen years old "upon establishing a research need that requires use of the Huntington's collections." See "Using the Library," The Huntington, accessed September 27, 2021, https://hunting ton.org/.

35. Krista McCracken and Skylee-Storm Hogan, "Laughter Filled the Space: Challenging Euro-Centric Archival Spaces," *International Journal of Information, Diversity, & Inclusion* 5, no. 1 (2021): 97–110.

36. Jane Anderson and Kimberly Christen, "Decolonizing Attribution: Traditions of Exclusion," *Journal of Radical Librarianship* 5 (2019): 113–52; Ann Laura Stoler, *Along the Archival Grain: Epistemic Anxieties and Colonial Common Sense* (Princeton: Princeton University Press, 2009), 9; Rhonda Harris Taylor, "Claiming the Bones Again: Native Americans and Issues of Bibliography," *Social Epistemology* 15, no. 1 (2001): 21–26.

37. Shayne Del Cohen, "Where Are the Records?," in *Tribal Libraries, Archives, and Museums: Preserving Our Language, Memory, and Lifeways,* ed. Loriene Roy, Anjali Bhasin, and Sarah K. Arriaga (London: Scarecrow Press, 2011), 169.

38. Rivard, "Archival Recognition," 123.

39. These collections can be found at the American Philosophical Society and the Newberry Library (Watson and Ayer), respectively.

40. Jessie Loyer, "Indigenous Information Literacy: Nêhiyaw Kinship Enabling Self-Care in Research," in *The Politics of Theory and the Practice of Critical Librarianship*, ed. Karen P. Nicholson and Maura Seale (Sacramento: Litwin Books & Library Juice Press, 2018), 146–56.

41. McCracken and Hogan, "Laughter Filled the Space."

42. Bernice Miller to State Historical Society of New York, January 9, 1973, folder 2, BMPC.

43. Sheila (Miller) Powless interview, *HOS*.

44. For an example of relationships with archivists, see Sheila (Miller) Moede to Polly Pierce, undated, folder 14, box 4, SIC. For asking authors to donate research papers, see Mega Jones, "Mohican Tribal History Listed in Library Archives," July 16, 1989, *Shawano (Wisc.) Evening Leader,* subfolder 5, Library Museum folder, HRC.

45. "Journal of John Sergeant, missionary to the Stockbridge Indians from the Society in Scotland for Propagating Christian Knowledge from January 1804 to July 1824, 003405," Finding Aid, Dartmouth Library Archives & Manuscripts, Dartmouth College, Hanover, New Hampshire.

46. Arlee Davids to Theresa Miller Puskarenko, "Five Year Plan for Library Museum Archives," memorandum, November 1996, Arvid E. Miller Library-Museum folder, box 5, DDC II; Nathalee Kristiansen, personal communication with author, November 7, 2022.

47. Leah Miller, interview with author, December 16, 2016.

48. The Stockbridge-Munsee Historical Library-Museum Committee, *Catalog of Materials: Stockbridge-Munsee Historical Library Museum* (Gresham, Wisc.: Muh-he-con-neew Press, 1980), xi.

49. For trainings, see S. M. Powless, "Overview"; David J. Grignon to Dorothy Davids, August 26, 1996, 1996 Historical Committee Meetings folder, CHLMC; Stockbridge-Munsee Historical Committee, "Meeting Minutes," October 24, 1996, 1996 Historical Committee Meetings folder, CHLMC.

50. For example, Duarte asserts that library classification systems misrepresent Native people so that they become "codified into an exceptional subclass," and Thomas Yen-Ran Yeh has shown that, as of 1971, the last-mentioned event under the Library of Congress's "American Indian History" subject heading was "Chippewa War 1898," effectively erasing American Indian history in the twentieth century. Though this has since been updated, Library of Congress subject headings still have many limitations. For more see Duarte, *Network Sovereignty*, 112; Thomas Yen-Ran Yeh, "The Treatment of the American Indian in the Library of Congress E-F Schedule," *Library Resources and Technical Services* 15, no. 2 (Spring 1971): 122–31; Tamara Lincoln, "Ethno-Linguistic Misrepresentations of the Alaskan Native Languages as Mirrored in the Library of Congress System of Cataloguing and Classification," *Cataloguing and Classification Quarterly* 7, no. 3 (Spring 1987): 69–90; Mary L. Young and Dara L. Doolittle, "The Halt of Stereotyping: When Does the American Indian Enter the Mainstream?," *Reference Librarian* 22, no. 47 (1994): 104–19.

51. Sandra Littletree and Cheryl A. Metoyer, "Knowledge Organization from an Indigenous Perspective: The Mashantucket Pequot Thesaurus of American Indian Terminology Project," *Cataloging and Classification Quarterly* 53, nos. 5–6 (2015): 640–57.

52. Jean Weihs, "A Tribute to Brian Deer," *Technicalities* 39, no. 3 (May/June 2019): 11–12.

53. Jessica Boyd, personal communication with author, November 7, 2022; Stephanie Bowman, personal communication with author, November 14, 2022.

54. Stephanie Bowman, personal communication, November 14, 2022.

55. Carlton Stevens, personal communication with author, November 7, 2022.

56. "Missionary Journals of John Sergeant, 1790–1809," finding aid, Harvard Library, https://hollisarchives.lib.harvard.edu/; "Timothy Pickering Papers," collection guide, Massachusetts Historical Society, http://www.masshist.org/. Both sources accessed January 27, 2020.

57. For more on Aupaumut's efforts to create peace and protect Native space, see Brooks, *The Common Pot*.

58. Christine DeLucia, "Fugitive Collections in New England Indian Country: Indigenous Material Culture and Early American History Making at Ezra Stiles's Yale Museum," *William and Mary Quarterly* 75, no. 1 (January 2018): 109–50.

59. Roger Williams, *A Key into the Language of America, or, An Help to the Language of the Natives in that Part of America, called New England: Together with Briefe Observations of the Customes, Manners, and Worships, &c. of the Aforesaid Natives, in Peace and Warre, in Life and Death: On All Which are Added Spirituall Observations,*

Generall and Particular by the Authour, or Chiefe and Speciall Use (Upon All Occasions,) to All the English Inhabiting Those Parts; yet Pleasant and Profitable to the View of All Men (London: Gregory Dexter, 1643).

60. Thomas Jefferson, *Notes on the State of Virginia* (Boston: Lilly and Wait, 1832), 158.

61. Christen, "Why the 's' Matters"; Michael Brown, *Who Owns Native Culture?* (Cambridge: Harvard University Press, 2003); Bruchac, *Savage Kin.*

62. Benjamin J. Barnes, "Becoming Our Own Storytellers: Tribal Nations Engaging with Academia," in *The Eastern Shawnee Tribe of Oklahoma: Resilience through Adversity*, ed. Stephen Warren (Norman: University of Oklahoma Press, 2017), 219.

63. Cara S. Bertram, "Avenues of Mutual Respect: Opening Communication and Understanding between Native Americans and Archivists" (master's thesis, Western Washington University, 2012), https://cedar.wwu.edu; Christen, "Why the 's' Matters."

64. For information on other tribes who have created clear policies in their tribal archive, see First Archivist Circle, "Protocols for Native American Archival Materials," First Archivist Circle, last modified April 9, 2007, http://www2.nau.edu.

65. "Policy for the Arvid E. Miller Memorial Historical Library/Museum for Both the Archives and Objects Contained Therein," 2015 HC Meeting folder, CHLMC.

66. The National Park Service maintains a list of different tribal protocols and contact information. See National Park Service, "Tribal Research Policies, Processes, and Protocols," National Park Service, last updated August 30, 2019, https://www.nps.gov.

67. "The Stockbridge-Munsee Historical Library Museum of the Mohican Nation," Library-Museum Records folder, BMPC.

68. Dorothy W. Davids to Patrick Frazier, September 2, 1981, folder 2, box 1, DDC II.

69. The Stockbridge-Munsee Historical Library-Museum Committee, "Catalog of Materials," vii.

70. "Catalog of Materials," 1.

71. "Catalog of Materials," 22.

72. "Catalog of Materials," xii.

73. Patrick Frazier to Dorothy W. Davids, September 11, 1981, folder 2, box 1, DDC II.

74. Dorothy Davids, "Remembering and Rambling through History with Dot Davids," folder 4, DDC II.

75. For another example of choosing not to digitize, see Evelyn Wareham, "'Our Own Identity, Our Own Taonga, Our Own Self Coming Back': Indigenous Voices in New Zealand Record-Keeping," *Archivaria* 52 (Fall 2001): 26–46.

76. Davids to Puskarenko, "Five Year Plan."

77. Christen, "Opening Archives."

78. See the Local Contexts Project, https://localcontexts.org/.

79. Christen, "Why the 's' Matters."

2. Mohican Oral History Projects

1. For other community oral history projects, see Lara Leigh Kelland, *Clio's Foot Soldiers: Twentieth-Century U.S. Social Movements and Collective Memory* (Amherst: University of Massachusetts Press, 2018).

2. Jim Oberly, "Outline for Nomination of Arvid E. Miller Historical Library and Museum for 2002 Governor's Archives Award," box 5, DDC II.

3. Stockbridge-Munsee Historical Committee, "Meeting Minutes," March 9, 2006, 2006 Historical Committee Meetings folder, CHLMC.

4. The Historical Committee worked with an outside company, Jeff Bass Creative Services, for the *Hear Our Stories* project to help with the process of interviewing, recording, and then transferring each file onto a DVD. Tribal members came up with all the questions and co-conducted the interviews with members of the Jeff Bass team. See Stockbridge-Munsee Mohican Historical Committee, "Tribal Council Agenda Request: 'Hear Our Stories'—Elder Videotaping Proposals," March 9, 2009, Tribal Council Papers, Arvid E. Miller Library-Museum; Stockbridge-Munsee Historical Committee to Tribal Council, March 9, 2009, 2009 Historical Committee folder, CHLMC.

5. While letters were sent out to 185 tribal members age seventy and over, only 41 chose to participate. There are several possible reasons for elders deciding not to participate in the project. Since all interviews were conducted on or near the reservation, it is possible that those who live off the reservation did not want to travel for the interview. Additionally, there may have been some who simply did not want to share their story or were uncomfortable being interviewed. See Stockbridge-Munsee Historical Committee, "Meeting Minutes," April 9, 2009, 2009 Historical Committee folder, CHLMC. For filming dates see Stockbridge-Munsee Historical Committee, "Meeting Minutes," March 23, 2006, 2006 Historical Committee Meetings folder, CHLMC.

6. *HOS.*

7. Alessandro Portelli, "What Makes Oral Histories Different," in *The Death of Luigi Trastulli and Other Stories: Form and Meaning in Oral History* (Albany: State University of New York, 1991), 56.

8. I conducted three oral interviews with Historical Committee members that were specifically focused on their work on the committee and their use of the Mohican tribal archive. The interviews are all about an hour in length; two were recorded orally, while one was recorded over Zoom. The interviews were conducted between 2017 and 2021. As I discuss in more detail later, the interviews were collaboratively shaped by Historical Committee members, who provided input on who should be interviewed and worked with me to create new release forms and practices for outside researchers.

9. Kevin P. Murphy, Jennifer L. Pierce, and Jason Ruiz, "What Makes Queer Oral History Different," *Oral History Review* 43, no. 1 (2016): 5.

10. Dave Besaw interview, *HOS.*

11. Swedberg Funeral Home and Crematory, Inc., "Dave L. Besaw," obituary, 2011, accessed April 17, 2021, https://www.swedbergfuneralhome.com.

12. Besaw interview, *HOS;* Robert Little interview, *HOS;* Eleanor Martin interview, *HOS.*

13. Stockbridge-Munsee Historical Committee, "Meeting Minutes," April 9, 2009.

14. Robert Jacobs interview, *HOS.*

15. Leona Bowman interview; Dorothy Davids interview; Betty Groh interview; Elaine Jacobi interview; Vaughn LaBelle interview; Little interview; Martin interview; Doug and Chenda Miller interview; Sherman Miller interview; Averil Jayne Pecore interview; all in *HOS.*

16. I am being intentionally vague here. Some of the oral histories that Dave Besaw, Bruce Davids, and Dorothy Davids either learned from their parents or witnessed themselves are spiritual in nature, and I do not believe it is my place to replicate those stories here in writing. See Besaw interview, *HOS;* Bruce Davids interview, *HOS;* D. Davids interview, *HOS.*

17. Aught Coyhis interview; D. Davids interview; B. Davids interview; Doreen Metzger interview; Pecore interview; and Sheila (Miller) Powless interview; all in *HOS.*

18. Interviewees' family members were sometimes present as well and helped encourage their relatives (typically their parents) to share certain items or stories from offscreen.

19. Patricia Miller interview, *HOS.*

20. Ruth Peters interview, *HOS;* Jacobs interview, *HOS.*

21. Sheila (Miller) Powless interview, *HOS.*

22. Roger Cuish interview, *HOS;* Fae Church interview, *HOS;* Peters interview, *HOS.*

23. Jacobs interview, *HOS.*

24. Opal Erb interview, *HOS;* Sheila (Miller) Powless interview, *HOS.*

25. Cuish interview, *HOS.*

26. Sheila (Miller) Powless interview, *HOS.*

27. Timothy B. Powell, "The Role of Indigenous Communities in Building Digital Archives," in *Afterlives of Indigenous Archives: Essays in Honor of the Occom Circle,* ed. Ivy Schweitzer and Gordon Henry (Hanover, N.H.: Dartmouth College Press, 2019), 36.

28. Coyhis interview, *HOS.*

29. Jacobi interview, *HOS.*

30. Earl Plass interview, *HOS;* Beverly Herring and Dorothy Kriha interview, *HOS;* Jacobs interview, *HOS;* Douglas Marr interview, *HOS;* Martin interview, *HOS;* Ernie and Virgil Murphy interview, *HOS.*

31. Blood quantum is a system established by the U.S. government that determines tribal citizenship based on what percentage of "Indian blood" one is estimated to have. Today, the blood quantum system is viewed by many as colonial, and many tribal nations are revising their constitutions to determine citizenship in other ways. For more on blood quantum, see Malinda Maynor Lowery, *Lumbee Indians in the Jim Crow South: Race, Identity, and the Making of a Nation* (Chapel Hill: University of North Carolina Press, 2010).

32. Stockbridge-Munsee Historical Committee, "Meeting Minutes," March 9, 2006; Stockbridge-Munsee Historical Committee, "Meeting Minutes," February 28, 2008, 2008 Historical Committee Meetings folder, CHLMC.

33. Youth of the Mohican Nation, *Stories of Our Elders,* 2nd ed. (Gresham, Wisc.: Muh-he-con-neew Press, 2010).

34. Youth of the Mohican Nation, 4–11.

35. Youth of the Mohican Nation, 20.

36. "IMLS Invests $5.2 Million in Library Services for Tribal Communities, Native Hawaiians," *Institute of Museum and Library Services,* August 20, 2020, accessed April 20, 2021, https://www.imls.gov/.

37. Stephen Warren, ed., *The Eastern Shawnee Tribe of Oklahoma: Resilience through Adversity* (Norman: University of Oklahoma Press, 2017).

38. William Bauer, "Oral History," in *Sources and Methods in Indigenous Studies,* ed. Chris Andersen and Jean M. O'Brien (New York: Routledge, 2017), 161; "Chickaloon Native Village," Log Number: MN-245530-OMS-20, accessed April 20, 2021, *Institute of Museum and Library Services,* https://www.imls.gov/.

39. Stockbridge-Munsee Department of Education and Cultural Affairs, "Memoirizing Our Mohican Lives: Elders Write Their Stories," 1997 Historical Committee Meetings Folder, CHLMC, 5.

40. Jacobs interview, *HOS;* Coyhis interview, *HOS.* For more military experiences see Clarence Chicks interview, *HOS;* and Little interview, *HOS.* For more experiences of discrimination see Little interview, *HOS;* and Martin interview, *HOS.*

41. Alfred Miller interview, *HOS;* B. Davids interview, *HOS.*

42. For secondary sources on relocation see Ned Blackhawk, "I Can Carry On from Here: The Relocation of American Indians to Los Angeles," *Wicazo Sa Review* 11, no. 2 (Autumn 1995): 16–30; Donald L. Fixico, *Termination and Relocation: Federal Indian Policy, 1945–1960* (Albuquerque: University of New Mexico Press, 1990); Donald L. Fixico, *Indian Resilience and Rebuilding: Indigenous Nations in the Modern American West* (Tucson: University of Arizona Press, 2013); Kasey Keeler, *American Indians and the American Dream: Policies, Place, and Property in Minnesota* (Minneapolis: University of Minnesota Press, 2023); Douglas K. Miller, *Indians on the Move: Native American Mobility and Urbanization in the Twentieth Century* (Chapel Hill: University of North Carolina Press, 2019); Nicolas G. Rosenthal, *Reimagining Indian Country: Native American Migration and Identity in Twentieth-Century Los Angeles* (Chapel Hill: University of North Carolina Press, 2021).

43. Bowman interview, *HOS;* Chicks interview, *HOS.* For similar narratives see B. Davids interview, *HOS.*

44. D. and C. Miller interview, *HOS.*

45. D. Davids interview, *HOS.* For more stories of relocation and movement see D. and C. Miller interview, *HOS;* P. Miller interview, *HOS.*

46. Church interview, *HOS.*

47. This builds on Bauer's argument that while oral histories, particularly the stories of daily lives, "may appear mundane; taken together they stitch together an American Indian collective memory." Bauer, "Oral History," 160.

48. Aroha Harris, "History with Nana: Family, Life, and the Spoken Source," in *Sources and Methods in Indigenous Studies,* ed. Chris Andersen and Jean M. O'Brien (New York: Routledge, 2017), 133.

49. For more on the historical context of personal narratives see Mary Jo Maynes, Jennifer L. Pierce, and Barbara Laslett, *Telling Stories: The Use of Personal Narratives in the Social Sciences and History* (Ithaca, N.Y.: Cornell University Press, 2008).

50. Ann Cvetkovich, *An Archive of Feelings: Trauma, Sexuality, and Lesbian Public Cultures* (Durham, N.C.: Duke University Press, 2003).

51. Portelli, "What Makes Oral Histories Different."

52. Murphy, Pierce, and Ruiz, "What Makes Queer Oral History Different," 10.

53. Dian Million, "Felt Theory: An Indigenous Feminist Approach to Affect and History," *Wicazo Sa Review* 24, no. 9 (Fall 2009): 61.

54. Church interview, *HOS*.

55. E. and V. Murphy interview, *HOS*. For similar stories of schools near the reservation see Pecore interview, *HOS*.

56. Jacobs interview, *HOS*; Verna Johnson-Miller interview, *HOS*.

57. Little interview, *HOS*. For more examples of narratives of education see Bowman, Chicks, Jacobs, and LaBelle interviews, all in *HOS*.

58. LaBelle, *HOS*; Plass interview, *HOS*. For other reflections on returns to New York, see Little, Marr, E. and V. Murphy, Peters, Betty Putnam Schiel, and Tom Rudesill interviews, all in *HOS*.

59. Church interview, *HOS*.

60. P. Miller interview, *HOS*.

61. Erb interview, *HOS*.

62. Cvetkovich, *An Archive of Feelings,* 8.

63. Sheila (Miller) Powless interview, *HOS*.

64. Metzger interview, *HOS*; Little interview, *HOS*.

65. Jacobi interview, *HOS*.

66. Barb Sommer and Dominique Tobbell, "Oral History Workshop: How to Do Oral History" (Institute for Advanced Study, University of Minnesota, March 28, 2014).

67. Jo Ann Schedler, interview with author, January 13, 2017.

68. Paula Hamilton and Linda Shopes, "Recreating Identity and Community," in *Oral Histories and Public Memories,* ed. Paula Hamilton and Linda Shopes (Philadelphia: Temple University Press, 2008), 103.

69. Stockbridge-Munsee Historical Committee, "Meeting Minutes," April 9, 2009.

70. Stockbridge-Munsee Historical Committee.

71. Sheila (Miller) Powless, personal communication with author, 2016.

72. Stockbridge-Munsee Community, "Authorization and Release for Recording" (Bowler, Wisc., 2016).

73. Portelli, "What Makes Oral Histories Different," 56.

74. For example, see Leah Miller, interview with author, December 15, 2016.

75. For example, in an oral history project initiated by Parks Canada with the Carcross-Tagish First Nation, Parks Canada attempted to gather oral histories from Indigenous peoples that would show an "Indian side" to a story about the Klondike Gold Rush. Instead, Carcross-Tagish community members "put forward a *parallel*

historical narrative describing their long use of the area and their connection to it as 'home.'" The narratives emphasized the Carcross-Tagish people's ongoing use of their territory connected to their cultural identity, and asserted their ownership of these lands, using the project to "challenge a national understanding of the historical significance of the Chilkoot Trail." Bauer also notes that when he conducted oral interviews with his own grandmother, who like him is a member of the Round Valley Indian Tribes, she refused to be recorded, asserting her choice to maintain control over her own words. See David Neufeld, "Parks Canada, the Commemoration of Canada, and Northern Aboriginal Oral History," in Hamilton and Shopes, *Oral Histories and Public Memories,* 160; Bauer, "Oral History."

76. Youth of the Mohican Nation, *Stories of Our Elders,* 20.

3. Archives as Arsenals for Community Needs

1. Jim Oberly, "Outline for Nomination of Arvid E. Miller Historical Library and Museum for 2002 Governor's Archives Award," box 5, DDC II.

2. Ruth Gudinas to Historical Committee Members, "Brief Conference Report," October 25, 2001, 2001 Historical Committee folder, CHLMC.

3. Mohican Historical Committee, "Many Trails of the Mohican Nation: A Conference on Mohican History and Culture," conference program, October 10–12, 2001, Many Trails of the Mohican Nation Conference 2001 folder, box 3, BMPC.

4. Dorothy Davids, "Book Project, Introduction," Mohican History Conference folder 4, box 5, Tribe and Community, DDC II.

5. Davids.

6. Mohican Historical Committee, "Many Trails of the Mohican Nation."

7. Stockbridge-Munsee Historical Committee, "Meeting Minutes," February 8, 2007, 2007 Historical Committee Meetings folder, CHLMC.

8. Quoted in Jody Ericson, "The Latest of the Mahicans," *Berkshire Magazine,* December/January 1991, 23.

9. Arvid E. Miller, "On Christianity in Our History," Writings folder 10, AEMC.

10. Dorothy Davids to Jeff Vele, "Rambling Maple Sugar," regular column submission for *Mohican News,* March 20, 2008, DDC II.

11. Kelly Wisecup, *Assembled for Use: Indigenous Compilation and the Archives of Early Native American Literatures* (New Haven: Yale University Press, 2021).

12. A. E. Miller, "On Christianity in Our History."

13. Historical Committee, *Quin'a Month'a* 1 (April 1972), Quin-a-Montha folder, Newsletters Collection, Arvid E. Miller Library-Museum; Ardie Adora Abrams-Miller, "Note," folder 9, box 3, series 4, SIC.

14. Dorothy W. Davids, "Information Requested for Rank and Tenure Appointment of Dorothy W. Davids to Associate Professor, Department of Education, University of Wisconsin–Extension," Commemoration folder, DDC.

15. Quin-a-Montha folder, Newsletters Collection, Arvid E. Miller Library-Museum.

16. Stockbridge-Munsee Historical Committee, "Meeting Minutes," October 25, 2001, 2001 Historical Committee Meetings folder, CHLMC; Stockbridge-Munsee

Historical Committee, "Meeting Minutes," October 24, 1996, 1996 Historical Committee Meetings folder, CHLMC.

17. Heather Bruegl, interview with author, January 21, 2021.

18. Dorothy Davids, *A Brief History of the Mohican Nation: Stockbridge-Munsee Band*, 3rd ed. (Bowler, Wisc.: Stockbridge-Munsee Historical Committee, 2017).

19. Davids, 3.

20. Davids.

21. Stockbridge-Munsee Historical Committee, "Meeting Minutes," August 10, 2016 (the author attended this meeting, and the notes are from her personal copy of the meeting minutes); Nathalee Kristianson, personal communication with author, November 7, 2022.

22. Leah Miller, interview with author, December 15, 2016.

23. Stockbridge-Munsee Historical Committee, "Meeting Minutes," August 10, 2016.

24. L. Miller interview, December 15, 2016.

25. Marisa Elena Duarte, *Network Sovereignty: Building the Internet across Indian Country* (Seattle: University of Washington Press, 2017).

26. "Stockbridge-Munsee Historical Project: Continuation of Research Phase; Initiation of Writing Phase," NEH Application folder, box 3, DDC II.

27. Dorothy Davids to Polly Pierce, December 1981, folder 14, box 4, series 4, SIC.

28. The Stockbridge-Munsee Historical Library-Museum Committee, *Catalog of Materials: Stockbridge-Munsee Historical Library Museum* (Gresham, Wisc.: Muh-he-con-neew Press, 1980); Youth of the Mohican Nation, *Stories of Our Elders,* 2nd ed. (Gresham, Wisc.: Muh-he-con-neew Press, 2010); Dorothy W. Davids et al., *The Mohican People: Their Lives and Their Lands* (Gresham, Wisc.: Muh-he-con-neew Press, 2008); Thelma Putnam and Blanche Jacobs, *Christian Religion among the Stockbridge-Munsee Band of Mohicans* (Gresham, Wisc.: Muh-he-con-neew Press, 1980); Kristina Heath, *Mama's Little One* (Gresham, Wisc.: Muh-he-con-neew Press, 1998); Eva Bowman, *Chief Ninham: Forgotten Hero* (Gresham, Wisc.: Muh-he-con-neew Press, 1999); Harry Bauman, *School Days: Memories of Life in Morgan Siding, 1925–1933,* ed. Jeri Bauman (Gresham, Wisc.: Muh-he-con-neew Press, 2006); Dorothy Davids, *Inner Dreams and Outer Circles,* ed. Beatrice Ganley (Gresham, Wisc.: Muh-he-con-neew Press, 2007).

29. Bowman, *Chief Ninham.*

30. Jolene Bowman, personal communication with author, November 7, 2022.

31. Jo Ann Schedler, interview with author, January 13, 2017.

32. Jo Ann Schedler, "Wisconsin American Indians in the Civil War," in *American Indians and the Civil War,* ed. Robert K. Sutton and John A. Latschar (Washington, D.C.: National Park Service, 2013), 66–87.

33. Schedler interview, January 13, 2017.

34. John A. Fleckner, *Native American Archives: An Introduction* (Chicago: Society of American Archivists, 1984), 4.

35. Daniel Heath Justice, *Our Fire Survives the Storm: A Cherokee Literary History* (Minneapolis: University of Minnesota Press, 2006), 7.

36. Frank G. Speck and Nekatcit, *The Celestial Bear Comes Down to Earth: The Bear Sacrifice Ceremony of the Munsee-Mahican in Canada as Related by Nekatcit* (Reading, Pa.: Reading Public Museum and Art Gallery, 1945).

37. Kristine Singleton and Molly Miller to Community Members, December 29, 1992, box 3, DDC II.

38. For Molly Miller's involvement, see Molly Miller, personal communication with author, April 20, 2022.

39. Dorothy Davids, "Storytelling & Ceremony Notes by Dot," box 3, DDC II.

40. Stockbridge-Munsee Historical Committee, "Meeting Minutes," August 3, 1995, 1995 Historical Committee Meetings folder, CHLMC; Dorothy W. Davids to Wisconsin Humanities Council, October 18, 1995, 1995 Historical Committee folder, CHLMC.

41. "Last of the Mohicans Dies at Milwaukee," *Sheboygan (Wisc.) Daily Press,* November 11, 1933, Wisconsin Historical Society, https://wisconsinhistory.org.

42. M. Miller, personal communication, April 20, 2022; Stockbridge-Munsee Community–Family Services Program, "Culture and Language Camp," Association on American Indian Affairs Summer Camp Grant Proposal Form, 2008, Language and Culture folder, LC.

43. For Masthay correspondence, see Rachel Wheeler and Sarah Eyerly, "Singing Box 331: Re-Sounding Eighteenth-Century Mohican Hymns from the Moravian Archives," *William and Mary Quarterly,* 3d ser., 76, no. 4 (October 2019): 649–96, digital companion published by the *Omohundro Institute,* oieahc.wm.edu. For other collecting, see Shawn Stevens, "'Walk' in Mohican," Language and Culture Committee folder, LC; Dorothy Davids to Roland Davids, March 2, 1981, folder 3, box 3, DDC II.

44. Shawn Stevens, "Mohican Language Project," Language and Culture Committee folder, LC.

45. Stevens.

46. Box 3, DDC II; HRC.

47. M. Miller, personal communication, April 20, 2022.

48. Ryan Winn, "Speaking Mahican: A Virtual Journey," *New Media-WI,* January 29, 2021.

49. Stockbridge-Munsee Community–Arvid E. Miller Library-Museum, "Help Save Our Languages," *IMLS Native American Library Services Enhancement Grant,* 2017, https://imls.gov.

50. Christopher Harvey, interview by Rachel Wheeler and Sarah Eyerly, "Singing Box 331 Digital Companion."

51. Winn, "Speaking Mahican." For Nicole Pecore, see M. Miller, personal communication, April 20, 2022.

52. Cutcha Risling Baldy, "The Flower Dancers: Reviving Hupa Coming-of-Age Ceremonies," *North Coast Journal of Politics People & Art,* August 2, 2018, https://www.northcoastjournal.com; E. Tammy Kim, "The Passamaquoddy Reclaim Their Culture through Digital Repatriation," *New Yorker,* January 30, 2019, https://www.new

yorker.com; "Project History," Wôpanâak Language Reclamation Project, *Wôpanâak Language Reclamation Project,* accessed November 14, 2021, wlrp.org.

53. Jolene Bowman, personal communication with author, November 7, 2022.

54. For more on the importance of information sharing and accessibility in the context of tribal sovereignty, see Duarte, *Network Sovereignty.*

55. For the full story of this repatriation, see Rose Miron, "Fighting for the Tribal Bible: Mohican Politics of Self-Representation and Repatriation," *Native American and Indigenous Studies* 5, no. 2 (Spring 2019): 91–122.

56. Timothy McKeown, "Notice of Intent to Repatriate a Cultural Item: The Trustees of Reservations, Beverly, MA," memorandum, February 2, 2006, HRC.

57. For more on Bibles as gifts and gifting in general in the colonial period, see Michael Witgen, *An Infinity of Nations: How the Native New World Shaped Early North America* (Philadelphia: University of Pennsylvania Press, 2013); Kevin A. McBride, "Bundles, Bears, and Bibles: Interpreting Seventeenth Century Native 'Texts,'" in *Early Native Literacies in New England: A Documentary and Critical Anthology,* ed. Kristinia Bross and Hilary E. Wyss (Amherst: University of Massachusetts Press, 2008); Phillip Round, *Removable Type: Histories of the Book in Indian Country, 1663–1880* (Chapel Hill: University of North Carolina Press, 2010); Ann Marie Plane, "'To Subscribe unto GODS BOOK': The Bible as Material Culture in Seventeenth-Century New England Colonialism," *Journal of the Bible and Its Reception* 3, no. 2 (2016): 303–29.

58. McKeown, "Notice of Intent to Repatriate."

59. Elaine M. Jacobi, "Our Great Spirit, Mohican Creator, 'Putahmowus,'" in *Reflections on the Waters That Are Never Still,* ed. Mark Shaw (Saline, Mich.: McNaughton & Gunn, 2015), 46.

60. "Has 198 Year Old Bible at Presbytery Session," *Milwaukee Sentinel,* October 14, 1915, folder 20, box 4, series 4, SIC; Dorothy Davids for the Stockbridge-Munsee Historical Committee, "Brief History of the Stockbridge Bibles: A Stockbridge-Munsee Perspective," *Quin'a Month'a* 9, no. 4 (March 1981), folder 7, box 3, series 4, SIC.

61. For theft of items, see Frederick Westfall to Ruth Gaines, January 31, 1930, MHSF. For sale, see Deed of Sale, May 4, 1930, MCP; Frederick Westfall to Mabel Choate, May 12, 1930, MCP.

62. See correspondence between Westfall, Choate, Virginia Baughman, and Ruth Gaines: MHSF and MCP. For quote on the legality of the sale see Deed of Sale, May 4, 1930, MCP; Frederick Westfall to Mabel Choate, May 12, 1930, MCP.

63. Davids, "Brief History of the Stockbridge Bibles"; Dorothy Davids to Polly Pierce, December 25, 1989, folder 6, box 3, series 4, SIC.

64. Margaret E. Guthrie, "The Return of a Pious Gift," *Milwaukee Journal,* June 2, 1991, HRC.

65. Laurence M. Channing to Gordon Abbott, October 27, 1975, box 4, DDC II; "Resolution No. 0739," memorandum, February 14, 1981, Tribal Minutes folder, Resolutions and Directives Collection, Arvid E. Miller Library-Museum.

66. Davids, "Brief History of the Stockbridge Bibles."

67. "Help Return the Stockbridge Bibles," box 4, DDC II; "Tribe Seeks Return of Treasured Bible," box 4, DDC II; "Stockbridge Bible Controversy," box 4, DDC II; "Mohican Tribe Resumes Efforts to Acquire 'Stockbridge Bible,'" *Berkshire (Mass.) Eagle,* February 1, 1982, box 4, series 4, SIC.

68. Stockbridge-Munsee Tribal Council and Stockbridge-Munsee Historical Committee, "The Stockbridge Bible: Documents Relating to Its Recovery by the Stockbridge Indians," folder 7, box 3, series 4, SIC.

69. Examples of these letters can be found in box 4, DDC II.

70. Nancy Lurie to Trustees, January 25, 1982, box 4, DDC II; Lee Dreyfus to Trustees, December 31, 1982, box 4, DDC II; Pete Seeger to Dorothy Davids, May 12, 1989, box 4, DDC II.

71. Dorothy Davids to Polly Pierce, April 26, 1982, box 4, DDC II.

72. The only external communication I have found from this time is in responses to letters sent from Mohican supporters. In some cases the trustees responded vaguely to letter writers, indicating that this was a matter they were still considering and that they were in contact with the Mohican tribe.

73. Trustees of Reservations, Meeting Minutes, June 17, 1982, folder 5, Legal Series, MHSF.

74. Trustees of Reservations, Meeting Minutes.

75. For a more in-depth discussion of this internal communication, see Miron, "Fighting for the Tribal Bible." Sources drawn from folders 4 and 5, MHSF.

76. Jack F. Trope, "The Case for NAGPRA," in *Accomplishing NAGPRA: Perspectives on the Intent, Impact, and Future of the Native American Graves Protection and Repatriation Act,* ed. Sangita Chari and Jaime M. N. Lavallee (Corvallis: Oregon State University Press, 2013), 19–54.

77. Trustees of Reservations, Meeting Minutes, September 26, 1989, folder 6, Legal Series, MHSF.

78. Asher E. Treat to R. C. Miller, October 19, 1989, box 4, DDC II.

79. R. C. Miller to Asher E. Treat, October 10, 1989, box 4, DDC II.

80. "Meeting with Trustees of Reservations," Minutes, July 17, 1989, box 4, DDC II.

81. "Meeting with Trustees of Reservations."

82. Trustees of Reservation, Meeting Minutes, August 2, 1989, folder 6, Legal Series, MHSF; Guthrie, "The Return of a Pious Gift."

83. The only institution that receives federal funding that is excluded from NAGPRA is the Smithsonian. This is because the National Museum of the American Indian Act, which was passed in 1989, already included repatriation regulations for the Smithsonian. These regulations were initially focused on human remains and funerary objects but were updated in 1996 to also include sacred objects and items of cultural patrimony. See Trope, "The Case for NAGPRA."

84. The act defines *cultural affiliation* as "a relationship of shared group identity which can be reasonably traced historically or prehistorically between a present-day Indian tribe or Native Hawaiian organization and an identifiable earlier group." Native

American Graves Protection and Repatriation Act, 25 U.S.C. 3001, November 16, 1990, nps.gov.

85. According to the National Park Service NAGPRA website, NAGPRA recognizes "Alaska Native villages that are recognized by the Bureau of Indian Affairs" as falling under the larger category "Indian tribe." For the full definition see National Park Service. "Frequently Asked Questions: Who may claim Native American cultural items under NAGPRA." National NAGPRA, accessed June 7, 2018, nps.gov.

86. Sangita Chari and Jaime M. N. Lavallee, introduction to Chari and Lavalee, *Accomplishing NAGPRA*, 7–18.

87. A significant number of items in museums continue to be classified as "culturally unidentifiable," a label that many tribal representatives have asserted is being used by institutions to avoid returning Native human remains and items. Delving deeply into this issue is beyond the scope of this book, but it is worth nothing that a 2010 amendment to NAGPRA does require institutions that receive federal funds to initiate further contact with Indian tribes and Native Hawaiian organizations when human remains are deemed "culturally unidentifiable" based on what lands the remains were taken from, but museums still have significant power in this process and the burden of consultation and proof is still relegated to Indian tribes and Native Hawaiian organizations. The amendment also does not apply to objects. See Clayton W. Dumont Jr., "Contesting Scientists' Narrations of NAGPRA's Legislative History: Rule 10.11 and the Recovery of 'Culturally Unidentifiable' Ancestors," *Wicazo Sa Review* 26, no. 1 (Spring 2011): 5–41; Native American Graves Protection and Repatriation Act.

88. Trope, "The Case for NAGPRA," 37.

89. The NAGPRA Review Committee can also resolve disputes between parties, and tribes can appeal to the committee if an institution denies their "cultural affiliation" claim. See Trope.

90. L. Miller interview, December 15, 2016; Sherry White, personal communication with author, October 24, 2022. This Historic Preservation Committee initially comprised Historical Committee chair Dorothy Davids, library manager Arlee Davids, and Steve Comer, a tribal member who lived on the East Coast and was able to represent the tribe in repatriation matters. Eventually, the tribe hired Sherry White as the cultural preservation officer (White became the tribe's historic preservation officer in 2004) and then Bonney Hartley, who as of this writing serves as the historic preservation manager and is now based on the East Coast with Jeff Bendremer, who serves as the tribe's historic preservation officer. See Dorothy Davids, "Repatriation Part One," folder 1, box 6, DDC II; Arletta Davids to Theresa Puskarenko, "Five-Year Plan for Library Museum Archives," December 17, 1996, Arvid E. Miller Memorial Library-Museum folder, box 5, DDC II.

91. Davids, "Repatriation Part One."

92. Sherry White, personal communication with author, January 5, 2023.

93. White, personal communication, January 5, 2023; White, personal communication, October 24, 2022.

94. Davids, "Repatriation Part One."

95. Walter R. Echo-Hawk and Roger C. Echo-Hawk, "Repatriation, Reburial, and Religious Rights," in *American Indians in American History, 1870–2001: A Companion Reader,* ed. Sterling Evans (Westport, Conn.: Greenwood Publishing Group, 2002), 177–93.

96. For the Communion set, see McKeown, "Notice of Intent to Repatriate." For the powder horn, see Frank Vaisvilas, "Wisconsin Stockbridge-Munsee Tribe's 19th Century Powder Horn Returns Home after 80 Years," *Green Bay (Wisc.) Press Gazette,* November 24, 2020, greenbaypressgazette.com. For moccasins and wampum belt, see Stephanie Zollshan, "Berkshire Museum Returns Items to Stockbridge-Munsee Community Band of Mohicans," *Berkshire (Mass.) Eagle,* February 10, 2022. For other Mission House items, see Bonney Hartley, personal communication with author, August 23, 2021. The tribe has successfully retrieved many items beyond those listed here.

97. Trope, "The Case for NAGPRA."

98. Frank Blackwell Mayer, "Frank B. Mayer Collection of Sketchbooks, Drawings, and Oil Paintings of Sioux Indians during the 1851 Treaty Negotiations at Traverse des Sioux and Mendota, 1851–1886," Edward E. Ayer Collection, Newberry Library.

99. The original ruling in the Kennewick Man cases is a classic example of the disregard for oral evidence presented by tribes. See Cathay Y. N. Smith, "Oral Tradition and the Kennewick Man," *Yale Law Journal* 125 (November 3, 2016), https://www.yalelawjournal.org.

100. Bernice Miller Pigeon and Lucille Bowman Miller to National Park Service, February 1, 1995, 1995 Historical Committee Meetings folder, CHLMC.

101. Schedler interview, January 13, 2017.

102. Stephanie Bowman, personal communication with author, November 14, 2022.

103. See HRC.

104. L. Miller interview, December 15, 2016.

105. Davids, *A Brief History;* "Stockbridge-Munsee Community," Great Lakes Inter-Tribal Council, glitc.org.

106. Davids, *A Brief History;* James Oberly, *A Nation of Statesmen: The Political Culture of the Stockbridge-Munsee Mohicans, 1815–1972* (Norman: University of Oklahoma Press, 2005).

107. "Time-Line 1972–1980s," History folder, DDC; Davids, *A Brief History.*

108. Associated Press and Shawano Leader, "Mohicans Win Land Case," February 2, 1994, *Shawano (Wisc.) Leader,* Boundary Case folder, HRC.

109. Associated Press, "Tribe Expects Lawsuit on Slots to Take Years," Boundary Case folder, box 3, DDC II.

110. Ryan J. Foley, "Court's Decision Shrinks Stockbridge Reservation," January 21, 2009, *Shawano (Wisc.) Leader,* Boundary Case folder, HRC.

111. Because the cases were only a few years apart and both considered the boundaries of the reservation as set out in the 1856 treaty, it is likely that the tribe presented similar evidence in both cases. "Tribe Offers Extensive Testimony in Defense of Keeping Pine Hills Casino Open," November 11, 1998, Boundary Issues folder, HRC.

112. National Archives at Chicago, "Record Groups 58–96," National Archives, last updated August 15, 2016, archives.gov.

113. McGirt v. Oklahoma, 591 U.S. 18-9526 (2020).

114. I'm drawing here on Daniel Heath Justice's understanding of Indigenous nationhood as articulated through his "peoplehood matrix," which includes "language, sacred history, ceremonial cycle, and place/territory." See Justice, *Our Fire Survives the Storm.*

115. L. Miller interview, December 15, 2016.

4. The Mohican Historical Trips

1. There are several documented examples of Mohican returns to their ancestral homelands, particularly Stockbridge, Massachusetts, since they were forced to leave their homelands in the late eighteenth century. These include the summer "pilgrimages" back to Stockbridge by Mohicans that Catherine Maria Sedgwick mentions in her 1842 novel *Hope Leslie;* groups of "thirty or forty Indians, men and women" who came down to Stockbridge in the winter from their homes in Oneida, New York, detailed in Timothy Woodbridge's 1856 *The Autobiography of a Blind Minister;* a 1936 visit from the Mohican sachem Uhm-Pa-Tuth; and a 1951 visit from Jim and Grace Davids, both of which were documented in local newspapers in Stockbridge, Massachusetts. See Catherine Maria Sedgwick, *Hope Leslie: Or, Early Times in the Massachusetts, Volume 1* (New York: Harper & Brothers, 1842), 127; Timothy Woodbridge, D.D., *The Autobiography of a Blind Minister: Including Sketches of the Men and Events of His Time* (Boston: John P. Jewett and Company, 1856), 37; "Uhm-Pa-Tuth Lays Pipe of Peace on Burial Ground of His Ancestors," *Berkshire (Mass.) Eagle,* May 1936, Rick Wilcox Personal Collection; "Indian Returns to Home of His Ancestors," July 31, 1951, SIC.

2. The only exception I have found for this is Ruth Gudinas, who was not an enrolled tribal member but was the lifelong partner of tribal leader Dorothy "Dot" Davids. Ruth served as the Historical Committee's secretary and was an active member of the committee until her death in 2014. See "Obituary: Ruth Anna Gudinas," *Shawano (Wisc.) Evening Leader,* September 10, 2014, http://www.shawanoleader.com/.

3. Trudi Coar, "Stockbridge Indians Come Home," *Berkshire (Mass.) Record,* September 1, 1989, box 4, SIC.

4. TTM Travelers, "A Special Report to The Stockbridge-Munsee Tribal Council: Our Trip to Stockbridge Massachusetts August 21–29, 1989," 1989 folder, HTC; Kristy Miller, "Excerpts of Journal" in 1972 Journal folder, HTC; Ruth Gudinas, "Trip to Stockbridge August 21–29 1989," 1989 folder, HTC; Bob Gardinier, "Iroquois, Mohicans to Share in Reburial: State Says Remains can be Reinterred on Peebles Island in July," *Native Circle,* July 11, 1996, HTC; Eileen Mooney, "Stockbridge Indians Discover Journey 'Home' Both Sad, Bitter," *Berkshire (Mass.) Eagle,* July 28, 1975, 1975 Other/Misc. folder, HTC; "Indians Visit Loudonville to Trace Tribal History," *Loudonville (Ohio) Times,* June 21, 1972, 1975 Other/Misc. folder, HTC.

5. K. Miller, "Excerpts of Journal."

6. Christine DeLucia similarly discusses the process of regrounding and the creation of what she calls "memorial geographies" in her work on Nipmuc returns to their ancestral homelands. See Christine M. DeLucia, *Memory Lands: King Philip's War and the Place of Violence in the Northeast* (New Haven: Yale University Press, 2018), 109.

7. Barbara Kirshenblatt-Gimblett, *Destination Culture: Tourism, Museums, and Heritage* (Berkeley: University of California Press, 1998).

8. *Time,* March 28, 1977, 54, quoted in Matthew Frye Jacobson, *Roots Too: White Ethnic Revival in Post–Civil Rights America* (Cambridge: Harvard University Press, 2006), 42. For the Mohicans, the connection to Alex Haley's *Roots* was quite direct: Dorothy Davids specifically mentions the television series based on the book in a proposal for funding one of the historical trips: "Alex Haley, through [unreadable] television series, exemplified an individual's long search for his historical roots. The Stockbridge-Munsee people watched this series, and like many others, identified with Haley's search." See Dorothy Davids, "Proposal, Historical Trip," Tribal/Community Service folder, DDC II. For *Roots,* see Alex Haley, *Roots: The Saga of an American Family* (New York: Doubleday, 1976); *Roots,* directed by Marvin J. Chomsky, John Erman, David Greene, and Gilbert Moses (Burbank, Calif.: Warner Bros. Television, 1977).

9. Jacobson, *Roots Too,* 19.

10. While I use the phrasing "chose to leave" broadly here, it is important to note that choice is always complicated within immigration. Certainly, some ethnic groups did not choose to leave their homelands but were rather forced or pushed out by violent or desperate conditions. Even for immigrant groups who came to what is now called America on their own accord, we don't know to what extent obligated wives and children always chose to leave their homes.

11. Renya Ramirez makes a similar argument in the context of Native people who live in urban spaces but maintain connections to their home and family on their reservations. See Renya K. Ramirez, *Native Hubs: Culture, Community and Belonging in Silicon Valley and Beyond* (Durham, N.C.: Duke University Press, 2007), 11.

12. Bergis Jules, *Architecting Sustainable Futures: Exploring Funding Models in Community Based Archives* (New Orleans: Shift, 2019).

13. Bernice Miller, "Our Trip to Stockbridge, Massachusetts," Stockbridge, Mass. folder, HTC.

14. Dorothy Davids, "Wherever We Were, Here We Are!," box 6, DDC II.

15. Gudinas, "Trip to Stockbridge"; K. Miller, "Excerpts of Journal."

16. Grace Wilcox, Polly Pierce, and current archivist Barbara Allen [these three were/are all archivists at the Stockbridge Library in Massachusetts—they are not tribal archivists] have all visited the Stockbridge-Munsee reservation. Rick Wilcox and Barbara Allen, personal communication with author, February 15, 2017; for Polly Pierce sending materials to the Historical Committee and advocating for the tribe, see correspondence between Pierce and Dorothy Davids (Stockbridge Library and Arvid E. Miller Library-Museum) and Margaret Raasch, "Story of the Historical Trip," box 3, DDC II.

17. Rick Wilcox, "Stockbridge Mohican Proprietors letter to Jaheel Woodbridge c. 1780 Op-Ed," Rick Wilcox Personal Collection.

18. Rick Wilcox, personal communication with author, August 24, 2021.

19. Vine Deloria Jr., *God Is Red* (New York: Grosset & Dunlap, 1973), 121.

20. Keith H. Basso, *Wisdom Sits in Places: Landscape and Language among the Western Apache* (Albuquerque: University of New Mexico Press, 1996), 7.

21. "Stockbridge-Munsee Search for Identity," *Shawano (Wisc.) Evening Leader,* March 15, 1974, HTC.

22. Quoted in Gardinier, "Iroquois, Mohicans to Share in Reburial."

23. Laura Harjo, *Spiral to the Stars: Mvskoke Tools of Futurity* (Tucson: University of Arizona Press, 2019), 33.

24. Leah Miller, interview with author, December 15, 2016.

25. Jo Ann Schedler, interview with author, January 13, 2017.

26. Gudinas, "Trip to Stockbridge."

27. Toni Toczylowski, "Mohicans Travel to Land Where Ancestors Lived," *Albany Times Union,* HTC.

28. K. Miller, "Excerpts of Journal"; Gudinas, "Trip to Stockbridge." For more recent examples of the expressed feeling, see Clarence Fanto, "For Stockbridge-Munsee Members, Return to 'Ancestral Homeland' Very Humbling," *Berkshire (Mass.) Eagle,* July 12, 2019, https://www.berkshireeagle.com/.

29. TTM Travelers, "A Special Report."

30. TTM Travelers.

31. Gudinas, "Trip to Stockbridge."

32. For example, Pauline Sharp, a member of the Kaw Nation Oklahoma, remarked that upon arriving at a special place, she and other tribal members experience a "special feeling." Narragansett tribal member Emeline Thomas Colbert expressed similar affective connections, recalling that "I couldn't explain that to anybody, the kind of feeling that I personally have when I go to the Great Swamp (a site of a massacre in Narragansett history). It's just like a vibration or an overall feeling of something around." See "Kaw Nation to Return to Ancestral Land in Kansas for Ceremony," *Indianz.com,* April 22, 2015; Christina DeLucia, "The Memory Frontier: Uncommon Pursuits of Past and Place in the Northeast after King Philip's War," *Journal of American History* 98, no. 4 (March 2012): 985.

33. Gudinas, "Trip to Stockbridge."

34. TTM Travelers, "A Special Report."

35. Gudinas, "Trip to Stockbridge."

36. TTM Travelers, "A Special Report."

37. Gudinas, "Trip to Stockbridge."

38. Steve Comer to "Folks," HTC.

39. This is similar to the process DeLucia calls "reclamation of Indigenous geographies." See DeLucia, "The Memory Frontier," 975.

40. DeLucia, 977.

41. The ceremony, led by Bruce Miller and Oscar Pigeon, was conducted mostly in what tribal secretary Ruth Gudinas refers to as "Winnebago," though the Ho-Chunk Nation typically refer to themselves as "Ho-Chunk" today. Though the Mohicans are actively working to recover aspects of their language, the language revitalization process had only begun when Gudinas made this record in 1989. Still, I presume it was important to have the ceremony conducted in a Native language rather than English. Oscar Pigeon is Library-Museum founder Bernice Miller-Pigeon's second husband (the Library-Museum is named for her first husband, Arvid E. Miller). Pigeon is Ho-Chunk, not an enrolled member of the Stockbridge-Munsee Band.

42. TTM Travelers, "A Special Report."

43. Bob Gardinier, "Indians: 2 Reburied in Waterford Park Ceremony," *Albany Times Union,* July 21, 1996, HTC.

44. The specific wording Bernice uses of a tradition passed from fathers is consistent with other sources: "The Indians being asked the reason of their Custom and Practice, say they know nothing about it, only that their Fathers and their Grandfathers and Great Grandfathers did so, and charged all their children to do so." See Ezra Stiles, *Extracts from the Itineraries and Other Miscellanies of Ezra Stiles, D.D., LL.D., 1755–1794,* ed. Franklin B. Dexter (New Haven: Yale University Press, 1916), 161–62, quoted in William S. Simmons, *Spirit of New England Tribes: Indian History and Folklore* (Hanover, Mass.: University Press of New England, 1986), 252. A source from 1872 recorded that upon arriving at a stream "we perceived our Indian looking for a stone, which having found, he cast to a heap, which for ages had been accumulating by passengers like him, who was our guide. We inquired why he observed that rite. He answered that his father practised it and enjoined it on him. But he did not like to talk on the subject." See E. M. Ruttenber, *History of the Indian Tribes of Hudson's River: Their Origins, Manners and Customs; Tribal and Sub-Tribal Organizations; Wars, Treaties, Etc., Etc.* (Albany: J. Munsell, 1872), 373.

45. Another source also corresponds with the wording Bernice uses, writing, "There is a large Heap of Stones, I suppose ten Cart Loads, in the Way to *Wanhktukook,* which the *Indians* have thrown together, as they have pass'd by, to throw a Stone to it: But what was the End of it they cannot tell: Only they say, their Fathers us'd to do so, and they do it because it was the Custom of their Fathers." See Samuel Hopkins, *Historical Memoirs, Relating to the Housatunnuk Indians* (Boston: S. Kneeland, 1753), VAULT Ayer 251, S811 H7, Edward E. Ayer Collection, Newberry Library. Also see Charles J. Taylor, *History of Great Barrington, Berkshire County, Massachusetts* (Great Barrington, Mass.: Clark W. Bryan & Co., 1882), 61; Ruttenber, *History of the Indian Tribes of Hudson's River,* 373.

46. "Welcome to Monument Mountain, Sacred Site of the Mohican People," trail signage at the base of Monument Mountain, Stockbridge, Massachusetts.

47. "Retracing the Steps of Our Ancestors," in 2006 folder, HTC.

48. Wilcox, personal communication, August 24, 2021.

49. Basso, *Wisdom Sits in Places,* 7.

50. D. Davids, "Wherever We Were, Here We Are!"

51. Maria Yellow Horse Brave Heart and Lemyra M. DeBruyn, "The American Indian Holocaust: Healing Historical Unresolved Grief," *American Indian and Alaska Native Mental Health Research* 8, no. 2 (1998): 60–82; Rachel Yehuda, Nikolaos P. Daskalakis, Linda M. Bierer, Heather N. Bader, Torsten Klengel, Florian Holsboer, and Elizabeth B. Binder, "Holocaust Exposure Induced Intergenerational Effects on FKBP5 Methylation," *Biological Psychiatry* 80, no. 5 (September 1, 2016): 372–80; Grace M. Cho, "Voices from the *Teum*: Synesthetic Trauma and the Ghost of the Korean Diaspora," in *The Affective Turn: Theorizing the Social,* ed. Patricia Ticineto Clough with Jean Halley (Durham, N.C.: Duke University Press, 2007), 156.

52. TTM Travelers, "A Special Report."

53. Ron Eyerman, "Cultural Trauma: Slavery and the Formation of African American Identity," in *Cultural Trauma and Collective Identity,* ed. Jeffrey C. Alexander, Ron Eyerman, Bernhard Giesen, Neil J. Smelser, and Piotr Sztompka (Berkeley: University of California Press, 2004), 62; Lara Leigh Kelland, *Clio's Foot Soldiers: Twentieth-Century U.S. Social Movements and Collective Memory* (Amherst: University of Massachusetts Press, 2018), 108.

54. Mooney, "Journey 'Home' Both Sad, Bitter." For more on the Gnadenhutten Massacre see Ron Harper, "Looking the Other Way: The Gnadenhutten Massacre and the Contextual Interpretation of Violence," *William and Mary Quarterly* 64, no. 3 (July 2007): 621–44; John P. Bowes, "The Gnadenhutten Effect: Moravian Converts and the Search for Safety in the Canadian Borderlands," *Michigan Historical Review* 34, no. 1 (Spring 2008): 101–17.

55. Mooney, "Journey 'Home' Both Sad, Bitter."

56. D. Davids, "Wherever We Were, Here We Are!"

57. D. Davids; Stanley W. Moulton, "Stockbridge Indians Back in Tribal Home on 1,600 Mile Historical Research Mission," *Berkshire (Mass.) Eagle,* June 28, 1972, 1975 Other/Misc. folder, HTC.

58. Gudinas, "Trip to Stockbridge."

59. TTM Travelers, "A Special Report."

60. TTM Travelers.

61. For another example of this, see DeLucia's conversation about Narragansett tribal members who have used returns to the Great Swamp, a site of trauma and loss, to ground their understanding of this place in larger geographies critical to collective memory. DeLucia, "The Memory Frontier," 985.

62. D. Davids, "Wherever We Were, Here We Are!"

63. TTM Travelers, "A Special Report."

64. Ann Cvetkovich, *An Archive of Feelings: Trauma, Sexuality, and Lesbian Public Cultures* (Durham, N.C.: Duke University Press, 2003), 7.

65. Cvetkovich, 7.

66. Dian Million, "Felt Theory: An Indigenous Feminist Approach to Affect and History," *Wicazo Sa Review* 24, no. 2 (2009): 53–76.

67. Cho, "Voices from the *Teum*," 156.

68. Jean O'Brien, *Firsting and Lasting: Writing Indians Out of Existence in New England* (Minneapolis: University of Minnesota Press, 2010).

69. This romanticization has probably been occurring for as long as the tribe has been absent from Stockbridge. In *Hope Leslie,* Sedgwick notes that during the summer "pilgrimages" back to Stockbridge, Mohicans were "regarded with a melancholy interest by the present occupants of the soil." Sedgwick, *Hope Leslie,* 127. This type of experience is not uncommon among other tribes who have returned to their ancestral homelands. For an example of Shawnee returns, see Benjamin J. Barnes, "Becoming Our Own Storytellers: Tribal Nations Engaging with Academia," in *The Eastern Shawnee Tribe of Oklahoma: Resilience through Adversity,* ed. Stephen Warren (Norman: University of Oklahoma Press, 2019), 218.

70. TTM Travelers, "A Special Report."

71. Mooney, "Journey 'Home' Both Sad, Bitter."

72. Mooney.

73. Jody Ericson, "The Latest of the Mahicans," *Berkshire (Mass.) Magazine,* January 1991, 24, HRC.

74. Kevin Conlon, "Indians' Skeletal Remains Buried on Peebles Island," *Schenectady Sunday Gazette,* July 21, 1996, 1996 folder, HTC.

75. Mooney, "Journey 'Home' Both Sad, Bitter."

76. Mooney.

77. B. Miller, "Our Trip to Stockbridge."

78. K. Miller, "Excerpts of Journal."

79. Gudinas, "Trip to Stockbridge."

80. Neal Boyer, "'Last' of the Mohicans Looking for the 'First,'" 1972 folder, HTC; Ericson, "The Latest of the Mahicans."

81. Trudi Coar, untitled newspaper article, 1972 folder, HTC.

82. Boyer, "'Last of the Mohicans'"; Coar, untitled article; Mooney, "Journey 'Home' Both Sad, Bitter."

83. Other tribal nations that maintain connections to their ancestral homelands are involved in similar efforts. For example, the Shawnee Tribe of Oklahoma has worked to protect sacred sites and reclaim human remains in both Ohio and Indiana. See Stephen Warren, "Introduction: The Eastern Shawnees and the Repatriation of Their History," in *The Eastern Shawnee Tribe of Oklahoma: Resilience through Adversity,* ed. Stephen Warren (Norman: University of Oklahoma, 2019), 6.

84. Woodbridge, *The Autobiography of a Blind Minister,* 37. It should be noted that this is not the Timothy Woodbridge who served as a missionary to the Mohicans in the eighteenth century.

85. Stockbridge Town Meeting Records, 1807–1832, Book 3, pp. 10–13, Stockbridge Town Clerk Office, Stockbridge, Massachusetts. Transcription provided by Rick Wilcox.

86. Thomas A. Weed v. J. H. Dunham, Esq. for the Town of Stockbridge, 1869, Berkshire Superior Court Records, pp. 500–505, Docket #167, Berkshire County Clerk, Pittsfield, Massachusetts. Transcription provided by Rick Wilcox.

87. bytheway, "Chief Wilcox, Sherry White and Barbara Allen honor Mohican life in Stockbridge," October 30, 2012, Rick Wilcox Personal Collection.

88. Richard B. Wilcox, "Indian Burying Grounds 2010 Report of Work," February 5, 2010, Rick Wilcox Personal Collection.

89. "Mohican Burial Ground," February 15, 2012, Rick Wilcox Personal Collection.

90. Fanto, "Return Very Humbling"; Jacob Posner, "Stockbridge Archaeological Dig Involves Community, Aims to Correct Historical Interpretation," *Berkshire (Mass.) Eagle,* July 11, 2021, https://www.berkshireeagle.com.

91. Wilcox, personal communication, August 24, 2021; Nancy Eve Cohen, "Artifacts, Dirt Floors from the Mohicans' Past Found at Archaeological Dig in Berkshires," *New England Public Media,* July 13, 2021, https://www.nepm.org.

92. Archaeological work for the ox roast site was ultimately funded primarily by a Cultural Research Fund grant from the Cultural Preservation Board in Stockbridge, and the search for the meeting house was funded by another grant from the National Park Service. See Fanto, "Return Very Humbling"; Wilcox, personal communication, August 24, 2021; Frank Vaisvilas, "Stockbridge-Munsee Mohican Officials Aim to Prove Feast with George Washington Happened," *Green Bay (Wisc.) Press Gazette,* April 19, 2021, https://greenbaypressgazette.com.

93. Wilcox, personal communication, August 24, 2021; Cohen, "Artifacts, Dirt Floors."

94. Posner, "Stockbridge Archaeological Dig."

95. Cohen, "Artifacts, Dirt Floors."

96. "Catskill Retail Development Stage 1B Cultural Resource Survey, Progress Report 2," December 4, 1995, 2003 Trip folder, HTC.

97. TTM Travelers, "A Special Report." For gathering historical archival evidence, see Stockbridge-Munsee Historical Committee, "Special Meeting," January 5, 1987, 1987 Historical Committee Meetings folder, CHLMC.

98. Stockbridge-Munsee Historical Committee, "Special Meeting."

99. It is important to note that the tribe's position on Schodack Island did slightly change after the 1987 trip. In 1988 the tribe rescinded its policy of opposing the development of Schodack Island State Park but emphasized that it still wanted this area to be treated with "much respect and dignity." The island does remain an undeveloped park as of this writing, but the addition of a campground, parking lot, and bathroom facilities on the island has been interpreted by other Indigenous peoples in the Northeast as disrespectful. For more on opposition to development from others, see John Sam Sapiel to Stockbridge-Munsee Tribal Council, April 26, 2000, Boston Harbor Islands/Stockbridge-Munsee Communications folder, HRC.

100. Cheryl Fields, "Journey to the Homeland," *American Jewish World,* August 2, 1996, 1996 folder, HTC.

101. Fields. As an additional note, NAGPRA did not apply to this case because the remains were deemed "culturally unidentifiable," leaving the Mohicans with little power to stop Wal-Mart from moving forward with their project. This is why the

tribe appealed to the chain store directly and, as outlined later in this chapter, worked with Haudenosaunee tribal members to rebury the ancestors together.

102. Virgil Murphy to David Glass, January 10, 1996, 1996 Historical Committee Meeting folder, CHLMC.

103. Sue Sturgis, "Wal-Mart's History of Destroying Sacred Sites," *Grist*, September 3, 2009; National Park Service, "NRHP_Link_2015 Spreadsheet," National Register of Historic Places Program: Research, http://www.nps.gov.

104. There are other instances where the Mohicans have fought land development plans in the Northeast that I do not include here for space purposes. To read more about one instance in which the Mohicans briefly participated (the redevelopment plans on Deer Island) see DeLucia, *Memory Lands,* 97–106.

105. Steve Moore, "Ancient Indian Village Found: Mohawk Indian Heads Team at South Berkshire Dig," *Berkshire (Mass.) Eagle,* August 4, 1991, box 4, SIC.

106. Gardinier, "Iroquois, Mohicans to Share in Reburial"; Valerie White, "Mohican Visit Leads to EG'bush Preserve," *The Courier,* July 25, 1996, 1996 folder, HTC; Mike Goodwin, "Ancient Remains Buried Again in Waterford," *The Sunday Record,* 1996 folder, HTC; Bob Gardinier, "Quiet Ceremony of Reburial: Native Americans Laid to Rest in Waterford Park," *Times Union,* July 21, 1996, 1996 folder, HTC; Conlon, "Indians' Skeletal Remains."

107. "Signature of Memorandum of Understanding between Stockbridge-Munsee Band of Mohican Indians and West Point Garrison Commander," 2003 folder, HTC.

108. Leader Staff Writer, "Stockbridge-Munsee Recognized by United States Military Academy," 2005 folder, HTC.

109. Leader Staff Writer.

110. Sangita Chari and Jaime M. N. Lavallee, introduction to *Accomplishing NAGPRA: Perspectives on the Intent, Impact, and Future of the Native American Graves Protection and Repatriation Act,* ed. Sangita Chari and Jaime M. N. Lavallee (Corvallis: Oregon State University Press, 2013), 7–18.

111. Advisory Council on Historic Preservation, "Section 106 Regulations Summary," Advisory Council on Historic Preservation, www.achp.gov.

112. Amy Dalrymple and Mike Nowatzki, "Company Showed 'Lack of Transparency' in Reporting Artifacts Discovery in Days Leading up to Pipeline Conflict," *Bismark Tribune*, November 1, 2016.

113. Advisory Council on Historic Preservation, *Consultation with Indian Tribes in the Section 106 Review Process: A Handbook* (Washington, D.C.: Advisory Council on Historic Preservation, 2012). For an example of when this justification was used to streamline a project see Gale Courey Toensing, "Aquinnah Wampanoag Sues Feds over Cape Wind," *Indian Country Today,* July 14, 2011.

114. Sherry White, personal communication with author, January 5, 2023.

115. Advisory Council on Historic Preservation, *Consultation.* Federal agencies can also terminate consultation at any time if they can show that they fulfilled the consultation requirements of Section 106. For an example of termination of consultation see Toensing, "Aquinnah Wampanoag Sues."

116. For requesting additional investigations, see Jake Fahrenkrog, email to author, April 24, 2018. For an example of a project that was streamlined for "public benefits," see the 2011 Cape Wind project, when the Aquinnah Wampanoag Nation filed a lawsuit against the Bureau of Ocean Energy Management, Regulations, and Enforcement and the Secretary of the Interior Department after they approved an offshore wind energy plant in spite of tribal contestation and lack of consultation required under Section 106. See Toensing, "Aquinnah Wampanoag Sues"; Cape Wind, "Litigation History of Cape Wind," Cape Wind, May 2, 2014, http://www.capewind.org.

117. If there are disputes between a federal agency and an American Indian nation, the Advisory Council on Historic Preservation (ACHP) reviews the site and provides recommendations to the federal agency, but the decision to shut down or move a project is ultimately up to the federal agency. The agency, the state historic preservation officer on the project, or ACHP (if they participate) can terminate consultation with tribes if an agreement on how to resolve adverse effects is not reached. See Advisory Council on Historic Preservation, *Consultation*.

118. Here it is important to note that federal agencies can and often do pay tribal consultants (typically, THPOs) for their time and consultation on these projects as well as their travel expenses. Some tribes have also created their own policies that require consultation or development fees, likely to avoid doing significant unpaid labor or having their land be exploited. The barriers I am emphasizing here are more about the physical distance the THPOs may need to travel and the time these consultations take. While some tribes have enough historic preservation staff to cover these extensive projects, others do not. For an example of tribal nations setting fees for construction permits on their lands, see Erin Mundahl, "Tribal Resistance to FCC Rule Change Could Slow Broadband Installation in Indian Country," *InsideSources*, March 23, 2018, http://www.insidesources.com. Though the article frames these fees as slowing down the implementation process of wireless features and wasting taxpayer money, American Indian nations have the right to charge money for structures being built on their lands.

119. White, personal communication, January 5, 2023.

120. Before Bonney Hartley established this office in September 2015, Sherry White was flying back and forth between Bowler and the East Coast for more than a decade to consult on various projects. Prior to that, the tribe often asked Steve Comer (a tribal member who lived on the East Coast) to serve as a tribal representative.

121. Bonney Hartley, personal communication with author, February 24, 2017.

122. Hartley.

123. Kenneth C. Crowe II, "Mohicans Reclaim a Key Part of Their New York Ancestral Lands," *Times Union*, May 8, 2021, last updated May 9, 2021, https://www.timesunion.com; Stockbridge-Munsee Community and Open Space Institute, "The Long Journey Home," https://www.storymaps.arcgis.com.

124. Stockbridge-Munsee Community and Open Space Institute, "The Long Journey Home."

125. DeLucia, *Memory Lands*, 108.

126. Wilcox, personal communication, August 24, 2021.

5. New Narratives for Public Audiences

1. This act is sometimes referred to as Title VII, since the Emergency School Aid Act is also known as Title VII (P.L. 92-318). See Department of Health, Education and Welfare, "Applicant Manual for Local Educational Agency Grants, Emergency School Aid Act" (Title VII P.L. 92–318, as amended by P.L. 93-380), United States Office of Education, University of Michigan Libraries; American Institutes for Research, "Overview: The Magnet Schools Assistance Program (MSAP) and This Evaluation," U.S. Department of Education, https://www2.ed.gov/.

2. In 1969 a Senate subcommittee issued the report "Indian Education: A National Tragedy, A National Challenge," which highlighted inequities in the education of American Indian and Alaska Native students and led to the passage of the Indian Education Act in 1972. Passed in the same year as the ESAA, the Indian Education Act established a comprehensive approach to Indian education that has been reauthorized through more recent legislation like the 2001 No Child Left Behind Act. See American Institutes for Research, "Overview"; Office of Elementary and Secondary Education, "History of Indian Education," U.S. Department of Education, https://www2.ed.gov/. The "National Tragedy" Indian Education report has also been credited with influencing the passage of the Indian Self-Determination and Education Assistance Act of 1975, which authorized certain agencies within the federal government to make grants directly to federally recognized tribes and amended the Johnson-O'Malley Act, giving Native communities a more direct role in how funds were used for their children in public schools. See Jon Reyhner, "A History of Indian Education Timeline," *Education Week,* December 3, 2018, https://www.edweek.org; Gerald R. Ford, "Statement on Signing the Indian Self-Determination and Education Assistance Act," January 4, 1975, The American Presidency Project, http://www.presidency.ucsb.edu.

3. John E. Coulson, "National Evaluation of the Emergency School Aid Act (ESAA): A Review of Methodological Issues," *Journal of Educational Statistics* 3, no. 1 (Spring 1978): 1–60.

4. Dorothy Davids, "Tentative Position Paper: Stockbridge-Munsee Community and Title VII," Bowler School Correspondence and Notes folder, box 3, DDC II.

5. Stockbridge-Munsee Historical Committee, "Spin-off: Timeline of Activities," Miscellaneous, Letters, History folder, DDC.

6. Dorothy Davids, interview with unknown, November 23, 2001, Interviews with Dorothy Davids folder, box 6, DDC II.

7. Dorothy Davids to Stockbridge-Munsee Historical Committee, Education Committee, and Other Interested Members of the Stockbridge-Munsee Community, Memo, May 20, 1974, folder 1, BMPC.

8. Davids interview, November 23, 2001.

9. Davids to Stockbridge-Munsee Historical Committee, Education Committee, and Other Interested Members of the Stockbridge-Munsee Community.

10. Davids to Stockbridge-Munsee Historical Committee.

11. Davids interview, November 23, 2001.

12. Dorothy Davids, "Information Requested for Rank and Tenure Appointment of Dorothy W. Davids to Associate Professor, Department of Education, University of Wisconsin Extension," February 8, 1980, Commemoration folder, DDC; District-Wide Advisory Committee, "Recommendation for ESAA Title VII Workshop, August 12–23, 1974 on the Stockbridge Reservation," Bowler School Title VII folder, box 3, DDC II.

13. Davids, "Information Requested for Rank and Tenure Appointment"; Dorothy W. Davids to Polly Pierce, December 23, 1974, series 5, box 4, SIC.

14. Bowler School District, "Extent of Minority Group Isolation," Bowler School Title VII folder, box 3, DDC II.

15. District-Wide Advisory Committee, "Recommendations for ESAA Title VII Workshop."

16. District-Wide Advisory Committee.

17. District-Wide Advisory Committee.

18. Leah Miller, interview with author, December 15, 2016.

19. "Caddie Woodlawn," Simon and Schuster, accessed December 24, 2022, https://www.simonandschuster.org.

20. Claire Glass Miller to Leah (Miller) Heath, December 15, 1976, Bowler School Correspondence and Notes folder, box 3, DDC.

21. Dorothy Davids to Polly Pierce, December 30, 1991, folder 15, box 4, SIC; Stockbridge-Munsee Historical Committee, "Spin-off: Timeline of Activities."

22. Stockbridge-Munsee Historical Committee, foreword, in *The History of the Stockbridge-Munsee Band of Mohican Indians*, 2nd ed. (Bowler, Wisc.: Muh-he-con-neew Press, 1993); Davids, "Information Requested for Rank and Tenure Appointment."

23. Stockbridge-Munsee Historical Committee, "Goals," in *History of the Stockbridge-Munsee Band*.

24. Stockbridge-Munsee Historical Committee, *History of the Stockbridge-Munsee Band*.

25. Stockbridge-Munsee Historical Committee, "Spin-off: Timeline of Activities."

26. Mary Ann Marchel, "'Before We Teach It, We Have to Learn It': Wisconsin Act 31 Compliance within Public Teacher Preparation Programs" (PhD diss., University of Minnesota, 2013); Ronald N. Satz, "Chippewa Treaty Rights: The Reserved Rights of Wisconsin's Chippewa Indians in Historical Perspective," *Transactions* 79, no. 1, Wisconsin Academy of Sciences, Arts and Letters, 1991.

27. Marchel, "'Before We Teach It.'"

28. Dorothy W. Davids and Ruth A. Gudinas to William J. Erpenbach, August 27, 1995, Miscellaneous, Letters, History folder, DDC.

29. Virgil Murphy to William J. Erpenbach, February 8, 1996, 1996 Historical Committee Meeting folder, CHLMC.

30. Ronald N. Satz to Virgil Murphy, no date, 1996 Historical Committee Meeting folder, CHLMC.

31. Dorothy Davids, "Educational Things," 2000, Rambling through History with Dot Davids folder 1, DDC II.

32. The curriculum authors note their intentions specifically, writing that they structured the curriculum in a similar manner to most Act 31 curricula, which begin with a study of the state's history. Their Appendix B breaks down how the curriculum specifically meets the states' requirements so that teachers can easily implement it into their classes. See Dorothy W. Davids et al., *The Mohican People: Their Lives and Their Lands* (Bowler, Wisc.: Muh-he-con-neew Press, 2008).

33. Davids et al.

34. Davids et al., 1.

35. For example, in 1992 a fourth-grade class at Bowler Elementary wrote a song that declared Stockbridge-Munsee people came to Wisconsin with "spears in their hands" and "rode on horses" all day long. When the Historical Committee challenged these stereotypical images, asking why the teacher allowed the students to construct these images and did not consult with any Stockbridge-Munsee teachers, the teacher defended her action, arguing that if she had told the children the word *spear* was bad, she would have been "imposing on them an adult image and forcing them to think that there was something negative about a spear . . . the only purpose [of the exercise] was to have fun, be creative and cooperate." In 2002 a first grader asked Dorothy Davids "how long she had been an Indian" during a classroom presentation she gave in the Bowler School District. See Dorothy W. Davids to Mrs. Wisnefske and Mrs. Werhane, March 2, 1992, 1992 Historical Committee Meeting folder, CHLMC; William Trautt to Dorothy W. Davids and Ruth A. Gudinas, March 20, 1992, 1992 Historical Committee Meeting folder, CHLMC; Dorothy Davids, "Gathering One's Wits," Rambling through History with Dot Davids folder 2, DDC II.

36. James W. Oberly is the author of *A Nation of Statesmen: The Political Culture of the Stockbridge-Munsee Mohicans, 1815–1972.* He has worked with the tribe on numerous projects over the last thirty years.

37. James Oberly, "The Mohican People: Their Lives and Lands—a Curriculum for 4th and 5th graders in Bowler and Gresham Public Schools," Mohican Curriculum Grant Proposal folder, box 6, DDC II; James Oberly to Ruth Gudinas, October 7, 2008, 2008 Historical Committee folder, CHLMC.

38. Oberly, "The Mohican People."

39. Jim Oberly, "Outline for Nomination of Arvid E. Miller Historical Library and Museum for 2002 Governor's Archive Award," Arvid E. Miller Memorial Library-Museum folder, box 5, DDC II.

40. Jo Ann Schedler, interview with author, January 13, 2017.

41. Stockbridge-Munsee Historical Committee, "Meeting Minutes," October 24, 2002, 2002 Historical Committee folder, CHLMC.

42. Stockbridge-Munsee Historical Committee, "Meeting Minutes," November 14, 2002, 2002 Historical Committee folder, CHLMC.

43. Ruth Gudinas to Members of the Stockbridge-Munsee Historical Committee, March 14, 2006, 2006 Historical Committee folder, CHLMC.

44. Native American Institute, "Proposal," Hudson River Valley folder, HRC.

45. Native American Institute, "Proposal."

46. New Netherland Museum, "Half Moon," http://www.halfmoonreplica.org/.

47. Native American Institute, "Meeting Minutes," May 5, 1997, June 2, 1997, Hudson River Valley folder, HRC.

48. Dorothy Davids to Richard Powell, September 15, 1997, Correspondence, Historical Work folder, box 3, DDC II.

49. Davids to Powell, September 15, 1997.

50. Native American Institute, "Meeting Minutes," March 11, 1998, September 1998, Hudson River Valley folder, HRC.

51. Dorothy Davids, "Mohican Seminar 2000," Rambling through History with Dot Davids folder 2, DDC II.

52. Nancy Eve Cohen, "Stockbridge Mohicans Partner with Williams College; Family Name 'Source of Pain' to Tribe," *New England Public Media,* February 1, 2021, https://www.nepm.org.

53. For example, in response to a request to participate in a Wisconsin documentary celebrating the state's sesquicentennial, the Historical Committee asserted that Native people do not see such events as cause for celebration and recommended that the Stockbridge-Munsee be included in other parts of the documentary in addition to a small section on their nation "since they are involved in politics, work, and play like other Wisconsinites." Instead, they were asked to discuss why "casinos are so important to Indian people" and "some concepts, like sovereignty." See Stockbridge-Munsee Historical Committee, "Meeting Minutes," November 21, 1996, 1996 Historical Committee folder, CHLMC.

54. The Mohicans are one of many Native nations with ties to the Hudson River Valley, yet it is unclear if the New Netherland Museum reached out to other nations in addition to the Mohicans before their curriculum was set to be implemented across the state.

55. Stockbridge-Munsee Historical Committee, "Meeting Minutes," April 9, 2009, 2009 Historical Committee folder, CHLMC.

56. Stockbridge-Munsee Historical Committee, "Meeting Minutes," April 9, 2009.

57. Stockbridge-Munsee Historical Committee, "Meeting Minutes," April 9, 2009.

58. Leah J. Miller to William T. (Chip) Reynolds, May 15, 2009, 2009 Historical Committee folder, CHLMC.

59. Stockbridge-Munsee Historical Committee, "Meeting Minutes," April 9, 2009.

60. New Netherland Museum, "Half Moon."

61. *Indians of the Hudson Valley: An Exploration of Indian Life: Before, during, and after European Contact, 1550–1750*, New Netherland Museum, "Half Moon," https://www.halfmoon.mus.ny.us/.

62. "Indians of the Hudson Valley."

63. Stockbridge-Munsee Historical Committee, "Meeting Minutes," February 28, 1992, 1992 Historical Committee folder, CHLMC.

64. Schedler interview, January 13, 2017.

65. Stockbridge-Munsee Historical Committee, "Mobile Exhibit on the Native American Patriots of the Revolution," April 1, 1975, Library-Museum Records, BMPC.

66. For examples of other exhibits, see Ana Fota, "What's Wrong with This Diorama? You Can Read All about It," *New York Times,* March 20, 2019, https://www.nytimes.com; Kate Abbott, "Mohican Storytellers Curate Their Past and Future at the Berkshire Museum," *btwBerkshires,* August 24, 2021, https://www.btwberkshires.com; Dick Lindsey, "Stockbridge-Munsee Focus on Correcting Historical Record through Collaborations with Berkshire Institutions," *Berkshire (Mass.) Eagle,* October 1, 2021, https://www.berkshireeagle.com.

67. Lindsey, "Stockbridge-Munsee Focus on Correcting Historical Record."

68. "Photos of Indian Museum Exhibit," 1987, Exhibitions/Research, MHSF.

69. Interestingly, in the video portion of the walking tour discussed in the next section, the video about the Mission House features tribal members walking through the walled-off portion of the museum. Perhaps, this was a subtle way of breaking down that divide and bringing Mohican people into the main portion of the house. As Ruth Gudinas noted in her account of the 1989 historical trip (discussed in chapter 4) the Mohicans have long been aware that their ancestors were not permitted to enter the house beyond the back room. See Stockbridge-Munsee Community, "Stop 8 at 19 Main Street: The Mission House," Footprints of Our Ancestors Mohican History Walking Tour of Main Street Stockbridge, https://www.nativeamericantrail.org (hereafter cited as FOA Walking Tour).

70. Hannah Van Sickle, "At the Mission House 'Mohican Miles' Gives Voice to Stockbridge's First Community," *Berkshire (Mass.) Edge,* July 2, 2021, https://www.theberkshireedge.com.

71. Upper Housatonic Valley National Heritage Area, Housatonic Heritage, last modified 2015, https://housatonicheritage.org.

72. Bonney Hartley, email to author, May 10, 2018.

73. Bonney Hartley, personal communication with author, February 24, 2017.

74. "'Footprints of Our Ancestors': Descendants Bring Stockbridge Mohican History to Life in Virtual Tour," *National Park Service,* July 24, 2019, https://www.nps.gov.

75. Stockbridge-Munsee Community, "Stop 1 at 50 Main Street Town Offices," FOA Walking Tour.

76. Stockbridge-Munsee Community, "Stop 9 at Across From 4 Main Street: Town Cemetery," FOA Walking Tour.

77. Stockbridge-Munsee Community, "Stop 11 West of Congregational Church, Main St.," FOA Walking Tour.

78. Stockbridge-Munsee Community, "Stop 11."

79. Stockbridge-Munsee Community, "Stop 4 at 39 Main Street: Captain Naunauphtaunk Home," FOA Walking Tour.

80. Stockbridge-Munsee Community, "Stop 6 at 23 Main Street: Jonas Etowaukaum Home," FOA Walking Tour.

81. Stockbridge-Munsee Community, "Stop 10 at 4–6 Main Street: Meeting House," FOA Walking Tour.

82. Stockbridge-Munsee Community, "Stop 1."

83. Stockbridge-Munsee Community, "Stop 3 at 46 Main Street: Library and Archives," FOA Walking Tour.

84. Stockbridge-Munsee Community, "Stop 3."

85. Quoted in Jacob Posner, "Stockbridge Archaeological Dig Involves Community, Aims to Correct Historical Interpretation," *Berkshire (Mass.) Eagle,* July 11, 2021, https://www.berkshireeagle.com.

86. Hartley personal communication, February 24, 2017.

87. For an example of mission signage, see Stockbridge-Munsee Historical Committee, "Meeting Minutes," September 8, 1994, 1994 Historical Committee folder, CHLMC; Stockbridge-Munsee Historical Committee, "Meeting Minutes," January 26, 1995, 1995 Historical Committee folder, CHLMC. For highway signage see Jon Campbell, "After Balking, New York to Honor Interstate 87 Mural Deal with Native Tribes," *Democrat & Chronicle,* January 22, 2021, https://democratandchronicle.com. For trail signage see New York State Department of Environmental Conservation, "Recognizing Indigenous and Enslaved People at Mawignack Preserve in Catskill," January 26, 2021, https://content.govdelivery.com/.

88. "Welcome to Monument Mountain, Sacred Site of the Mohican People," trail signage at the base of Monument Mountain, Stockbridge, Massachusetts.

89. Heather Bellow, "'Long Overdue' Changes on Monument Mountain to Honor Mohicans," *Berkshire (Mass.) Eagle,* April 8, 2021, https://www.berkshireeagle.com.

90. Van Sickle, "At the Mission House."

91. L. Miller, interview with author, December 15, 2016.

Conclusion

1. Society of American Archivists, "SAA Council Endorsement of Protocols for Native American Archival Materials," Society of American Archivists, last modified August 13, 2018, http://www2.archivists.org; Association of College and Research Libraries, "ACRL Speaks Out," last modified August 2019, http://www.ala.org.

2. Sandy Rodriguez, Ruth Tillman, Amy Wickner, Stacie Williams, and Emily Drabinski, "Collective Responsibility: Seeking Equity for Contingent Labor in Libraries, Archives, and Museums," https://www.laborforum.diglib.org; Stephanie Bredbenner, Alison Fulmer, Meghan Rinn, Rose Oliveira, and Kimberly Barzola, "'Nothing about It Was Better than a Permanent Job': Report of the New England Archivists Contingent Employment Study Task Force," February 2022, New England Archivists, https://www.newenglandarchivists.org; American Library Association, "The State of America's Libraries 2022: A Report from the American Library Association," April 2022; Makala Skinner and Ioana Hulbert, "A*CENSUS II All Archivists Survey Report," *Ithaka S+R,* last modified August 22, 2022, https://www.ala.org; Association of College & Research Libraries, "ACRL Legislative Agenda 2022," accessed January 11, 2023, https://www.ala.org/acrl.

3. Brian Carpenter, "Archival Initiatives for the Indigenous Collections at the American Philosophical Society," Society of American Archivists: Case Studies on

Access Policies for Native American Archival Materials, February 2019, https://www2 .archivists.org/.

4. Cline Library, "Indigenous Peoples in Special Collections and Archives," Northern Arizona University, http://libraryguides.nau.edu/; Jonathan Pringle, "Northern Arizona University's Cline Library and the Protocols," Society of American Archivists: Case Studies on Access Policies for Native American Archival Material, April 2019, https://www2.archivists.org/.

5. Zoe Ducklow, "Sisiyutl House Plank Coming Home to Vancouver Island after 127 Years Away," *Vancouver Island Free Daily,* September 6, 2020, https://www.van couverislandfreedaily.com/; Pringle, "Northern Arizona University's Cline Library"; Lynn Malerba, Melissa Tantaquidgeon Zobel, and Tamar Evangelestia-Dougherty, "Mohegan Tribe, Cornell Partner to Repatriate Fidelia Fielding Diaries," *Library Journal,* March 4, 2021, accessed March 12, 2022, https://www.libraryjournal.com; Jill Radsken, "An End and a Beginning," *Harvard Gazette,* accessed January 3, 2023, https:// www.news.harvard.edu; "Repatriation of Samson Occom's Papers to the Mohegan Tribe," Dartmouth Library, accessed January 3, 2023, https://www.library.dartmouth .edu.

6. "Mahican Indians," Library of Congress Authorities, accessed January 9, 2023, https://lccn.loc.gov; "Stockbridge Indians," Library of Congress Authorities, accessed January 9, 2023, https://lccn.loc.gov.

7. See X̱wi7x̱wa Library, "Indigenous Knowledge Organization," University of British Columbia, accessed January 10, 2023, https://xwi7xwa.library.ubc.ca/; Dominique Foisy-Geoffroy, *Between Duty to Remember and Imperatives of Reconciliation: Procedures for Writing Culturally Sensitive Titles for Descriptions of Indigenous Materials at Library and Archives Canada* (Ottawa, Ontario: CRKN Access to Knowledge Conference, 2019), https://www.crkn-rcdr.ca/.

8. Brian Carpenter, "Finding Mrs. Mahone and Indigenous Experts in the Archives," *American Philosophical Society,* June 5, 2019, https://www.amphilsoc.org.

9. Krista McCracken and Skylee-Storm Hogan, "Laughter Filled the Space: Challenging Euro-Centric Archival Spaces," *International Journal of Information, Diversity, & Inclusion* 5, no. 1 (2021): 97–110.

10. American Philosophical Society, "Protocols for the Treatment of Indigenous Materials," American Philosophical Society, accessed December 3, 2021, https://www .amphilsoc.org.

11. Will Hansen, Alison Hinderliter, Alan Leopold, Analú López, Rose Miron, John Powell, Alice Schreyer, Blaire Topash-Caldwell, "Access to Culturally Sensitive Indigenous Materials in the Newberry Library Collections," Newberry Library, January 14, 2021, https://www.newberry.org. For more on TK labels, see "TK Labels," Local Contexts, https://www.localcontexts.org.

12. The Library of Congress, "About this Collection," Ancestral Voices Collection, https://www.loc.gov.

13. The Library of Congress, "Rights and Access," Ancestral Voices Collection, https://www.loc.gov.

14. "TK Labels."

15. Keara Duggan, "Case Study: Northern Arizona University and the Hopi Cultural Preservation Office," cited in Cara S. Bertram, "Avenues of Mutual Respect: Opening Communication and Understanding between Native Americans and Archivists" (master's thesis, Western Washington University, 2012).

16. Elizabeth Joffrion and Natalia Fernández, "Collaborations between Tribal and Nontribal Organizations: Suggested Best Practices for Sharing Expertise, Cultural Resources, and Knowledge," *American Archivist* 78, no. 1 (Spring/Summer 2015): 192–237.

17. Carpenter, "Archival Initiatives"; Pringle, "Northern Arizona University's Cline Library."

Index

Index by Denise E. Carlson

Page numbers in italics refer to photographs and other illustrations.

ROSE MIRON is director of the D'Arcy McNickle Center for American Indian and Indigenous Studies at the Newberry Library and affiliate faculty in the Center for Native American and Indigenous Research at Northwestern University.